BAWDS AND LODGINGS

BAWDS AND LODGINGS

A History

of the London Bankside Brothels

c. 100-1675

E. J. BURFORD

PETER OWEN · LONDON

ISBN 0 7206 0144 4

PETER OWEN LIMITED
20 Holland Park Avenue London W11 3QU

First British Commonwealth Edition 1976
© 1976 E. J. Burford

Printed in Great Britain by
Daedalus Press Stoke Ferry King's Lynn Norfolk

CONTENTS

Introduction   9

I   Roman Beginnings   11

II   'Wymmon that fair & freoly is to fyke'   24

III   William the Bastard Conquers England   36

IV   Accordynge to the Old Custumes   53

V   A Plague of Plantagenets   63

VI   'All Harlottys and Horrys and Bawdys that Procures'   83

VII   'Lewd men and women of Euill Life Dwellinge in the Stewes'   89

VIII   'The Perylous Infirmitie of the Brennynge'   113

IX   'It is made but a laughing matter and a trifle'   130

X   'Englisshe Women be hotte as goattes'   140

XI   'Vulva Regit Scotos . . . ac tenet ipsa Britannos'   147

XII   'Elizabeth was King. Now is James Queen.'   164

XIII   The End of the Beare's Colledge   177

Bibliography and References   185

Index   199

ILLUSTRATIONS

1   Roman architrave

2   The Isis jug

3   The Ordinance of 1161

4   Early illustration of a brothel

5   Prostitutes enticing a customer

6   Medieval stewhouse

7   Interior of a brothel

8   Prostitute, bawd and client

9   Prostitutes and clients round a table

10   Coronation procession of Edward VI

11   Map of Southwark, 1618

12   *The Cardinal's Cap,* No. 49 Bankside

13   *The Anchor,* No. 1 Bankside

The illustrations are reproduced by courtesy of the following: The Guildhall Museum (1); The London Museum (2, 10); The British Museum (3); The Courtauld Institute (5, 6, 9); The Warburg Institute (8); The Corporation of London Record Office (11); The Greater London Council (12); Messrs Courage and Co. Ltd. (13).

The illustrations of the London jug and the knights' jug on pp. 66 and 68 are reproduced by courtesy of Dr Gerald Dunning; the illustration of Fish Pond House on p. 158 by courtesy of the Wellcome Trustees. The drawing of Bankside on pp. 142, 143 is by Bill Crook.

ILLUSTRATIONS

1.
2.
3. The Dominoes' Dish
4.
5.
6.
7.
8.
9.
10.
11.
12.
13.

INTRODUCTION

In the otherwise not very momentous year of Our Lord 1161 the 'Mooste Cristen and Mooste Excellent Prince Henry Plantagenet the Secund after the Conquest King of England and Wales Duke of Normandy and Anjou Count of Maine and Aquitaine', grandson of King Henry I and great-grandson of William the Conqueror, found time during a Parliament held at Westminster to append his signature to a grandiose document consisting of some thirty-two Latin rubrics and fifty-two English paragraphs. It bore the sonorous title ORDIN-AUNCES TOUCHING THE GOUERMENT OF THE STEWHOULDERS IN SOUTH-WARKE UNDER THE DIRECTION OF THE Bpp OF WINCHESTER.

By means of this ordinance the King put into operation the first officially licensed brothels in England, and possibly the first under royal recognition in all Europe. The King was legalizing some ecclesiastical Customs that had been in operation at least thirty years previously, controlling a group of whorehouses on the Bankside in the London borough of Southwark. These Customaries now also bore the signatures of the Most Noble and Reverend Theobaldus, 'Archibisschope of Caunterburie', and his 'Archideacon' Thomas à Becket. There was no fanfare of trumpets.

On 'the Twenty-first day of Aprill in the year of Our Lord 1546 Henry Tudor by the Grace of God Eighth of that name King of England and Ireland' solemnly and 'with an harolde and a trumpette' caused to be proclaimed the annulment of his illustrious predecessor's ordinance, demolishing at a stroke four hundred years of the most picturesque and picaresque history of 'the Banck-syde in the Libertie of the Clincke' of the Bishops of Winchester in the ancient Borough of Southwark over the River of Thames.

It is my intention in this book to explain what caused Henry II to take such action at that time and for that place; and what caused another Henry some four hundred years later to bring it to an end. For this purpose it will be necessary to return to those far-off days when Julius Caesar first came to our island and decided that it should at some time be included in Rome's expanding empire. But even the great Caesar could never have foreseen what a certain facet of that empire's civilization was to create on a dank, dismal piece of no-man's-land on the southern side of the unimportant – at least to Caesar – River of Thames.

9

In the course of this book, events familiar to every schoolchild will be mentioned. But, more important, our chief concern will be the events thought insignificant or embarrassing by the authors of the history books: events that pertain to the sexual customs and concerns of ordinary Englishmen and women of high and low estate. For through an examination of what occurred on a stretch of riverside at Southwark we begin to gain an understanding of a crucial but hitherto neglected aspect of the social history of England.

I

Roman Beginnings

The fact that there have been whorehouses and prostitution in Britain since Roman times will surprise nobody. It would, however, be a very curious quirk of history if the first brothels are shown to have been established in an obscure military outpost on the south bank of the River Thames, opposite the civilian settlement later to be known as Londinium.

Julius Caesar reported in 54 BC that Britain was a green, lush and rich island, making it certain that the Romans would attempt another invasion at a suitable time. The known savagery of the inhabitants deterred them for many years. For instance, Augustus Caesar had intended to come in 27 BC, but Horace (in his *First Satire*) remarks that Caesar would have needed special protection because it was too dangerous to travel amongst the ferocious and cruel Britons. However, another source[1] says that Augustus had a venereal disease and disliked the discomforts of travelling.

When therefore the Divine Emperor Claudius decided in AD 43 that this tempting piece of land should be attached to his own domains he made the preparations with typical Roman thoroughness. He chose the clever commanding officer of his troops in Pannonia, Aulus Plautius, to be *Magister Militarium* (Field Marshal) and gave him three legions from the Army of the Rhine, adding a contingent of the Emperor's own Praetorian Guard. These were a stiffener to the morale of the Pannonian legions who were reluctant, to the point of mutiny, to move from their comfortable and peaceful quarters in Dacia, the present-day Rumania. As an additional stiffener he appointed Vespasian, commander of the crack Legio II 'Augusta', as second-in-command. To boost their morale still further the troops were provided with a battalion of elephants.

The objective was annexation and not merely a punitive expedition, nor was the invasion unexpected. The pro-Roman King Cymbeline (Cunobelinus) in a long reign ending in AD 43 had encouraged Roman tradesmen, craftsmen and travellers to come to Britain, so that some knowledge of Roman ways and of the Latin tongue existed. British nobles were often to be seen in Rome having a good time on money borrowed from Roman moneylenders, as well as British slaves enjoying a much less comfortable life. Roman luxuries had long been imported through Cymbeline's new capital, Camulodunum (Colchester, in Essex), thus adding to its riches, glory and stability.

The invaders could also count upon a useful fifth column. Many British kinglets, nobles and their sons had been exiled, and even Cymbeline's own son Adminius was a refugee in the Rome of Emperor Caligula in about AD 40. The exiles were heavily in debt to Roman usurers, including Seneca, so that invasion was the only way they could hope to regain their estates and pay their debts.

It is logical that the first permanent Roman settlement was in Southwark. It was at the end of the line of march from Rutupiae (Richborough in Kent) to the site of their first major military obstacle after they had spent the first days searching for an elusive British army which they found waiting for them at this spot on the broad river Tamesis, whence a network of tracks branched out all over the island. At this point the legions rested awhile, while their engineers threw up a pontoon bridge with the materials they had carried with them against this very contingency, for Julius Caesar had warned them of it a century earlier. In fact, he may very well have put up a bridge himself, for Dion Cassius[2] (writing about a hundred and fifty years later) said that 'Aulus Plautius' British troops forded the river at places they knew: his Germans swam across, and the more heavily weighed down armoured Roman soldiers crossed by a bridge a little further up.' In any case, whenever it was built, the bridge at this point determined the line of the ancient Stane Street and ultimately the line of Southwark High Street to this day.

At the bridgehead they established their commissariat and stores, because Southwark – and not London – would have been their resistance base if the campaign had gone wrong. That it was a considerable place shortly afterwards is evidenced in the *Geography* of Claudius Ptolemaeus of Alexandria, which was written before AD 151. Ptolemaeus placed Londinium on the south side of the River Thames, which infers a settlement there, already important enough to make him, or his informant, think it was Londinium itself. When we consider that at least a cohort would have been stationed there, and that in that period a cohort comprised between 600 and 1,000 men, to which must be added the supporting establishments and the camp-followers, there would have been at least two thousand people in that settlement at any one time.

The place would have been given a purely functional name because it was a military bridgehead and was so to remain for

centuries. It required a name easily recognized and pronounced by
Rome's multinational and polyglottally illiterate soldiery; even their
Greek and Italian soldiers were illiterate, since education was the
privilege of the few. It was probably known by a name like *ad
caputem pontem* (by the bridgehead). Centuries later it was to be
called 'the head of the bridge' and sometimes 'the foot of the bridge';
this perhaps depended on whether the speaker was a Londoner or a
man of Southwark. While it was a military bridgehead it needed no
other name.

Hence the settlement would have been known as 'the village at the
bridgehead' or something of that nature. Here, on the hard shoulder
of land in the riverine marsh, adjacent to the camp, would soon have
been erected a row of soldiers' *lupanaria*. Every Roman legion had its
complement of camp followers who catered for both its alimentary as
well as its sexual nourishment. These brothels were indeed a necessity,
for until the end of the second century AD Roman soldiers were not
allowed to marry. These modest little edifices would have been popularly known as the 'whorehouses at the bridgehead', and conveniently
situated just off the military highway but near enough to be of easy
access for the soldiers' urgent sexual needs.

It is possible to reconstruct with reasonable accuracy some aspects
of life in Southwark and Londinium in Roman times, on the basis of
analogy to contemporary written material in Latin as well as artifacts
excavated from ancient Roman sites elsewhere, although such
remains in Southwark itself are very rare. This is not unexpected for
most buildings in those days, except for temples or official residences,
were of flimsy construction and have left no trace of their existence.

We can visualize a signpost at the turn-off from the highway
indicating 'the way to the brothels' to guide newcomers; more than
likely such signposts would also bear that most ancient international
sign – the palm of a hand – fully understood by every illiterate in the
mélange of nations which made up the empire and its armed cohorts.
The brothels would assuredly have been patronized by the sailors
from the war-galleys disembarking at the nearby landing point almost
outside the establishments, which would have been open for their
convenience twenty-four hours a day.

At first these houses would have been of timber framework with
thatched roofs and brightly coloured plaster walls within, standing
on earth or clay foundations. Inside would have been little cells each
with a narrow wooden bunk and straw pallet. There would have been
no ceremony or preliminary lovemaking; the clients would take their
pleasure – or rather, relieve their tensions – quickly and depart to
make way for the next man in the queue. Later these cabins would be
replaced by a row of terraced brick tenements as in other Roman

cities. These would be very different from the elegant whorehouses of their homeland, but the 'poor bloody infantry' had never had access to such places in any case. The better-class establishments, soon to be erected in Londinium, would be out of bounds for NCOs and men, even if they could have afforded them.

From these little relieving stations the customers left, in Seneca's words, *'redoles adhuc fuliginem fornices'* ('with the stink of fornication on their clothing') but this would not have occasioned any comment, recourse to whorehouses being an acceptable part of Roman manners. The playwright Plautus described such low-class brothels and the hard life of the unlucky girls compelled to serve in them. The whores were usually slaves especially bought for the purpose at the nearby slave-markets, which were usually near the water-side. For example, immediately adjacent to Queenhithe, just across the river from Bankside, there was in Roman times a large open space where goods landed from the vessels were stored, sorted out and made ready for further despatch. In these yards the slavers would unload their unhappy freight into special slave-compounds, for slave-trading in Roman times was a large and highly lucrative business. In the compound men, women and girls were washed and made ready for auction. Here the brothelmasters and other buyers were encouraged to examine and handle every part of their bodies. They saw paraded naked before them the loveliest specimens of womanhood of all nations, for every Roman victory meant hordes of slaves on the world markets. For example, Titus, one the conquerors of Britain and later to become emperor, exported almost the whole of the Jewish population of Palestine into slavery. It is a certainty that after his conquest of Palestine in AD 71 hundreds of Jewish girls found themselves facing the ultimate degradation in Roman brothels in that last dim outpost of the empire, the bleak, cold and wet island of Albion.

These open spaces were known in medieval times as 'Romelands' and were found at all ancient Thames harbours: at Queenhithe, the Tower, Dowgate and Billingsgate, and doubtless at all of them were slave-markets. Queenhithe's history is known from King Alfred's time in 899 and the origin of its name is disputed, but it may very well derive from *cwen-hythe*, the harbour at which women slaves were landed. The Romelands were later railed off and used as markets; in 1546 they were the subject of a lawsuit in Chancery, where they were declared to be the property of 'the commons of London . . . from tyme oute of mynde.'

Once sold, these slaves had no rights whatsoever. The *leno* (whoremaster) or *lena* (bawd or brothelmistress) was their absolute master. Each one would spend the rest of her life on her back, day and night, submitting to every sexual vagary forced upon her body by exigent men, until she died. If she were not lucky enough to be bought by some admirer for his personal pleasures, she would die of exhaustion or disease before the age of thirty.

For Roman men brothel-visiting was a way of life, as it was for the Greeks. Eubulus, in his burlesque *Plangion* (c. 350 BC), provides a useful picture of a slave-compound, while giving some homely advice: 'It is simpler to go openly and look at the pretty girls lined up by the riverside, quite naked or covered only by a transparent tunic. You can choose one in complete safety and without worrying about any family complications.'

The women who followed the soldiers were treated little better than the pack animals, but unlike the animals, the women were for use and abuse at any time. Some may have formed sentimental attachments, but for most life was hard and ugly, and they could echo the cynical answer of the slave, who on being asked whether he had ever been in love, replied that 'he had never had a full belly in his life, so he couldn't say.'

This small spit of land would soon have attracted round it all the ancillary entertainments of a low-class nature. Taverns, bars, gambling joints, cockpits, and bear- and bull-baiting rings were a feature here for centuries. These in turn would have attracted the lowest elements in society: criminals, petty thieves, gangsters, murderers and confidence tricksters, as well as runaway slaves and fugitives of every description. The very nature of the surrounding land – marshy, dank and uninhabited – made it a natural hiding-place and refuge.

It was probably regarded as part of the *pomerium* of London. This was a swathe of no-man's-land outside the walls of Roman cities which was deliberately left clear so that approaching enemies could be quickly spotted and dealt with. Roman commanders in Britain had learnt from bitter experience, beginning with Boudicca's ferocious swoop on Londinium in AD 61. If Southwark was part of the *pomerium* of London this might account for its later status of a 'Liberty', an area in which people could not only seek refuge and asylum, but in which all sorts of activities, banned or restricted elsewhere, could be carried on without interference, and certain kinds of sexual activity in particular.

From very early days this part of Southwark was a centre of sexual activity. Nearby, in the first century AD, there was very probably a shrine or temple to the goddess Isis. Some years ago the remains of a very substantial Roman building with stone foundations and tessellated floors were uncovered on the south side of what is now Southwark Cathedral. While it may have been a public building, it may equally have been a temple to serve the worship of one of the popular sex gods, Isis, Apollo or Hermes. A pottery jug of that date, inscribed 'LONDINI AD FANUM ISIDIS' ('In London, at the Temple of Isis'), was found nearby in 1912.[3] It was either a temple utensil, or for use in drinking in a local wineshop by members of a Guild of Worshippers, on the specified 'Days of Drinking' when these devotees carried out their religious tasks in the temple. These duties consisted, amongst others, of acting as *phallophores*, bearers of the gigantic phalli which were part of all such rituals. Similar vessels and the activities of similar guilds are known elsewhere. Isis, the principal goddess of Egypt, wife of the great god Osiris and mother of Horus, was essentially a women's deity. Women were her most constant and fervent devotees, from empresses down to the lowest slave-prostitute. Her ceremonies were characterized by the lewdest behaviour and the most lubricious festivals and sexual orgies ever devised by man or woman. To the Temples of Isis resorted whores of high and low degree, as well as women seeking sexual gratification, for these temples were places of assignation. The cult of Isis persisted in England until as late as AD 350.

Further evidence of public sexual practices in Southwark is the small silver statue of the Egypto-Roman god, Harpocrates (who is also linked with Hermes), found in the Thames on the south side of London Bridge. He was earlier a manifestation of the god Horus, and he was renowned for his sexual prowess. He is usually depicted as a man (sometimes dressed in a Phrygian cap) with a penis two or three times his height. In the House of the Vetii in Pompeii there was a statue in the vestibule showing him weighing his enormous penis in an apothecary's scales. His picture was to be found often on the walls and ceilings of Roman brothels, to welcome the client and exhort him to maximum endeavours.

In passing, it must be said that this Pompeiian brothel, for all the magnificence of its vestibule, atrium, ante-chambers and reception rooms in the front had only a row of very small cramped *cellae*, each with a small wooden bunk, short and narrow, tucked away at the rear of the house.

Harpocrates-Hermes had his temples too – associated also with Mercury, the most popular Roman god in Britain – where the rites were of the most blatant phallic character. In the annual procession, gigantic phalli were carried by stalwart *phallophores* – priests or laymen – amidst scenes of utter drunkenness and unbridled lust; crowds of crazed women would dance and cavort, exposing themselves stark naked and copulating publicly with all comers. (The Christian apologist Firminius Lanctantius said of them, '. . . they worshipped the sexual organs, calling them God.')[4] The poet Catullus[5] described one of these ceremonies, where females would hang garlands on the god's enormous penis, as many as they had had lovers the previous night. Often the penis would be completely ringed and covered from sight with the offerings of a single woman. Terracotta models found at North Saqqara in Egypt in 1971-2 show Harpocrates' enormous penis supported on the shoulders of four acolytes. There is another figure of the god, with a wooden phallus inserted into a hole, so that it can be slid backwards and forwards to adjust its length to suit the worshipper's foibles. Such scenes could be witnessed at the same festivals in Londinium. (One must add, however, that the London statuette shows Harpocrates as a boy, not greatly endowed, and is of a late date when the cult had become somewhat more innocuous.)

There were other gods who had their cults in London – like Attys, who was usually portrayed with his tunic pulled to one side to expose his enormous penis and testicles and a pendulous belly, demonstrating simultaneously lechery and gluttony – and other joyous festivals in the Roman calendar, such as the *Tutunus* and *Mutinus*. Both were phallic in character and lubricious in observance.

Once a site was made holy to one religion, it usually remained a sacred place with shrines and temples to other, later gods being erected there. Thus there is a strong possibility that the site of the temple to Isis was used during the Saxon period for a temple to the goddess Freya or Frigg, Odin's wife and a goddess of love – indeed a lineal successor to the Roman goddess Venus. Freya's day (Friday) equates with Venus's day (*dies veneriis*), and as late as 1326 there was a Fridayfeld in neighbouring Lambeth,[6] which clearly infers Saxon rites. It is known that very many parish churches are built on sites of Saxon origin, and it it thus conceivable that St Swithin's monastery, which was built in 852-860, stands on the site of Frigga's temple. Frigga was being worshipped right up to end of Saxon paganism and even into the early Middle Ages. If this were the case, it goes a long way to explain how the bishopric of Winchester became involved in the control of sexual affairs on Bankside later on.

Then, when between AD 50 and AD 150 the Romans built a permanent fort in the north-west suburbs of Londinium, another brothel area sprang up to serve the troops there, possibly leaving the Southwark 'houses' to cater for various civilian classes such as freedmen, petty traders, travellers, lower officials, even slaves – and of course criminal elements using whorehouses for nefarious purposes, not the least of which would have been the overthrow of the existing order. The link between whorehouses and anti-government plotting is very ancient; it can be traced back to Joshua and Jericho.

Under different emperors the laws regarding brothels fluctuated between laxity and severity, but at no time did dishonour attach to the men who patronized such establishments, or often to those who owned or managed them. Panders and procurers could and did become Roman citizens, rendering a public service on the practical principle enunciated by that stern old Republican, Marcus Porcius Cato (234-149 BC), the Censor: 'Blessed be they as virtuous, who when they feel their virile members swollen with lust, visit a brothel rather than grind at some husband's private mill.'[7]

On the other hand, much odium attached to any woman compelled to accept money for prostituting her body, although at times it became fashionable – as well as lucrative – to do so. Indeed the official register of prostitutes kept by the official in charge of public health and sanitation, the *aedile*, 'in accordance with the custom which obtained amongst the early Romans' (Tacitus), was designed to discourage ladies of high rank from adopting the profession. The *aedile* in Londinium probably had his headquarters inside the Cripplegate fort, at or near the cross-roads now known as Addle Street and Wood Street. Addle Street perhaps derives from an earlier *Via Aedilia*, for in ancient times it was known as *Adelstrete*, supposedly after the Saxon appellation for a noble. The early Teutons may have taken over the word *aedile*, the official who in most cases would have been lording it over them. Since Addle Street was linked with Love Lane and Maiden Lane, streets of brothels whose inhabitants had to visit the *aedile* regularly to pay their special taxes and renew their licences, there is probably a direct link with Roman Londinium. Another authority[8] thinks 'addle' derives from the Saxon word for dirt or filth, which applies equally well to the business being carried on there.

When adopting the profession of prostitute the woman had to tell him under what *nom de guerre* she wished to trade and what category of client she intended to cater for. The *aedile* was supposed to try to dissuade her, but if she persisted he issued her with a *Licentia Stupro*, a licence to carry on a shameful practice. Over the entrance to her premises she had to put a tablet inscribed with her professional name and her scale of charges. Naturally there were some expenses connected with the granting of a licence, first and foremost the *Lenonium Vectigal* which had been originated by Caligula (5 BC-AD 41). One paragraph of this directed that the prostitute had to pay out a portion of her daily earnings. In practice this worked out at about an eighth of her earnings.

It is pertinent to mention at this point that the first brothels in the West were established about 600 BC in Athens by the great statesman and philosopher Solon as a non-profit-making public health service to all male citizens, at a nominal charge of one *obol* (a penny) a time. The Roman state, however, had no scruples about making profits from fornication; indeed the better the class of whore the greater the revenue to the state. It was an annual tax, periodically adjusted by means of a census of the whores.

Some prophylactic measures may have existed from an early time to control the *morbus indecens aie cunnientis* (the filthy disease of the cunt). The *morbus turpis* (the shameful disease) was brought to Rome about 183 BC when General Manlius' victorious troops returned from their campaigns in Asia Minor bringing with them thousands of Syrian girls, who, when sold onto the market, were said to have caused an epidemic of the *morbus indecens*, manifested by a venereal sore known as the *ulcus turpe* (the shameful ulcer), and most probably syphilis. About 150 BC rules were introduced in the army about washing the genitals and frequent bathing.

The Emperor Commodus (180-192) instituted the *Lenonum Vectigal et Meretricum et exoletorum* (Tax on Bawds and Whores and male prostitutes). The income from this tax was colossal and was disbursed according to the prevailing emperor's ethical scruples or political needs. Alexander Severus (222-235) forbade the monies to be paid into the sacred treasury and ruled that the revenue must be used for improvements in the public services. Others used the money for less honourable purposes. The first Christian emperor, Constantine the Great (274-337), called the tax the *Chrysargyrum* (gold and silver) because it brought in such a vast amount in these precious metals. He levied this *lustral* (tax) through his *lustrali* every five years. Theodoric II (*c.* AD 460) abolished the tax on the *lenonia* (the brothels and brothelkeepers) but collected it ruthlessly from the whores themselves – so much so that many parents were compelled to send out their daughters to prostitution in order to pay the tax due on another daughter's whoring. [9]

However remote the seat of power may have been, the *aediles* and *lustrali* in Londinium would have levied zealously all such taxes from the whores and *lenos* of the Bankside. The Emperor Lucius Septimius Severus, who spent some time in Britain (and in fact died in York), made a mild and naturally ineffectual attempt to check the growth of prostitution, and before him the Emperor Hadrian (117-138), reputed to have had homosexual inclinations but otherwise of exemplary character, had tried to ban the brothels and stop mixed bathing in the *thermiae* (hot baths) in public because it encouraged prostitution. He was quite unsuccessful and his successor, Julian the Apostate, restored the *status quo ante*.

All these imperial vagaries prior to AD 404 were reflected onto the lives of Britain's brothelkeepers and whores; after that date none of the imperial laws could be enforced in this country, but it is certain that the terms of the old laws were maintained as long as central government lasted.

The registration process gave the whore a legal existence and enabled her, like any other tradesman, to sue anyone who tried to bilk her. But it also compelled her to submit to frequent inspections and she was forbidden to wear the *stola* of the Roman matrons and had to limit herself to wearing the *toga*. This did not stop *stola*-clad ladies from engaging in unladylike competition. The poet Horace in his *First Satire* observes tartly: '*Magno prognatum deposco Consule Cunnum velatumque stola*', which may be translated that whores dressed in matrons' *stolas* for the convenience of great ones such as consuls. (It is also a very early use of the word *cunnus* to describe a whore.)

The laws failed to prevent the spread of venereal disease. Eubulus, in *Plangion*, has a phrase '*nummulo emer voluptatem, neque clandestiniam venerea, turpissimus morborum omnium, persequi superbiae, non amoris causa*', which, translated, reads 'for a few pence you can buy enjoyment at a brothel without any risk, as with clandestine fucking, of catching the most shameful disease.'

The historian Gaius Plinius, better known as Pliny the Elder (AD 23-79), anxious to remove the blame for originating the disease from virtuous Rome, refers in his *Natural History* to venereal sores which he calls 'lichen' and says the disease was brought to Rome by the 'dirty Egyptians'. Syphilitic nodules on the body were commonly known in Rome as 'figs' (*ficus*) and there was a special phrase 'goats' figs' (*caprificus*), meaning the disease caught from *caprae* (goats), a slang term for whores. In Martial's *Carmen No. 50* a young man asks the god Priapus whether a girl is playing him up because 'she is full of figs'. This was written in about AD 100. Ovid and Catullus also mention the disease, and more than two hundred years later D. Magus Ansonius (*c.* AD 340) in his *Epigrammata No. 108* refers to a citizen trying desperately to get rid of his putrid ulcers on his penis by washing.

Undoubtedly, while the Bankside brothels were under military supervision some hygienic rules would have been enforced if only to prevent impairment of the soldiers' martial capacities through venereal indisposition; presumably the task fell later upon the *aedile's* inspectors.

Despite all the exactions of taxes, pay-offs to inspectors and other harassments, brothelkeeping was from the start a very lucrative business. Brothels were bought and sold like any other business. An advertisement on a wall in Pompeii offers the five-year lease of a bath house and *venereum* (brothel) with nine bars and shops, owned by the Lady Julia Felix. Similar announcements must have been seen in Southwark. It was a constantly expanding business because prostitution was too deeply rooted in the Roman ethos ever to be eradicated. Moreover it was impossible to forgo the immense revenues in taxes or imperil the immense fortunes enjoyed by the great whoremasters and their landlords, amongst whom were senators and high dignitaries. Hence, as Londinium grew ever more prosperous, so did its southern satellite.

In the later Roman period Roman-British houses were built of brick, with tiled roofs and mosaic courtyards and fine pictures painted on the plastered walls. For the poor there were rows of multi-storied brick-built tenements. It is certain that the Bankside brothels would also have improved their amenities and some would have merited the description (given by a modern American madam) of being 'old-fashioned, respectable, clean and inexpensive, fit to be patronized regularly by respectable middle-class fathers of families', to pass the time away enjoyably in this otherwise dull, remote, provincial town far away from fashionable Rome.

Throughout the Roman occupation Southwark High Street was the principal road in the country and with the expanding economy, prosperity and peace, the number of travellers increased. All the way from the coast the route was lined with inns and taverns: the *hospitia* (places for hospitality), the less comfortable *diversoria* (places for turning off the roadside briefly) and *cauponiae* (low-class hostels for workers and slaves). All had one thing in common: a prostitute was available at all times. Slave girls served and entertained the customers and even bakers and cookshops had slaves for this purpose. There were also independent whores, known as *meretrices, ambulantrices* or 'night-moths' (*noctiluces*).

There were twopenny whores called *diabolares* (two obols) and even cheaper ones who would take anything from a farthing upwards. Numerous quayside inns and cookshops catered for the officers and crews of ships moored at the bank and quayside brothels slaked the sexual thirsts of matelots and merchants, for according to Pliny's *Natural History* sailors would not allow a whore on board because she would induce foul weather. If they found one on board they usually threw her overboard to drown. The all-night *popinae* (bars) also had their quotas of whores.

Throughout the four hundred years of Roman occupation a great number of ocean-going merchant vessels and warships came up the river to discharge at Queenhithe on the city side, or at the 'harbour' on the Southwark bank side, and this is perhaps the most persuasive argument in favour of the continuous existence of these whorehouses. It is perhaps not without significance that at Rome the brothel quarter was the Trastevere quarter (*trans-Tevera* – on the other side of the Tiber), thus bearing the same relationship as Southwark to Londinium.

It is a great pity that none of the graffiti such as decorated the walls of streets and brothels in Rome and Pompeii and other Roman cities will ever be found on Bankside. They would help greatly to ascertain the sort of pidgin-Latin used by Southwark's inhabitants and their equally rude and cheerful humour. The *lingua franca* of the polyglottal illiterates must have contained many words coined from German and Flemish and these may have included the origins of the commonest English word to describe sexual intercourse. Sexual activities, carried on under the *fornices* (arches) of the theatres, circuses and public places in the empire became known as 'fornication'. This was debased by the Teutons into *vokken*, and *fukken* in Dutch; into *ficken* in German and into English as 'fucking'. The Latin word *futui*, which is identical, passed into French as *foutre* and is commonly used to this day.

The historian Tacitus in his book *Germania* describes the Londinium of about AD 61 as a place with '*copia negotiatorum et commeatuum maxim celebre*' ('crowded with merchants and provisions of all sorts'). Where there were many merchants there would be many brothels. These tired and dusty travellers usually stopped near the city gates to have a wash, a meal and some drinks, then paid a visit to the nearest brothel for the other kind of refreshment. For this reason inns and brothels were usually to be found in the vicinity of the gates, just inside or outside the walls. Each would have its sign painted or sculpted over the lintel, like that of the famous *Ad Sorores IIII* (At the Four Sisters) in Rome. None such have been found on Bankside, but just across the river in Aldgate a stone architrave depicting three women, two reclining in voluptuous poses while the third, half-naked, stands by what appears to be a table, preparing a meal, was excavated in the last century.[10] This may very well have been the sign over the door of a brothel situated near the ancient Ald-gate, which is known to have existed from Roman times to guard the main route to the east.

Whether the *aedile* residing in Londinium also excercised jurisdiction over Southwark is not known, although it is most probable that he collected the taxes there as well. It cannot be regarded as certain because later it is found that the laws of London, as laid down by its governing authority, do not apply to Southwark. Southwark, being more exposed, was not easily defensible; it was burnt down and destroyed several times in its recorded history, but its destruction was never a military threat to Londinium. Its simple buildings could be quickly restored after each attack. It is also essential to remember that not until 1327 was any sort of organized government imposed on Southwark, and even then the Bankside (which was in the Bishop of Winchester's Liberty) was not included.

The Romans were soon to leave. In valediction it is apposite to record that they gave Britain and the Britons not only Roman order and civilization but also organized, legalized and institutionalized prostitution – and as a sort of bonus, venereal disease. The legions are gone, but the last gift is with us still.

NOTES

[1] Richard Lewinsohn, *History of Sexual Customs*, p. 77.*

[2] Dion Cassius, *History*, cap. 1x. 23.

[3] This jug is in the London Museum. See also J. Gwynn Griffiths, 'The Isiac Jug from Southwark', *Journal of Egyptian Archaeology*, Vol. 59, August 1973, pp. 233-6.

[4] Lanctantius (AD 260-340), *De Justitia*, Lib. I, v, p. 485.

[5] Catullus, 'Carmine', No. xxxiv, in W. H. Kelly (ed.), *Erotica*, Bohn, London, 1887.

[6] English Place Names Society, *Surrey*, Vol. XI, p. 279.

[7] Tacitus, *Annales*, Book II, p. 85.

[8] E. Ekwall, *Early London Street Names*.

[9] Zosimus, *History*, I, cap. 38, pp. 115-6.

[10] This architrave is in the Guildhall Museum.

* Where full bibliographical details are not given, they may be found in the Bibliography.

II

'Wymmon that fair & freoly is to fyke'

To reconstruct in the same manner the early Saxon period in Southwark is much more difficult because not only are Saxon remains and
artifacts almost non-existent there, but being in the main illiterate they
left no documents. Moreover, it is still a subject for debate whether
the Saxons ever occupied Londinium or Southwark or whether both
lay 'empty' during the 'missing century' after the Romano-British
forces had been beaten at the battle of Crecganford (Crayford) in
Kent in AD 457 by Hengist and Horsa, and had fled incontinently
through Southwark into Londinium, leaving the victors in control of
the riverside and in occupation of all Kent and a great part of Surrey.
This author believes that organized civilian life continued, although
at a low level, within the battered walls of Londinium until written
history begins again about 600, by which time it was reputed to be the
chief town of the East Saxons. Traffic between the various Saxon
kingdoms was sporadic and unfriendly, thus the bridgehead settlement of Southwark, whose importance during Roman times was as a
communications centre, must have suffered at the least a considerable
decline during the early years of Saxon occupation.

The incoming Jutes and Angles were not footloose raiders but
settled tribes who were being forced out of their ancient homelands
by the pressure of other Teutonic tribes.[1] Hence they were seeking
new homes and, because of the weakening of the Roman power, had
found the English coasts wide open and vulnerable, occupied only by
squabbling factions. Of course, they countered resistance with contemporary savagery, burning and slaughtering when it was necessary
and accepting bribes when it suited them not to attack. Indeed, their
later reputation for savagery may be unjust. It is impossible accurately to assess how ferocious they were or how much damage they
inflicted on civilians as distinct from their attacks on monks and
monasteries. History was written long after the events by Christian
monks lamenting the destruction of these edifices by pagans. By
contrast, the poorest elements in the British population may well have

24

welcomed the invaders as liberators, in a sense, from the harsh slavery under which they had suffered at the hands of cruel and rapacious Romano-British masters. At worst, if they became enslaved to Saxons, their new masters were not much higher in social status than they.

The Saxons had no siege artillery to overcome any defended walled town, so perhaps London remained unconquered, a quasi-independent entity surrounded by Saxon tribes. The invaders had primitive ideas of social and domestic comfort and could not comprehend the complexities of organized town life, being content with the necessities provided by the cultivation of their lands and homesteads.

Gradually, however, as conditions became more settled, London began to recover. Its natural position ensured that it would remain a commercial community and as the invaders settled in their newly-conquered lands they would have needed merchants and traders. As London recovered, then so did Southwark. There is no reason to think that the Thames was closed to ocean-going merchant vessels – the Saxon kinglets on either side of the river could control only their own frontages, and not always efficiently at that – and the 'harbours' at Queenhithe and Bankside would still have been needed, however small the volume of cargoes. Certainly by 604, according to Bede, London was 'a trading centre for many nations who visit it by land and sea.' Those coming by land from the south, and a proportion of those coming by sea, would have passed through Southwark.

What was the fate of our chief concern, the Bankside brothels, we do not know. However, we do know that during this early period brothels were unknown in northernmost Europe. Each Saxon village had its local whore, whose house was usually set aside from the main settlement. She probably drew her clientele chiefly from the older and more sedate menfolk, as well as randy youngsters and occasional strangers, although a later story mentions that husbands also had occasion to visit the *horhous*.

In the year 565, says the *Anglo-Saxon Chronicle*, 'Aethelberht succeeded to the kingdom of Kent and ruled 53 years'. The Kentish kingdom, founded by Hengist and Horsa, was the most advanced of the districts, since its rulers were influenced by the remains of Roman order and civilization and were in regular contact with their relations on the other side of the English Channel. It also included Southwark from an early time. It is measure of the degree of civilization and organization of the rulers of Kent that by 597 they had invited St Augustine to come and Christianize their subjects. With the help of King Aethelberht and his Christian wife, St Augustine quickly 'converted' the Kentish pagans, although it is doubtful whether more than a handful of these illiterates consciously knew what they were doing. A directive from their king would have been enough, on the age-old principle that when father turns we all turn. Pagans elsewhere resisted the disciplines of the new religion (the Londoners chased out Bishop Mellitus in 616 after fifteen years of his exhortations) because they found it onerous, but by about 670 this new and stricter brand of Christianity had spread all over the country; at least the kings had been Christianized and accommodation had been reached with the older forms of local British Christianity existing in the West Country.

Until the Augustinian form of the new ethic had been established the various forms of Saxon and Gothic tribal customs had had the force of law, and insofar as they concerned sexual matters one of the earliest-known, that of the Visigoths (*c.* 450),[2] provided that whores should be publicly scourged, and later, that their noses must be slit (a savage custom, be it noted, that still prevailed in this country until Hogarth's time!). In the meantime most of the German tribes had accepted the Arian form of Christianity, so that the early Gothic law[3] required that 'girls and women who were constantly incontinent', that is, whores, must be put to death.

The existence of whores and whorehouses is attested by the words for these conveniences in the earliest vocabularies; indeed the word 'whore' comes from *hore* or *hure* or more correctly *hore-cwen* (a filthy woman), whence also *hore-hus* (a brothel). The Saxons also had a simple word for intercourse, *fyken*, which basically means to breed, and sounds very familiar today, although this word could also mean flirtatious or forward behaviour of a low sexual sort.

The cucking-stool as a punishment for whores is of very early provenance, being mentioned by Tacitus[4] as prevalent among the *Teutones* about AD 100, as also was that of drawing on a hurdle and suffocation in mire and excrement. Nonetheless even these harsh tribal laws could not eradicate such breaches of custom, which were not yet a religious sin.

Saxon marriage laws were not clearly defined; wives could be bought from their fathers, or indeed elsewhere when it suited. *Troth-plight* (true pledging) permitted acceptable sexual intercourse or *haemed,* and an exchange of the *wed* at the ceremony called a *wedding* could follow at some convenient date. The *wed* was actually the payment or pledge – much later a ring – registering the sale, being a pledge for value received; the same word also meant 'wages'.[5] Lower down the scale women were literally bought and sold into marriage as well as into prostitution at the whim of their fathers. (Wives were still being sold in English provincial markets as late as 1720.)

The protagonists of the new religion did not make sexual matters easier to understand. Their attitude towards marriage was still fluid; for instance, St Augustine himself could see no difference between *copula carnis* (fleshly intercourse between man and wife), and *copula fornicatoria* (intercourse with a whore). Both were sinful. Nonetheless he had great understanding of human frailty, pleading with God: 'Give me chastity and continence, but not yet!'[6] Elsewhere in his *Confessions* he said that if prostitution were to be suppressed 'capricious lusts will overthrow society'. Incidentally this saintly man sheds light on another Saxon aberration, according to a text printed in 1493 by Wynken de Woorde: 'For seynt Austin sayeth . . . that avoutry [adultery] is greter synne than fornycacyon, and woors and more vyle is a manne to synne wythe hys owne moder then [than] wyth a nother womman.'

But Christian marriage did give women status and some sense of security, hence a very large proportion of genuine converts were women and whores.

By at least the beginning of the seventh century Southwark seems to have been thriving again. There are some ninety-seven references[7] to it during the Heptarchy (the seven Saxon kingdoms which flourished between *c.* 550-750) with mentions of wharves and ships in London in the records of the Mercian kings who controlled London and Kent at various periods. There is a possible reference to Bankside in 672 in a grant by Frithwald, King of Surrey, of land, 'a separate part of ten hides by the part of London where the ships come into land . . . on the southern side.'[8] This may refer to the inlet just east of Bankside, much later called a 'harbour' in *Domesday Book* and later still known as St Saviour's Dock. There is also a record that the joint-kings of Kent, Hlothaere and Eadric (685-686), used to issue passports for visitors to go to Lunden-wic.

The first Saxon code of law known in England is that of Aethelberht (565-616), King of Kent and *Bretwalda* (High King) of all Britain. The laws, promulgated towards the end of his reign, refer mainly to adultery, rape and incest, but curiously enough do not mention prostitution or brothels, perhaps because in the early days of the Church in England they were not crystallized as misdemeanours for punishment. The penalties for other misbehaviours are based on the older pagan customs of pecuniary compensation, such as *wergeld* and *leudgeld*.[9] Paragraph 77 confirms that women could still be bought: 'If a man buy a maiden with cattle let the bargain stand if it be without guile'; and elsewhere the *weotuma*, the bride price, is mentioned. There were distinctions between those who were *wedded* and those living together as man and wife without ceremony. One can indeed infer that if a woman could be purchased, there was little need for professional prostitutes except for those unable to raise the *weotuma*.

Older tribal practices are evident in the law that if a man 'destroyed' another's penis he had to pay a threefold compensation, but if he only 'pierced' it and otherwise left this important piece of equipment serviceable the *bote* (compensation) would be only six silver shillings.

For the next one hundred and fifty years Southwark again disappears from recorded history, but assuredly it did not escape the ravages of warring kings and the later Danish incursions, finding stability again only in the more settled years of King Aelfred's reign. Like his forebears, the young Aelfred was something of a rake. According to John of Wallingford: 'He yielded his member . . . to uncleanness and iniquity upon iniquity . . . and strove with all his might to subdue . . . virgins and those who wished to lead a chaste life.'[10] But his defeats and humiliations at the hands of the Danes seem to have given him time for reflection and repentance and a chance to gain a thorough understanding of human frailties. Thus, after his victories and his assumption of power as monarch of all England, his laws reflected many commonsense attitudes. His scales of fines still followed the principles of rank and *wergeld* and *leudgeld* – although the costs had escalated since Aethelberht's day. Law No. 42 allowed a husband to fight and kill without *orwige* (penalty) if he found a man fornicating with his wife behind closed doors, or seducing his mother, daughter or sister. Nonetheless a *theow* (slave) who raped a female slave suffered the loss of his testicles to ensure that he would not repeat the offence, while also ensuring that he could still carry on his normal tasks.

Again we find references to *hore-cwen* (pronounced 'hoor-queen') and *hore-hus*. It is a sobering reflection that *cwen* (a woman) has come to form both 'Queen' and 'quean', making the distinction between highest and lowest merely one letter.

The mildness of the English laws is in sharp contrast with those across the water in Charlemagne's kingdom. This erstwhile pagan had five lovely queens and five beautiful concubines and the lubricious happenings at his court were known far and wide. Nonetheless it was his unamiable custom occasionally to collect all the '*filles de joie*', have them stripped stark naked and make them run races through the streets while the populace was incited to revile them and pelt them with filth. (Charlemagne also gained a certain respect in ecclesiastical circles for refraining from cooked meat during Lent and from uncooked meat by sleeping alone; a 'taste for raw meat' being a euphemism for whoring.)

The long years of war and destruction must have increased the incidence of prostitution in England, as elsewhere, although perhaps not to the level of Charles the Bald (*c*. 872) who, when besieging the city of Neuss, 'had one prostitute for every four soldiers'. One corollary of Aelfred's rebuilding of London and reopening the

Thames to shipping must have been an increase in the number of quayside whorehouses north and south of the river.

Sixty years after Aelfred's death his grandson, the young Prince Eadwig, or Edwy, came to the throne under the tutelage of the bigoted and ruthless Archbishop Dunstan. The King was in fact opposed to much of the Christian dogma put forward by Dunstan, for he was a courageous and passionate – and also profligate – young man and deeply in love with his beautiful young cousin Aelgiva. He soon fell foul of the prelate. John of Wallingford narrates: 'after the coronation and celebration of the mass, the thanes and earls were sitting . . . at a grand and sumptuous feast. When they were finished eating and were at their cups . . . the king jumped up and went to his chamber for wanton purposes. The thanes waited a long time . . . at last the bishop . . . and Abbot Dunstan went to his chamber . . . they found the crown fallen from his head and the king seated between two women, one named Aethelgiva and her daughter, and the king was embracing them wantonly and shamelessly by turns.'[11]

As a result the young girl's face was seared with hot irons and she was murdered by the Archbishop's minions. Shortly afterwards the young King was ousted and killed. He was succeeded by a lad of sixteen who became King Edgar, and to quote an early chronicler,[12] 'theigh this Edgar were smal and litel of stature, yet he wolde overcome euerich man, were he euer so strong, that wolde wyth hym fyte.'

Edgar (959-975) was a strong ruler and an excellent soldier and was the first English king to maintain a long reign in peace. But he was a man of violent temper and, though he promulgated the first set of English laws based on Christian tradition, was utterly profligate sexually.

One of his more notorious exploits was the abduction and rape of the nun Eadgifu, with whom he lived in open concubinage for seven years despite the interdiction of the Church. An unknown apologist[13] tries to soften the impact by claiming that she 'was not a myncheon [nun] as people reherce but she toke the habite [of a nun] . . . for cause that this kynge Edgar hadde inordinate luffe to here, and yitte the kynge toke hys plesure of here, wherfor seynt Dunstan caused the kynge to do penaunce.'

Penaunce or no, the King carried on his sexual wilfulness to the extent of murdering his best friend because his wife's beauty had attracted the King's attention and he would not be withstood. Passing through Andover one day he was so taken by a passing girl that he demanded her body straightaway from her mother – who by a stratagem substituted a beautiful maid. On this occasion the King made the best of it and his accidental bedmate became one of his favourites.

Edgar's laws covered every aspect of the lechery he himself had committed; clearly his laws were for others, and assuredly any penances imposed on him by the wrathful Dunstan could not be as arduous as later Christian apologists would have us believe. To ensure a safe reception for his soul in the hereafter he built and endowed a large number of nunneries. To some he is known as Edgar the Peaceable, but the later Danish king of England, Canute – who is probably a reliable informant – described him as a lecherous tyrant.

Edgar's laws spell out a long and involved series of punishments for sexual offences – seventeen paragraphs are devoted to them – but on the whole they are tempered with mercy, being content with rigorous fastings and lamentations coupled, of course, with appropriate payments. They also give us many new words to describe old sins and sinners.

Whores are *cifes* or *ciefes*, the latter word also meaning a concubine. Consequently fornication is *cifeshad*, committed by a *cifesgemann* (a fornicator of either sex). The word *hore* appears occasionally with *horing* being whoredom or prostitution. Adultery was *forleat* or *forlege* and the adulterer was a *forlicger* engaged in illicit copulation, otherwise a *haemed-thing*. He was a marriage-breaker, an *aew-breca* or *spus-brycge* (spouse-breaker). An *aew-bryce* was a married woman.

Shortly after Edgar's death there is a description of *Suthvirki* in the Icelandic saga known as the *Heimskringla* (*c*. 1008)[14] wherein it is stated to be 'a very considerable trading place' linked to London by a magnificent wooden bridge wide enough to take two carts. (This is in fact only the second mention of Old London Bridge, the first having been in 975 when a poor old woman was drowned for practising witchcraft, by being thrown off the bridge.) Southwark was then occupied by the Danes who were attempting to capture London from Aethelred the Unready, and the saga describes how the bridge was pulled down, thus drowning a large number of the Danes and removing the danger.

About a hundred and fifty years prior to these events, between 850 and 860, the Bishop of Winchester, later to be St Swithin, had built a monastery in Southwark a few hundred yards from the Bankside, and this later became the nunnery of St Marie Overie. This very early connection of the Bishops of Winchester with Southwark is of considerable importance to this history, marking the first substantial edifice of stone thought to have been erected in this area.

The Danes, like the Saxons, have always had a bad press, ignoring the fact that they too were originally settled traders – indeed great merchants ranging the whole continent – clever enough to take *danegeld* to leave the English cities and English merchants alone.

They too were seeking a new homeland and taking it in the accepted traditions of the day.

The Southwark maidens would undoubtedly have been pleased to deal with the wealthy and lusty Danish soldiers – indeed in proof of Danish sophistication is the testimony of John of Wallingford. Referring to Aethelred's Danish mercenaries stationed in East Anglia, he says: '[they] caused much trouble to the natives of the land, for they were wont, after the fashion of their country, to comb their hair every day, to bathe every Saturday, to change their garments often and set off their persons with many such frivolous devices. In this manner they laid siege to the virtue of the married women, and persuaded even the daughters of the nobles to be their concubines.'[15]

The same chronicler remarks that the Danes paid dearly for these outlandish customs later on, 'for on a Saturday, when they were naked, the Saxons destroyed them . . . from the least to the greatest sparing neither age nor sex . . . some [English] women had their breasts cut off or were buried alive and their children dashed against posts and stones.'

Wooden houses burnt by the Danes in Southwark could be immediately rebuilt and there was no lack of 'living furniture' at any time. The Danes would certainly have had regard for the maintenance of any institutions of pleasurable convenience on Bankside during the lulls in the fighting; and as can be seen from the gory tale above, the customers' nationality did not concern the whores or their masters. It was the cash that counted.

Less than ten years later the Danish king, Canute, became King of England. He ascended the throne in 1016 and proved to be a strong and enlightened ruler, wise enough to make a distinction between Edgar, 'the leccherus tyraunte', and that tyrant's good laws. He declared to his English subjects at a Great Folk Moot at Oxford in 1019 that he would govern England by the laws of King Edgar. He maintained the principle of a sliding scale of fines commensurate with the degree of sin and the degree of the sinner, one of the few exceptions being for the rape of a virgin for which the offender 'forisfacet membra sua' ('had his penis cut off');[16] somewhat later he changed this to permanent exile 'because the punishment was ineffective.'

He manifested a certain sense of humour when he ruled that foreigners who refused to stop fornicating were 'to leave the country with their possessions and their sins', which is as nice a piece of ancient sophistry as can be found anywhere.

This erstwhile pagan took his Christianity seriously only when it suited his convenience and he purposely made the laws on adultery more tolerable. He was after all living in adultery himself with his

English mistress, the noble Lady Edith, who ruled his Danish kingdom loyally and with great efficiency during those periods when he cohabited with his 'wedded' English queen, Emma, widow of Aethelred the Unready.

The town of Southwark returns to written history in the collection of documents called by the historian William Maitland,[17] who discovered and collated them, the *Burghal Hideage*, a hideage being a record of the extent of the 'hides' of land within a borough. In them there is a reference to the 'head of the bridge', which must refer to the gateway on the southern side – perhaps a reminder of the ancient Roman gate at that point, and to 'a strande' which can be no other than Bankside. Indeed it is most probable that this was the time when the strand became known as Bankside, following the renewal of the wooden wharfings after the many Danish raids. In *Domesday Book* the St Saviour's Dock there is described as 'a harbour': '*de exitu aquae ubi naves applicabant*' ('the water outlet in which the ships used to moor alongside').

More important is the confirmation that Southwark was a recognized borough (a fortified village or town) and thereby already enjoyed some special privileges, partly in view of its military importance and also because of its independence of London and hence of London law. These fortifications helped to safeguard the military installations, but Southwark's civic importance was recognized by the fact that as early as 1000 there was in Southwark a well-established Saxon mint with a large output of coin of the realm.[18] Such a vital manufactury would not have been situated in an unsafe or unsettled place.

Edward the Confessor, King of England (1042-1066), owned large tracts of land in Southwark and a number of properties on the Bankside. His powerful henchman-cum-adversary Earl Godwin not only had a palace just across from London Bridge but also owned some messuages on Bankside – indeed one authority[19] says that the 'Clink belonged to Earl Godwin in 1047'. Certainly his ships and forces were anchored off Bankside during his confrontation with the King in 1052, and it is thought that one of the reasons why his 'band continually diminished the longer he stayed'[20] was because his men could not resist the temptations of the Bankside whorehouses just across from where their ships were moored.

About this time there is a very curious reference, attributed to the year 1058,[21] to a prostitute of London: 'Seated on a jaded mule, her locks falling over her shoulders, holding a little gilt rod in her hand . . . by means of indiscreet clothing she excited the travellers' attention in the high ways.' If this date is accurate, it is almost the first description of a harlot soliciting blatantly in the streets of London.

Roman architrave, *c.* AD 100-150, found in Aldgate.

The Isis jug, *c.* AD 100, found in the Thames off Bankside.

Ordinaunces Touchinge the Gouerm.te
of the Stewhoullders in Southwarke
vnder the Direction of the B.PP: of
Winchester, instituted in the Tyme of
Henrye the Second:

An Acte, or Ordynaunce was made is hereafter dj=
peareth in this Acke, in the Parliamt: condenat
holden, in the vnj: yeares of the raigne of
Kinge Henrye the Second, With all the Assent of the
Comons, And so Confyrmed by the Kinge and all
the Lordes of the Parliamt: And in the same yeare,
and tyme of Parliamt: there so holden Theo=
baldus then beinge Archbff: of Canterburye and
Thomas a Thorkett then beinge Archdeacon of the
same:

these Ordayne, and make for the Lordes Bayliffes their
Stewardes and Constitutions, to be kept for stewes
within theseid Lordshipp: and frauncrigh, Accordinge to
the oulde Customes, that hath bene vsed, and accusto=
med, tyme out of mynde, whiche nowe of late were
Altered, to the greate displeasure of God, and greate
hurte vnto the Lordes, and otter vndoinge of all the
poore Tennants their dwellinge, and also to the
greate multiplyinge of horrible sinne, vppon the
simple woemen which ought to have their free =
goinge, and Comynge, at their owne libertyes, as it
Appeareth by the oulde Customes there approbate

out yt

3 The Ordinance of 1161 for the 'Government of the Stewhoulders'. Harley MS. 293.

Edward the Confessor, the son of King Aethelred and Queen Emma, spent most of his early life in France. There, it would seem, he developed a taste for comfortable living and when he came to the throne he encouraged the importation of luxuries such as carpets, tapestries, gold and silver utensils and fine materials.[22]

No doubt some of these refinements seeped down into the whorehouses, for these were the places of relaxation and revelry for the nobility and gentry in each generation. The 'light ladies of the Bank' would be presented with the latest materials, advised of new fashions, given presents of jewellery at times and taught new phrases and habits by their foreign customers. Their premises too would have been gradually improving in structure and amenities. Not all were still built of mud and thatch; indeed some are thought to have been built of stone at a very early date.

It is impossible for a modern generation to imagine the lives of men and women in these 'dark ages' of Anglo-Saxon development. The social structure was sharply differentiated and the status of women varied considerably according to station. There were great and independent noblewomen, freedwomen, and a mass of slave women. The whores were still mainly slaves and their treatment was in sharp contrast with the respect ostensibly shown to the high-born free women, whose names reflect a certain degree of culture. For example, Eadburga: Citadel or Fortress of Happiness; Eadgythe (Edith, a very popular name): the Gift of Happiness; Elfgiva: the Gift of the Fairies; Elfthrida: the Strength of the Fairies, meaning high spiritual and moral character; and perhaps the best known of all, Godiva (Godgiva): the Gift of God.

The Anglo-Saxons seem also to have possessed some knowledge of sexually-transmitted diseases. There is a manuscript in the Leningrad Museum written about AD 800 entitled *de Mulieram Affectibus* (Of Women's Diseases) which is thought to be included in the compilation of the Saxon *Leechbook of Bald* (*c.* 900-950),[23] which includes much older medical material and is more than simple magic and folklore.

Dr F. Buret[24] refers to a Swiss MS dated before AD 1000, *de Curruptione Omnium Statuum et Imminente Interitu Mundi* (On the General Corruption and Imminent Destruction of the World) which contains the phrase *'et leprosa sodomorum tertient contagione'* ('the disease of Sodom is highly infectious') and is of the opinion that it refers to venereal disease rather than the moral cancer of the spread of sodomy.

The *Saxon Leechdoms*[25] contain a number of 'Recipes' which appear to refer to venereal diseases. There are 'Leechdoms for the perilous disease', 'Leechdoms against the evil blotch', 'Leechdoms against lust' and 'Leechdoms for the "fig" disease'. There are leechdoms advising '. . . how the *congressus sexuum* is not holesom for a dry body . . . swiving [copulation] most severely hurteth them who have the disease of foul humours.' A reference to the 'vlesshly lues' (fleshly contagion) perhaps refers to syphilis.

Some of these leechdoms, especially those connected with female illnesses, appear quite disgusting to the modern observer; for example a 'recipe' to induce menstruation requires: '. . . take as fresh horses tord, lay it on hot gledes, make it reek strongly between the thighs up under the raiment that the woman may sweat much.'

One such leechdom which conceivably would have been useful to the future clients of Bankside was that 'against women's chatter . . . a root of radish at night; that day the chatter shall not harm thee.' It is instructive that the old leeches were reduced to making the man deaf rather than attempting to curb the tongues of the chatterers.

Even in those early days there was close contact between English and Continental leeches. The best-known practitioners of the medical sciences were the Jewish physicians from the famous school at Salerno in Italy. Some of these would undoubtedly have been called in to attend to the later Saxon and Danish kings.[26] Some would certainly have had knowledge of venereal diseases and some idea as to treatment; later there were to be several practising in Southwark.

The only specific reference to whores in this later Saxon period is in King Edmund's Laws (939-946) but a better evidence of their existence in many Saxon cities, including London, is a street with the unmistakable Saxon provenance of 'Gropecuntelane'.

When the Confessor died in 1066 his successor King Harold Godwinsson was defeated at Senlac, near Hastings in Sussex, and killed. The fleeing remnants of his army were chased as far as the gates of London by five hundred of William of Normandy's cavalry, who, being turned back by the grim hosts of Londoners, 'burnt Southwark to the ground'. This probably means that they destroyed all the buildings, such as the inns, churches and houses lining the High Street; it is highly unlikely that they would have then wasted time in destroying the Bankside *maisons de débauche*. With the coming of the Normans and their Flemish mercenaries the Bankside is about to enter written history and enjoy notoriety – if not exactly fame – for another five hundred years.

NOTES

1 Bede, *Historia Ecclesiastica*, Lib. I, 15.

2 David Wilkins, 'Lex Visigothoria' in *Leges Eadgari*, Lib. III, cap. 18.

3 Ibid., 'Constitutiones regni Seculi', Tit. xlviii.

4 Tacitus, *De Germania*.

5 Old Teutonic *wadjom*, cognate with Latin *vadvas*, a pledge or surety, or Latin *vadium*; eventually through *gage* to *wage*, a payment for services rendered.

6 St Augustine, *Confessions*, Lib. 8, cap. 7: '*da mihi castitatem et continentiam, sed noli modo.*'

7 Ralph Lindsay, *Etymology of Southwark*.

8 Benjamin Thorpe, *Ancient Laws and Institutes*, Vol. I.

9 Ibid.

10 John of Wallingford, *Chronicle*, in Joseph Stevenson (ed.), *Church Historians of England*, Vol. II, p. 539.

11 John of Wallingford, *Historia Britannicae-Saxonicae* (ed. Thomas Gace), quoted in Stevenson op. cit.

12 Ranulph Higden, *Polychronicon* (ed. J. R. Lumby).

13 Harley MS. 2261, British Museum.

14 Snorre Sturlasson, *Olaf Saga*, translated by R. M. Perkins.

15 John of Wallingford, in Stevenson, op. cit., p. 558.

16 William Alexander, *History of Women*, Vol. I, p. 233.

17 William Maitland, *History of London*.

18 R. H. M. Dolley, 'Notes on the Anglo-Saxon Mints in Sudbury and Southwark to the time of Aethelred II', *British Numismatic Journal*, Vol. 8, 1955-7, pp. 264-9.

19 M. Concanen and A. Morgan, *History and Antiquities of St Saviour's Southwark*.

20 *Anglo-Saxon Chronicle*, E.E.T.S. Orig. Ser. 208.

21 Walter de Hemingburghe, *Chronica*, cited by G. F. Fort, *History of Medical Economics*.

22 See Thomas Wright, *Vocabulary of Anglo-Saxon English*.

23 MS. Royal 12 D xvii, British Museum.

24 F. Buret, *Syphilis in Ancient and Prehistoric Times*, Vol. II, p. 81.

25 T. O. Cockayne (ed.), *Leechdoms Wortcunnings & Starcraft of Early England*.

26 One wonders whether the curious reference forbidding Christians to fraternize with ('*convivia eorum particiare*') Jews, dated about 730, made by the Archbishop of York, concerns Jewish Physicians (see *Archaeologia*, Vol. VIII, p. 390). The only other Jews in England at the time could have been Jewish slave-traders, whose activities in Europe in this period are noted by Joseph Jacobs in his *The Jews in Angevin England*.

III

William the Bastard Conquers England

Duke William of Normandy's army consisted of some twelve thousand men, of whom half were Norman cavalry and the rest Flemish and other mercenaries. Their military services were to be paid for in lands won from the conquered. By his conquest, William became the sole master and sole owner of all property in England. Labelling all those who had supported Harold as traitors who must forfeit their estates, he began his confiscations immediately.

Writing five hundred years later, John Howes[1] gives a vivid description of this time: 'It appeareth that ymeadtly afftre the Conquest the people of the lande were so oppressed by ransomes ffynes Taxes & spoyles that they were not able to satysfie the desyer of the hungrye ravenynge Normans, whoe subdued them by such tyrranye that all the Wealthe of the lande was to lyttel to satysfie theire gredye desyre. Whervppon the Lande was pestred withe a multitude of ydell people & yt was longe before they could be suppressed.'

The historian Maitland[2] states that the Normans were as cruel as the Anglo-Saxons and the Danes, 'lopping-off hands and feet, gouging out the eyes of rebels, and massacring whole populations.' By the time they had finished, half of northern England lay devastated and depopulated. Even while he was being crowned at Westminster on Christmas Day 1066, William's followers were burning down houses of English citizens outside. However, by an astute arrangement with the rich oligarchs of the City of London, William granted them a new Charter, confirming the City's ancient rights, granting all burgesses 'both French and English [to be] all law-worthy . . . as in the days of King Edward . . . that every child shall be his father's heir.'

Having thus neutralized the only formidable bastion – and building the Tower of London next-door to be doubly sure – William was secure. He commissioned the *Domesday Book* to show every last animate and inanimate thing within his new domain. It was done with extreme thoroughness; significantly, London was exempted. However *Domesday Book* does contain some nuggets of useful infor-

36

mation touching on Southwark and Bankside. The Bankside properties and the monastery belonging to Edward the Confessor have already been noted, but in addition there were sixteen messuages on the Bankside which brought the Crown eighteen shillings and twopence a year.

There was a considerable revenue from tolls on the vast catches of herrings landed on the bank, and there must also have been customs dues paid by visitors landing at the wharves. *Domesday Book* states: 'The men of sudwerche testify that in the time of King Edward no one received toll on the strande or bank of the river ["*le strande vel in vice aque*"] except the king.' An indication of how considerable a sum this could be is the disclosure that 'Count Eustace had to pay for his fifteen houses in Suduuerca six shillings and two thousand herrings.' William also secured the properties of his arch-enemy Earl Godwin.

What sort of man was the new ruler? He was certainly hard and cruel, but he was not sexually profligate. According to one account,[3] however, he did own some brothels in Rouen; this would not have occasioned any comment then or afterwards, but it does demonstrate that even a chaste Christian king thought nothing of owning houses of prostitution.

Perhaps the most penetrating portrait is that by William of Malmesburie:[4] 'He [William] was of just stature, of ordinary corpulence & of a fierce countenance; his forehead was bare of hair. . . . He was majestic whether sitting or standing, although the protuberance of his belly deformed his royal person. . . . His anxiety for money is the only thing on which he can deservedly be blamed: this he sought all opportunities of scraping togther he cared not how, and he would say or do . . . almost anything . . . where hope of some money allured him.'

The pickings were enormous. He began to parcel out the loot to his friends and relations and then to his knights and Flemish mercenaries. In this way freebooters became landed nobility overnight, with all English men and women to prey on without let or hindrance. Only Londoners were relatively secure.

Large estates in Southwark, as well as the earldom of Kent, went to William's half-brother Bishop Odo of Bayeux. In 1090 Odo passed these estates on to the Abbot of the Priory of Bermondsey, and he in turn, in 1107 granted to the Bishop of Winchester the stretch of land along the waterside, extending to the end of Bankside, at a rental of eight pounds a year. The worthy and pious Bishop Gifford of Winchester clearly knew what he was leasing. It was the responsibility of the *hlaford* (lord of the manor) to administer ecclesiastical correction to the 'light-tayled huswives of the bank' for the sins of *cifeshad* (fornication) and whoredom, as well as overseeing the 'light' houses themselves. And Bishop Gifford had now become the *hlaford*.

It is possible that this particular responsibility had begun in the days of St Swithin of Winchester, whose monastery had been built in this area in the ninth century. It was near the site of this monastery that Bishop Gifford began to build his great new palace, which was to be finished in 1127.

Under his new palace Gifford would have had built a place of confinement for recalcitrant priests, or for petty malefactors sentenced thereto by the Bishop's own Courts leet. Much later, this 'prison lying under the Manor House of the Bishop of Winchester' became known as 'The Clink'.

These estates were later to become known as 'the Liberty of the Bishops of Winchester'; indeed they may have been so designated even at this early date, but contemporary records are lost. The bishops began to alienate many plots in this new domain almost immediately, but they continued to collect the ground rents (with a brief interruption by Henry VIII) until the time of Charles II. They also collected the fines and fees from the brothel licensees paid into and through their Courts leet, as well as such profitable side-lines as indulgences and couillages. Thus they cannot be exonerated for their part in the organization of this sin against their own Christian dogma.

For the better and more efficient accounting of his vast new revenues, William brought over from Rouen a number of his Jewish financial advisers and administrators. They were to play an impressive and vital part in the establishment of the nation's commerce, internally and externally, albeit that at all times they were the king's chattels and all the wealth they amassed was eventually the king's. They were the petty usurers for the arch-usurer, the king, and, of course, they attracted the obloquy and hatred for his activities.

Whereas the economics of Anglo-Saxon England were too primitive to be able to utilize the Jews' financial acumen, the new feudal situation required experienced financiers with international connections. These French Jews helped to maintain the spread of learning and of some of the sciences to William's new dominions. They were, it would seem, not unconnected with the special business (naturally on the king's behalf) which is the subject of this book.

In 1087, King William died prematurely from a ruptured stomach[5] which his 'vast belly' (he had grown enormously fat during his reign) suffered when his horse jumped suddenly and thrust him hard into the high pommel of his saddle.

His son, William Rufus, so-called because 'he was a thickset corpulent man with a ruddy complexion,'[6] was crowned at Westminster on 9 September, 1087. He was then about thirty years old. He was a man of vastly different character to his father and in many respects more broadminded and tolerant. He has been greatly traduced by the Church historians but his real spirit is inadvertently shown by a vignette from William of Malmesburie, intending of course to denigrate: 'at home and at table he gave loose to levity and mirth. He was a most facetious railer at anything he had done amiss . . . and made it a matter for jest. He knew not how to judge the value of goods.'

He was in fact an atheist and not only mocked his churchmen but had the effrontery to compare them with his Jews, and even once encouraged a debate during which he appeared to support the Jews' arguments, thus inciting the churchmen to a frenzy. 'In William's day', says William of Malmesburie, 'the Jews of Rouen and London stood erect before the princes of the land.' The King was refreshingly cynical, as is evidenced by his reply to Bishop Lanfranc when accused of going back on his word: 'Who can be expected to keep *all* his promises?'

William Rufus was vain, often bad-tempered and given to blasphemy; his favourite pastimes were hunting and military exercises. He and his court were licentious to a degree hitherto unknown in England, and he exasperated his detractors by his foppish dress, which was aped by the gilded youth in his court, who spent their nights in revelling, dicing and loose talk, and their days in sleeping. On this account he was accused of sodomy although there is no evidence of it beyond the fact that he had no known mistresses and fathered no bastards. He was a strong ruler, and thus did not endear himself to his barons. From such a monarch, the Bankside houses of prostitution had nothing to fear.

Such was the hatred of the Church and the barons against him, that it came as no surprise when he was murdered by an arrow shot into his back while he was hunting in the New Forest. His brother Henry, who was also in the forest at the time and who was assuredly privy to the assassination (if he had not actually connived at it), rushed to seize the throne – incidentally usurping the right of his older brother Duke Robert. William was buried in the Old Minster at Winchester 'without religious rites because he was regarded as a sodomite'.

Henry had no cause for self-righteousness. A sexual profligate of no mean order, he had at least six mistresses and some sixteen illegitimate children.[7] 'Others attribute to him three gross vices: avarice . . . cruelty [in that he plucked out the eyes of his kinsman the Earl of Morton] . . . and wantonness, for like Salomon he was perpetually enslaved by female seductions.'

Another contemporary[8] describes him as 'of middle stature, his hair was black but scanty near the forehead . . . he was facetious in proper season . . . [he was] not prone to personal combat, [saying] "My mother bore me to be a commander, not a soldier".'

Some insight into Henry's attitude both to the Church and to sexual matters can be gained by an examination of his handling of the controversial matter of *cullagium*. The Concilium Juliobonens had passed an ordinance in 1080 on the celibacy of priests, which commanded '*ordere propter eorum femmes nulla pecunia emendatur exigatur*' (that no money was to be exacted in respect of women being kept by priests). Priests, though technically celibate, were in the habit of keeping *focarii* or 'hearth girls'. These *focarii* were also known as concubines – *meretrix foco assideus* (fire-tending whores) – who lived in the priest's house and kindled other fires as well. The licences required by the priests to keep *focarii* were known as *cullagium*, or in England *couillages*.

In 1129 Henry I held a Great Council in London to confirm the banning of *focarii*, as agreed beforehand with Archbishop William of Canterbury, Archbishop Thurston of York and all their Suffragan bishops. The King agreed to ensure the correct fulfilment of the ordinance of 1080. The King, however, had realized immediately that here was a potential source of immense revenue and it is scarcely surprising to read that 'he deceived the archbishops and took money from innumerable priests and allowed them to keep their *focarii* and this deception was not only clear, but depressed his subjects.'[9] It also depressed the archbishops.

The Bankside brothels remained free from Henry's interference though. In the next year, 1130, there appears in a very rare document, a single surviving Pipe Roll,[10] a passage which mentions that dane-geld was still being collected, expressed in units of five hides 'for Sudewerca', which is also described as a 'borough'. This is a most important discovery because it establishes that as a borough South-wark still had the special rights of asylum, so that the Bankside brothels were in a certain sense *hors de la loi* – a vital factor in their survival. Certainly Henry left them alone; perhaps the collection of moneys for paying off non-existent Danish raiders compensated him instead of a levy on the whores.

Henry's other vice was gluttony. It was to prove fatal: he died in 1135 from a surfeit of poisoned lampreys. The unlucky surgeon who performed the post-mortem remarked on the stench from the King's body, and himself died shortly afterwards from an infection.

King Stephen's reign began as it was to continue, inauspiciously. The *Anglo-Saxon Chronicle* relates that there was nothing but strife and evil, for when the nobles saw that the King was a good-humoured, kindly, easy-going man 'who inflicted no punishments', they committed all manner of crimes and 'inflicted unspeakable tortures on the people and caused thousands to starve to death. . . .

Never did a country endure greater misery, and never did heathen act more vilely than they [the nobles] did.'

The Crusades had begun in 1097, but not until Stephen's reign were English men conscripted into this senseless slaughter. In consequence great numbers of widows and orphans augmented the multitude already caused by the English barons' carnage. The ranks of prostitutes swelled mightily and the numbers of *focarii* multiplied out of all proportion. So great was the destitution and degradation of the womenfolk in this era that at the great medieval fairs, according to Walter de Hemingburghe,[11] 'women of doubtful virtue abounded. Actresses, joculatores [female minstrels], laundresses . . . were all regarded as prostitutes. The price was a packet of lace-needles.'

It was calculated at this time that there were seven women to every man. The number of destitute women was also increased by the ecclesiastical laws ordering married priests to put away their wives and practise strict celibacy. These women had no other choice than to become *focarii* or ambulant whores. A few of the wealthier ones went into nunneries, but as they entered from compulsion and not from conversion, and were in the main sophisticated women, some of these religious sanctuaries soon became quasi-brothels.

These civil wars and the Crusades brought an epidemic of venereal disease, most probably syphilis. Dr Buret says that there were syphilis epidemics in England in the years 542, 945 and 1160.[12] It is to be noted that by 1130 the bishops of Winchester were already administering a set of rules in some Bankside brothels, one rule providing heavy penalty for any woman found suffering from the *nephandam infirmitatem* (the filthy disease), the first time it is mentioned in England. It is thought to be the same as the 'burning sickness', otherwise syphilis.

In 1154 Henry II, the grandson of Henry I, ascended the throne. The first of the Norman line to speak English, he was a highly intelligent and efficient administrator of both his English and Norman domains, but like his grandfather and great-grandfather his lust for money was overpowering. He was the first to adopt the name of Plantagenet. As to the man himself, Sir Richard Baker[13] says that 'he was somewhat red of face and broad-chested, short of body and fat therewithal. . . . His incontinency was not so much that he used other women besides his wife but he used the affianced wife of his own son.' The chronicler Holinshed is more outspoken: 'He was oute of mesure given to fleshly lust, for not contented with the use of his wife he kept many concubines; but namely he delighted most in the company of a damsel whom he called "Rose of the World" – the common people called her Rosamund – for her passing beauty being verily a rare and precise piece in those days.'[14]

She was in fact Rose, the daughter of Walter Lord Clifford, and she bore Henry two sons before she was poisoned by the jealous Queen Eleanor. Not that Eleanor was any better in terms of morality than her husband. She is supposed to have yielded her maidenhead first to the Earl Marshal. She finally departed to the Holy Land, where, says Sir Richard Baker, 'she carried herself not very holily but led a licentious life . . . the worst of which was . . . carnall familiarity with a Turk.'

The King spent much of his time in France, where his responsibilities included organizing his own whorehouses in Rouen. Thus he cannot have been totally unprepared when his attention was drawn to the Bankside Stewes in 1161. By the ordinance which he then issued he gave Southwark's brothels a status and protection which they were to enjoy for some four hundred years.

The original ordinance has not survived but three copies exist, all of much later date. The oldest, and most complete, is that in the Bodleian Library in Oxford. The two manuscripts in the British Museum follow the terms of the ordinance fairly closely; both are of a later date, one, the Harley MS. 1877 probably about 1580 and the other, the Harley MS. 293, about 1600 or a little later, judging by the calligraphy, in both cases a Tudor secretarial handwriting.

The Harley MS. 1877 is headed: 'HERE FOLLOWETH the custumaries of the said Lordship made of olde tyme in Articles wh'ought to be enquired of att every Court holden w'in the Manoir and Lordshipp of Southwark appertaining to the Bishopp of Winchester and his successors.'

All the subsequent conditions are set out but not in the same order as in the earlier Bodleian manuscript. All the Latin rubrics are faithfully rendered but not all of the subsequent meetings of the Great Court leet. The most significant addition is the final phrase: 'These Art[icles] for th'ordering of the Stue[s] began thus "To the honour of god and accordyng to the laudable custumes of the Lande".'

Here it is made clear that there were customary regulations made in very ancient days by the Church for the control of these Bankside brothels, which were dealt with by the Bishop's own Courts leet, the records of which have unfortunately not survived. More important, however, is the reference to 'the laudable custumes of the Lande', which not only discounts the hypocritical excuse about God's honour but infers that similar institutions were to be found elsewhere in the kingdom.

The Harley MS. 293, which is written in a very fine hand, bears the title 'Ordinaunces touching the Gouerm.te of the Stewhoulders in Southwarcke vnder the Direction of the Bpp of Winchester instituted in the Tyme of Henrye the Second.'

It then follows faithfully the paragraphs and wordings of the Bodleian manuscript, except that the scribe felt that the Latin rubrics were not needed, and after carefully inscribing in capital letters the first rubric, he omits all the rest. Of course, by that time (*c.* 1600) the regulations were officially dead, and all laws and proclamations were being issued in English. (There is however reason to believe that until about 1603 some of the ancient terms were included in leases granted by Lord Hunsdon to bawds in Paris Gardens.)

The Bodleian MS. e MUS 229 is a proper copy of the original. It was written early in the reign of Edward IV [15] for it includes amendments made in the thirty-seventh year of Henry VI (1459). It also contains the texts of the questionnaires to be answered respectively by the brothelmaster and the whore on the occasion of the regular inspections by the bailiff. All these questions are based upon the paragraphs of the ordinance and are clearly meant as cross-checks.

Each paragraph is in English, but is usually headed by a Latin rubric. At the end of the document is a record of a series of Great Courts leet held between 1422 and 1461 – all in the reign of Henry VI – dealing with administrative methods designed to ensure justice and prevent corruption on the part of the bailiffs, constables and other court officials, and also to prevent collusion between the officials and the denizens of the brothels. These were meetings of the Great leet; the ordinary leets were held at intervals of about a month and summarily disposed of the usual petty misdemeanours and infractions of the ordinance. Unfortunately none of their records before the thirteenth century have survived.

These regulations are for the first time set out here in full. The originals are inscribed on parchment leaves written in the old English script and have been bound into a small book which is catalogued MS. e MUS 229 in the Bodleian Library at Oxford. The first few leaves deal with ecclesiastical matters unrelated to the ordinance, and these pages have been omitted here. Some of the paragraphs have Latin rubrics and these have been included where they occur, and they infer that the original customaries of the Church were written in Latin and then translated so that the brothelkeepers and the prostitutes could understand them.

For easy reference the author has numbered each rule although in the original they are not so numbered. Also, to aid comprehension the archaic phrasing and some of the words in some paragraphs have been reconstructed into modern English without, however, affecting the meaning.

'THIS acte and ordinaunce was made as here aftir apperith in this boke in the Parliament holden in Westminster in the viii yere of the reigne of kyng henri the secund by all the assent of the Comons And so confermyd by the kyng and all the lordes of the seid Parliament and in the same yere and tyme of Parliament there so holden Theobaldus than beyng Archbisshop of Caunterbury And Thomas Beket than beyng archideacon of the same.

WE ordeyne and make to the seid lordys avayle dyvers ordinaunces and constitutions to be kept for evermore within the seid lordship and fraunchise accordyng to the olde custumes that hath ben usyd and accustomed there oute of tyme of mynde which nowe of late were broken, to the gret displesuir of god and gret hurte unto the lorde And utter undoyng to al hys poire tenaunts there dwellyng and also to the gret multiplicacion of orrible synne with the syngle women which ought to have theire free goyng and comyng atte theire owne libertees as it apperith by the olde custumes thereof afore made oute of tyme of mynde for theschewyng [the eschewing] of thise inconvenientes and of alle othir inconvenientes and of alle othir therof comynge.

1. FIRST therfore we ordeyne and make accordyng to the seid olde custumes conteyned in the custumary That there be no steweholder nor his wife let not [prevent] no single woman to go and come atte alle tymes when thei list [when she wishes] And as ofte tyme as thei [do] to the contraire to forfaite to the lorde atte every courte holden within the seid lordship when thei be presented by the constables there [in the sum of] iii*s* iiii*d* [three shillings and fourpence].

2. ALSO WE ordeyne and make that there shal no gret housholder shal kepe no women to borde but that they be voyded [sent away] bytwene this and Whitsontide nowe next comyng after the date of this present writing uppon payne to lese [of losing] to the seid lorde atte every defaut so made C*s* [one hundred shillings].

3. ALSO WE ordeyne and make that no gret housholder kepe opyn his dores uppon no halydayes [holy days] accordyng to the olde custumes and custumarie nother [neither] to kepe non of theire women within their houses ayenst [against] their wylle uppon the peyne of L*s* [fifty shillings].

4. ALSO WE ordeyne and make that the bayllif of the seid fraunchise for the tyme beyng shal see all the single women voyded every halyday oute of the lordship aforeseid accordynge to the olde custume theruppon made And that he begynne in the same so for to do onthishalf [shall start to evict them by reason of the old custom] the fest of Whitsontide nowe nexte comyng uppon payne of x*li* [ten pounds] to be forfayted to the seid lorde And if any stewe holder or hys wife lette hym [try to stop the bailiff] that than thei and either of them to be brought in to the prison and to forfayte unto the seid lorde

xl*s* [forty shillings].

5. ITEM WE ordeyne and make that the Baillif and Constables of the
same fraunchise iiii tymes in the yeir that is to sey every quarter
once shal make a due serche in every gret house if there be any syngle
woman founde and kept there ayenst her wille that wolde borde and
leve her synne and never come there no more. Hit shalbe than lefull
[it will then be lawful] to the seid bayllif and constables and other
honest men of the seide lordship to avoyde [eject] the seide women
oute of the seide lordship withoute any lette [hindrance] or intirupcion
[interference] of any gret housholder or of his wife for any manner
accion cause or any matter ayenst them or any of them to be taken or
commensid in any wise [no action may be taken against the official or
the honest men for any reason whatsoever, in such case when carrying out their official function].

6. ITEM WE ordeyne and make [known] that there shal no gret housholder lene [lend] nor trust to noo single woman above the summe
of vi*s* viii*d* [six shillings and eightpence] and if they or any of them do
the contrari thereof than [then] their accion or accions condempna-
cion and condempnacions thereof shal utterly stonde voide and
annullid accordyng to the olde custume thereof hadde and made [if
any stewholder contravenes this, any action or complaints will be null
and void].

7. ITEM WE ordeyne and make that noo man or woman dwellyng
withynne the seid lordship and fraunchise of what degree so ever
he or they be of [no matter what their status] shal not commense nor
take noone accion ne processe none ayenst other no no matter ne
cause in noon court of the kyng but only withynne the seid lordis
court and there to be determined and endid without matters recevyng
oute of the seid court that hit be uppon an obligacion above the
summe of xl*s* [nobody may start an action or process in any claim concerning more than forty shillings in the lord's court] uppon the peyne
of forfayting to the seid lorde atte every tyme that they or any of them
so do to the contrary to that byhalf x*li* [ten pounds].

8. *Quod sit uxor lotrix & hostilarius vir in hospicio t'm et no' plures*
FIRST that noo stewholder that holdeth and kepeth any stewhous
have nor kepe any woman dwellyng with hym buth hys wif and a
wasscher and a man to [be] his ostiler and noo woman for hostiler.

9. *Quod xiiij denar' solvend' qualt.septimana pro cam*[era] *cinuslt'
mulieris*
ITEM that the women that ben at comon bordell be seyn every day
[for] what they be: an a woman that liveth by hir body to come and to
go so that she pay her duete [so long as she pays her dues she must be
free to come and go] as olde custume is, that is for to say for every
woke[week] xiiij*d* [fourteen pence] for hir chambre at alle tymes [and]

shal have fre [free] licence and liberte without any interupcion of the steweholders.

10. *Quod hiis q' retinent aliquos in domibus suis ppt' debita*

ITEM if any of theym that holdeth any stewehous tary [restrains] any man agains his wille withynne his hous as prysonner for any dette that he owyth to hym or for any other cause but if the stewholder bring suche personnes to the lordes prisonne [he must take the man to the prison] as the lawe wol [requires] there for to answere as the court wol awarde to every partie that wol say anythynge, agains hym. He that otherwise doth shal pay xxs [twenty shillings] at every tyme and as often as he weketh [weakens] this ordinaunce.

11. *Quod mulieribus religiosis et uxor' non recipiend' in hospiciis stuffar'*

ITEM that no steweholder receyve any woman of religious or any mannes wif if it be knowe but that thei do the lord' officers to wete [must inform the court officials] under payne of xij*d* [twelve pence] [if] suche defaulte is founde.

12. *Quod mulieribus que secrete vellent custodiri quasi incogniti*

ITEM if an woman come on to this lordshep and wold be kept privee withynne and it be not the steweholders wil, thei shal doo the officers for to wite [they must inform the officials] upon the peine of xls [forty shillings] and the same woman shal be take [arrested] and made a fyne of xxs [twenty shillings] and be lette [put] thries upon de cokyngestoele [thrice on the cucking-stool] and than forswere the lordship.

13. *Quot hiis qui habent bona alicinus in custodia & noluerunt reddere ea*

ITEM if any man come into this lordship to any stuehous and lette [leaves behind] any harneys [harness – bandolier, sword, buckler etc.] with the wif or with the hostiler [ostler] or any other woman therein that he must have deliveraunce of his harneys agayn at his goynge or elles de goodman [gentleman] brenge the hostiler of the woman that hath withdrawe it [that withholds it] to prison and same [hold at disposal] the herneys to my lord and make gree [reach agreement] with the partie.and if the hostiler or the woman goo awey with the herneis the goodman shal answere therfore [the gentleman will be held responsible] and make a fyne of xxs [twenty shillings].

14. *Quot mulieres que attrahunt homines per vestimenta vel aliter*

ITEM if any woman of the bordel lette any man [hinder any man] but sit stille at the dore and lette hym go or come chese [choose] whither they wol [wherever he wishes] or if she drawe any man by hys gowne or bi his hod or by any other thynge she shal make a fyne to the lord of xxs [twenty shillings].

15. *Quod uxoribus custodiencui stufas que simili modo attrahunt homines*

ITEM if ther be any stueholders wif that draweth any man in to hir hous without his wil, hir husbond and she shal be amercyed [fined] to the lord in xl*s* [forty shillings].

16. *Quod impedibientus officiar' facere septimat'im scrutinia sua*

ITEM that the lordes officers that is for to wete [that is to say] the constables bailly and sturbeour [court warden] every woke [week] whanne theym shal like best shal serche every hous in the stues an if any man or woman lette theym [stop them] he or she shal be amercyed unto the lord in C*s* [one hundred shillings].

17. *Quod hiis qui h[ab]ent mulieres ad mensam contra consuetudinem*

ITEM that no stueholder holde any woman that lyveth by hir body to borde [board] but thei go to borde ellis where theym list [must be allowed to board wherever they wish] upon peyne of xx*s* [twenty shillings] at every time that this ordinance be broke.

18. *Qd' hiis qui non custodiunt horas sua' diebus fest' in absencia*

ITEM that no woman be founde withynne the lordship on holy dayes from Michelmesse unto Candelmesse aftyr viii of the clokke by the morwe [after 8 a.m.] unto xi of the clokke at noon [11 a.m.] and that they be voided [ejected] at i of the clokke aftyr noon [1 p.m.] unto v of the clokke at nyght [5 p.m.] uppon the peyne contayned in custume of the manoir: and from Michelmesse unto Candelmesse that thei be not founde ther on halydayes [holy days] from vi of by the morwe [6 a.m.] unto xi of the clokke at noon [11 a.m.] and thanne be voyded by i of the clokke aftyr noon [1 p.m.] and not come there unto vi of the clokke at night [6 p.m.] uppon the same peyne.

19. *Qd' mulieres qui habent pprios amasios suos contra consuetudinem*

ITEM if there be any woman that livyth bi hir body holde any paramour agains the use and custume of the manoir she shal be iii wokes [weeks] in the pryson and make a fyne of vj*s* viij*d* [six shillings and eightpence] and than be sette oones [once] on the Cukstole [cucking-stool] and forswere the lordship.

20. *Quod mulieribus que filificant contra consuetudinem*

ITEM if therbe any woman that liveth by hir body that spinneth or cardeth with the stueholder or elles cast any stone or make any contenaunce [makes a face or grimace] to any man goyng by the wey out by wator or by land she shal make a fyn of iii*s* iiii*d* [three shillings and fourpence].

21. *Quod mulieres que obiurgat' contra consuetudinem*

ITEM if ani woman that liveth by hir bodi chide with any man or make a fray, she shal be in prison iii dayes and iii night.and make a fyne of vi*s* viii*d* [six shillings and eightpence].

22. *Qd' hiis qui custodiunt hostia sua aperta diebus festivalibus*

ITEM if any stueholder open his dore on hooly dayes from the tyme of matyns onto noon, or from ii of the clokke at after noon [2 p.m.] unto betwix v and vi agains night. [until 5 or 6 p.m.] he shall be amercyed [fined] at every time that that default is founde.

23. *Qd' mulieribus no' absentibus per noctem tempore parliamenti*

ITEM if any woman be founde withynne the lordship after the sonne is goo to rest [sunset] the kynge beynge at Westminster and holdyng there outher [either] parliament or Counseill, unto the sonne be uppe uppon the morwe [dawn] after the custume of the Manoir, she shal make a fyne at every tyme she so doth of vj*s* viij*d* [six shillings and eightpence].

24. *Qd' Officiar' qui concelat aliqua Premissory*

ITEM if any officer such as constable borsholder [purse-holder or treasurer] or bailly consele any of the defaultes above rehercyd [set out] buth that thei present theym at every [and if they fail to present them] court.Suche offycer shal be put in ward and kept in prisonne unto the tyme that he make a fyn at the lord' wil [as the Lord of the Manor may decide].

25. *Qd' hiis qui capiunt hostilar ultra dimidium annu' contra con-suetudinem*

ITEM if any stueholder take any hostiler [ostler] in any wise lenger than from half yere unto half yere with raisonnable hire for his service he shal make a fyn to the lord of xx*s* [twenty shillings].

26. *Qd' Officiar' qui permittunt aliquos ad ballium vel manucap-cionem*

ITEM that no constable Borsholder nor bailly lette any man or woman to baille maynprise or ondirborwe [not to allow bail, main-prise or release against security from a third party] but bringe hym to the lordes place to prysonne like as thei owe for to do [as is their duty] upon the peyne of lesynge [losing] as often tyme as thei so doo vi*s* viij*d* [six shillings and eightpence].

27. *Qd' mulieribus que racapiunt argentum ad concubend' cum viris et no fac'*

ITEM if any woman take any monee to lye with any man but she ly stille with hym [if she takes his money she must stay with him] til it be the morwe tyme [next morning] and thanna arise [if she does not do so] she shal make a fyn of vi*s* viij*d* [six shillings and eightpence].

28. *Qd' hiis qui tenent vel occupant batellas contra consuetudinem*

ITEM if any stueholder holde or occupie any bote in any maner wise agains the custume of the manoir.he shal make a fyn of vi*s* viij*d* [six shillings and eightpence].

29. *Quod mulieribus custodientibus stufas et non habentibus viros*

ITEM if any sengle woman holde or kepe any stuehous wythynne the lordship agayns the custume of the manoir.she shal at everi cort make a fyn of xxs [twenty shillings] unto the tyme that it be reformed.

30. *Qd' mulieribus impregnat' invent infra aliquas stufas*

ITEM that no stueholder nor noo tenaunt wythynne the lordship receyve any woman that livet by her body if she be knowe with childe. after raysonnable warnynge uppon de peyne peyenge to the lord xxs [twenty shillings] and the woman to pay vis viiid [six shillings and eightpence].

31. *Qd' ballina tradente aliquos in ballium sine licencia Cur'*

ITEM that the bailli late no woman nor man [allows no man or woman] to baille or unto mainprise withoute the leve of the court uppon peyn of payenge a fyne to the lord of Cs [one hundred shillings].

32. *Qd' hiis qui custodiunt mulieres habentes nephandam infirmitatem*

ITEM that noo stueholder kepe noo woman withynne his hows that hath any sikenes[sickness]of brennynge[burning]but that she be putte oute uppon the peyne of makyng a fyne unto the lord of xxs [twenty shillings].

33. *Qd arest et p'ptitis faciend' per certis denar*

ITEM that noo baille nor constable shal take for arrest but iiiid [fourpence] at the most.and that the clerc for the plaint iid [twopence] but if hit be for a gret some [a large amount] or for a gret trespasse [a serious crime] oppon of a fyne to the lord.

34. *Qd' hiis qui custodiunt licista' apertas infra domum contra consuetudinem*

ITEM if any man wythynne the lordship holde any breche that goth assault [commits a breach leading to assault] withynne the same lordship he shal make a fyne for it to the lord of iiis iiiid [three shillings and fourpence].

35. *Qd' mulieribus utentibus vestiment qui vocatur aprannes*

ITEM if any comon woman were [wear] any apron she shal forfayt hit and make a fyne after the custume of the manoir.

36. *Qd' hiis qui vendiunt victualia extra hospic' no' ingress.*

ITEM that any man kepynge a stewe hous sel nor retaille out of the same hous breed, ale, flessh, fissh, wode cole candel nor any outher vitaill upon peyne of a fyn to be made an to the lord at the discrecion of the steward and the constables.

On the reverse of folio 28 appear three Latin rubrics without any corresponding details in English:

37. ITEM. *De hiis qui multiplicat' auream et argentii* (Concerning those uttering false coin of gold and silver).

38. ITEM. *Meretrices et meretricantibus cum eos baudis* (Whores and

whoring and their procuresses).

39. ITEM. *De committibus obiurgatibus & causantibus ligitum inter hospices* (Concerning the causes of quarrelling [cursing] and complaints in the brothels).

Of these three items only 37 is of major interest for it is the first time that a serious crime is mentioned in direct connection with the whore-houses. Coin-clipping was a common offence in the medieval period, especially during periods of war and inflation. It comes as no surprise to learn that the Bankside brothels harboured amongst their comple-ment of variously talented criminals the men who engaged in this racket.

Item 38 is most probably to be read in conjunction with the restric-tions on outside whores in Item 11, which in the years after 1161 had become something of a national problem. The missing particulars probably set out the means to prevent and punish what was by then a highly organized prostitution racket controlled largely by foreign bawds, who favoured the Bankside 'sanctuary' because of its legal advantages.

Item 39 almost certainly had reference to Items 13, 19 and 20 dealing with brawls, affrays and disturbances. The use of foul lan-guage and swearing (as well as blaspheming, which is the ostensible principle here involved) was regarded as heinous, especially in Tudor times when there were a number of ordinances prescribing heavy punishments for this offence, even to cutting out a man's tongue. The mention in Item 16 of the official entitled the 'sturbeour', which must mean a court officer specially dealing with disturbances, will be evidence of the prevalence of all sorts of hooliganism. The longer these stews existed the more the area and the behaviour of those resorting to it deteriorated. Moreover, affrays which started in the stews had the bad habit of spreading into the neighbouring areas and not infrequently causing raids over London Bridge into the City of London.

The Harley MS. 1877 alone mentions a number of additions and amendments to the regulations. The only major one concerns the 'perilous disease of the brennynge'. Sometime in the intervening centuries (the most likely time being about 1500) the penalty had been increased to the staggering sum of one hundred shillings. This is a clear pointer to the great fear of the disease, and also to its great prevalence.

The same manuscript also mentions two administrative changes, both putting extra financial burdens on the inmates of the stews. One is headed 'Stewards' and reads :

ITEM The Stewards and Constables to the Lordes bailey there shall
have and take of every comon woman within the Lordshipp for
quarterage at every of the four quarters of the yere iij*d* [threepence]
and of every hostiler in the same Lordshipp iiij*d* [fourpence] towards
hys dynner and of the lorde by the hande of the Bailiff vj*s* viij*d* [six
shillings and eightpence] for the said dynner.

The other is headed 'Bayliffe' and reads:

ITEM Hee shall have and take of every woman that is comon or is
taken with any comon hostel four tymes in the yeare at every tyme
iij*d* [threepence] for her quarterage.

Some staggering increases in the fines are also recorded; for keeping a woman of religion (Item 11) the penalty is increased to £10,
such is the magnitude of the offence. It may be a reflection of growing
indigency amongst nuns who may have drifted into that way of life,
and hence an attempt to stop them being recruited into the licensed
brothels. The fine for wearing an apron (Item 35) has in the interim
been fixed at twelve pence.

Incidentally, the eighteenth-century historians Manning and
Bray[16] also mention another curious regulation which is not mentioned elsewhere, nor do they give it provenance. It is that 'No man
within the lordship to keep a bitch on heat [against a] fine of vj*s* viij*d*
[six shillings and eightpence].' Unfortunately, some of their pro-
nouncements are taken from untrustworthy sources without checking,
and this seems to be one of them. It does not appear in the three
extant manuscripts which are the basis of this work, but one must not
exclude the possibility that other manuscripts may have been in
existence or that they may have had another source. The regulation
itself seems pointless.

In the next chapter we shall discuss Henry's regulations in more
detail. Before doing so it is worthwhile to stress again that his ordinance of 1161 was only giving extra weight to rules and customs that
had been in operation for some time beforehand. It is clear that recognized licensed brothels existed on the Bankside long before the
emergency in 1161 which caused the King to enact a law. One might
hazard that these rules dated back to the syphilis scare of 945 and had
fallen somewhat into disuse, or that the ecclesiastical sanctions which
had worked well enough hitherto no longer had the desired effect.
They now needed the extra muscle given by a royal proclamation.

It needs to be made clear, too, that the salvation of poor women's souls or the displeasure of God had little to do with these enactments. Rather it was the inconveniences suffered by the clients, young and old, when by indiscriminate fornication they had acquired a venereal disease. Perhaps the creation and legalization of this red-light district was some sort of attempt at prophylaxis, a sort of *cordon sanitaire* by which the diseases might be controlled. Areas of prostitution were certainly in existence in some large cities in England by 1240 and certainly none of them could have existed without the knowledge of, and perhaps also the connivance of, the Church; and all of them would have been in existence long before they are first mentioned in writing.

NOTES

1 *John Howes MS. 1582* (ed. S. V. Morgan).
2 William Maitland, *History of London*.
3 Paul Dufour, *Mémoires Curieux sur l'histoire des Moeurs et de la Prostitution*, Brussels 1853 edition, p. 469.
4 William of Malmesburie, *Chronicles of the Kings of England* (ed. J. A. Giles).
5 Ibid., p. 31.
6 Ibid., chap. 'William Rufus'.
7 J. P. Malcolm, *Anecdotes of London Manners*. The mistresses were Ausfreda, Sybylla Corbett, two named Edith, Nest ap Twdr and Matilda.
8 Henry of Huntingdon, *Historia Angliorum* (ed. T. Forester).
9 Ibid.
10 Joseph Hunter (ed.), *Magna Rotuli Scacciarum*, 31 Henry I (1130), pp. 50-51.
11 R. C. Hamilton (ed.), *Chronica Domini Walterus de Hemingburghe*, Vol. I.
12 F. Buret, op. cit., Vol. II.
13 Sir Richard Baker, *A Chronicle of the Kings of England* (1643).
14 Rafael Holinshed, *Chronicles of England Ireland and Scotland* (1586), (ed. J. Johnson).
15 It was probably made for William Corum, Steward of the Bishop of Winchester (1461-1485).
16 O. Manning and W. Bray, *History of London*, Vol. III 'Southwark'.

IV

Accordynge to the Old Custumes

In the preceding chapters we have examined some of the causes of the 'grete multiplicacyon of orrible synne amongst the syngle women' which had led the King to have the matter debated in Parliament and to enshrine what had hitherto the oral customs of the bishopric of Winchester into the law of the land.

Prostitution is a consequence of urbanized life, and its history goes back to very ancient times, when heavy religious pressures were placed upon men to adopt some form of marriage – with its consequent responsibilities. In such circumstances a system is devised whereby men can slake their sexual desires without incurring obligations. If he pays a strange woman for the service, she has no claim on him and he can return again and again on the same cash terms without taking on any legal or moral responsibility for her. By this means the complications of marriage are replaced by a simple monetary transaction. The man pays for a plain, uncomplicated act of coition, performed without any of the paraphernalia attaching to romance. From his point of view it is extremely convenient.

In the countryside the situation was different. There were always women to be used sexually: slaves, concubines, daughters, or indeed any female in the family. But in the urban districts the problem – at its most basic – was lack of room. The establishment of special houses for sexual purposes was thus the logical outcome. That supremely logical people, the Sumerians, record a brothel in the city of Erech (or Uruk) next to the temple of the god Anu, some three thousand years before Christ. This was a special building dedicated to the goddess Ishtar, the lustful daughter of the great god himself.[1]

This brothel, the Ka-Kum, housed three grades of prostitutes, the highest of which performed only in the temple rites. Those in the next category had the run of the temple grounds and slaked the lusts of visitors in the god's name. The third and lowest grade were ambulant, and it seems that even as early as this they were reviled and abused for carrying out their business.

53

Some 2,500 years later, in the empire of King Nebuchadnezzar of Babylon, a certain rich citizen, Nabu-Akhe-Iddin, hired out his female slaves to a brothel run by one Kal-Ba, cannily reserving for himself 75 per cent of the profits. (Kal-Ba must surely be the first brothelkeeper on record.)

Thus Solon's establishment of cheap public brothels for lustful Athenians was a very late achievement. (There was, of course, at least one brothel in Jericho in Joshua's time.) The Romans restored the municipal type of brothel and it was left to King Henry II to return the brothel to the control of the ecclesiastical authorities, although not quite on the Sumerian model.

By this act of recognition, the King and the Archbishop of Canterbury gave certain advantages to the licensed brothelkeepers or stewholders. It was much easier for them to carry on business in a protected premises in a protected area. The regulations and penalties, although set out in great detail and with seemingly terrifying (or at least terrifyingly expensive) punishments, were of little practical consequence. Most infractions would be hard to prove, and all could be nullified with a little judicious bribery.

One side-effect was that women working for a licensed bawd were safeguarded against accusations of witchcraft, or at least of consorting with Satan. They were now, with Church permission, copulating with honest burghers or, at any rate, normal human beings. In the popular mind there had always been a connection between whores and witches; aged whores and madams were particularly vulnerable to such charges. Indeed in the laws of King Eadward the Elder (son of King Alfred) witches, whores and magicians are linked together.

Henry II's regulations differed from the old Roman ones in a number of ways, particularly in that the whores themselves were not individually licensed nor were they compelled to wear a distinctive garb. (Rule No. 8 says only that 'they must be seen every day for what they are'. While this infers some kind of distinctive dress or sign, it was not to be an apron [rule 34]. In later centuries the apron became the sign of a cheap whore in certain areas of London.) There is, however, early mention of 'hoods of ray' (striped) in the City of London's ordinances and this was probably the distinguishing sign.

Nor were they slave-bound to the brothelmasters; in fact their freedom of movement was guaranteed. Indeed, at first sight the houses were not real brothels but rooming houses in which individual whores could carry on their business, with the rental of the rooms being fixed. From their earnings they also had to pay for their food and victuals at places outside the brothel house; the stewholder was forbidden to stock any such items for sale to them or their clients. Bed without board was the scheme for both whore and customer. Nor, strangely enough, was there a fixed tariff of charges to which she must adhere, or a professional name which had to be displayed. There is evidence, however, that both such requirements were later enforced.

In order to prevent the whoremaster establishing a lien on the women, he was forbidden to lend them more than six shillings and eightpence. This was evidently a sum which she could make up easily and quickly to absolve the debt. The rule ensured too, that she could not build up such a debt as would render her liable to imprisonment if unpaid. There is no doubt that such a regulation was impossible to uphold;[2] for any number of reasons a brothel-girl needed money and (as in all ages) the moneylender was the whoremaster.

Not only were the houses to be closed on the holy days, but the whore was allowed to leave the precinct if she wished – perhaps to attend divine service. At this time almost all the whores would have been communicants: they were not refused Holy Communion, only Christian burial! There is some confusion in the rules on this point, for another instructs the bailiff to expel all whores on the holy days; perhaps the answer is that she could stay in the Liberty if she did not ply her trade that day.

She was not allowed to solicit custom by cries or gestures or to grab the potential customer by his gown or harness. She was supposed to sit quietly by the door and await events. That this rule was a non-starter is evidenced by the great number of cases of this nature which came up before the Courts leet for centuries afterwards. The whore was forbidden to chide or make a grimace at any passing man or to throw stones at him. The existence of this rule testifies to the prevalence of the practice; the penalty was severe: three days and nights in prison and a fine of six and eightpence.

All over the world whores cry out for custom, importune men brazenly and loudly and quarrel with their competitors and clients alike. When a potential client moves off, he is abused or even pelted with whatever missile comes to hand. The Bankside would have been no different; it was, after all, a dockside area with dockside manners. Certainly any man who tried to bilk a prostitute, by running for the nearest wherry at the stairs, would have been the recipient of a mouthful of abuse and a volley of stones – perhaps even the contents of a chamberpot – and lucky not to have left a part of his garment in her wrathful hands. If he was unlucky enough to lose his harness and his sword or weapon, he was in trouble, for he would be heavily fined for allowing it. If he created a breach of the peace leading to an assault he was fined three shillings and fourpence.

The whoremasters' wives sometimes indulged in a little trading with their bodies 'on the side', hence the rule that if they enticed any-one 'against his will' both she and her husband jointly would have to pay the enormous sum of forty shillings. By showing that these men could prostitute their wives, it also shows what sort of men the King and the Church were licensing to keep brothels. From such people every sort of trickery and deceitfulness was to be anticipated. Although forbidden to keep any sort of victual on his premises, there was nothing to stop him from owning the next-door tavern, cookshop or bakery.

Perhaps the strangest rule is that forbidding a whore to have a paramour 'against the use and custom of the manor'. The punishment was exceptionally harsh: a fine of six shillings and eightpence, plus three weeks in prison, plus once on the cucking-stool and then ejection from the Liberty. Seemingly, copulation for money for as long as her strength held out was permissible, but copulation for love was reprehensible enough to merit a condign punishment. Since the moral or ethical principle seems questionable, the reason must have been economic. Time spent on free fornication meant less revenue for the whoremaster, the bailliff and the bishop. There does not appear to be any penalty levied on the paramour, who would undoubtedly have been a ponce or a pimp. Perhaps he was punished under the other laws as a 'vacabund' or a 'mislyvver'.

The whore was not permitted to spin or card wool in her spare time: it was contrary to the strict laws governing the craftsmen in their guild. This raises the question as to how much spare time they had and whether they worked on Sundays. The rule appears to have been that the whorehouse must be closed 'from matins till noon' and then from 'two till six'; whether this was a meal break is an intriguing point.

Then there is the curious rule that once she had taken a man's money, the whore must lay with him all night. This can only have applied to the last customer of the day. To ensure this, the brothel-keeper was forbidden to keep a boat, and the boatmen were ordered to moor their boats at night only on the northern (City) side of the Thames. There can be no moral reason for this rule; it was clearly a means to prevent river traffic after nightfall, thus hampering the movements of malefactors and, of course, political plotters. While the guards at the gates on London Bridge could check all movements, it was impossible in pitch darkness to control small silent boats at night.

There has always been a link between prostitution and politicians. Hence the wise rule that when Parliament was sitting, or the king and his council were just across the water at Westminster, no whore was to be found in the bishop's lordship 'after the sun went to rest and until the sun came up again in the morning'. (Centuries later Charles II was enraged to discover that his parliamentary supporters were in the brothels when they should have been in the other House. One of the

King's vital measures was lost as a result. Still later, John Wilkes and Charles James Fox were able to rush straight from the whorehouse to Parliament to make long and brilliant speeches. Instead of being tired out by their nocturnal exercises, they seem to have derived from them great stimulation. Both were fiery exponents of freedom and liberal ideas – but not, curiously, for women.)

The rule that no single woman should keep a stewehouse 'against the custom of the manor'[3] must infer that women were not totally forbidden to keep a brothel house, but only in such cases as provided for in the customs of the Liberty. A woman might be left a property, or a widow might inherit and run one. (Female owners of properties on Bankside, as well as females running the brothels, are certainly to be found in the later records.) The rights of inheritance were always safeguarded from the earliest times.

The brothelkeeper was not allowed to have any other women on the premises save his wife and one washerwoman, and he could keep one male ostler. He was not to recruit any married woman or nuns – at least not knowingly. If any whore wished to stay in his house he had to inform the bailiff. If he kept her clandestinely, and it was discovered it would cost him forty shillings. If she had come without his knowledge, the poor woman was fined twenty shillings, put three times on the cucking-stool and expelled from the lordship. (It is important to note that it was a cucking-stool: the ducking-stool came much later and was not such a harsh punishment. Cucking meant immersion in mud and filth, ducking merely a dowsing or repeated dowsings.)

There is a curious lack of information about how the women were recruited. Were they to apply to the bailiff (as their forebears had applied to the *aedile*) or did they fix it with the brothelmaster who then informed the authorities? This rule, No. 12, does infer that there were independent prostitutes outside the Liberty who sought to enter it to enjoy its business possibilities and protection. It is inconceivable that any brothelkeeper would have remained content with merely extorting an enormous rent; he would certainly have wanted additional pickings from whores and clients. Keeping clandestine whores was another way to fiddle extra money, and no doubt the constable could always be squared.

Indeed, as there were only eighteen brothels licensed, the demand for rooms must have been enormous; and since the chance of getting a room was so restricted, it meant that high 'key money' could be extracted from a fresh whore, and ensured also that the resident ones would be well-behaved and obedient, so as not to be evicted. Under the regulations the harlot had many rights, but she was not really able to exercise them. Although she was not tied to the brothel she could

The cucking-stool used at Sandwich, Kent.

not legally practise her profession anywhere outside the Liberty, at that time. (Not until *c*. 1240 was another 'assigned place' recognized, in Cocks Lane in the City ward of Farringdon Without.)

At this point it is pertinent to point out a remarkable omission in the ordinances. There is no mention as to the fees or rents payable by the 'gret Stewehoulder' to the lord of the manor, at least at this initial period. (Later it could be expected that the stewholder could sub-let or sell his lease to another person.) Nowhere does it say that the brothelkeeper would be expelled from the Bankside for any breach of the regulations. Presumably this ultimate deterrent lay in the lord's power, but the circumstances for making it operative are not spelled out; nor the method adopted for his replacement. Probably the highest bidder got the privilege.

Another regulation forbids the brothelkeeper to detain any man within his house 'for debt' or 'for any other reason'. Clearly brothel-masters had other ways of placing their customers in their debt. Withholding (or even stealing) their harness was one way of securing payment; even in those days no respectable civic dignitary would have wanted his wife to hear about his visits to the whorehouse. The delightful contemporary tale 'The Husbande Shut Oute'[4] tells how an errant wife turns the tables on her blameless husband by shutting him out of the house after curfew and maliciously telling the watch, 'Hee cometh nou fram the hore-hous; thus hee was wont mee to serue!'

The male ostler's contract was to be limited to six months only (rule 25). At first sight this seems curious, but the clue to this may perhaps be found in a later amendment to the clause which precluded the employment of an old soldier 'if he had served overseas' and increased the penalty to 100 shillings. The reason is most probably that, at a time when kings were always chronically short of trained and able-bodied men for their armies (and soldiers were badly treated and badly paid), such men sought well-paid jobs in civilian life in order to escape the press-gangs. Old soldiers were eminently suited for employment in whorehouses, where the services of a stalwart chucker-out were daily in demand, especially in a rough quarter like Bankside.

Perhaps the most important item of all this legislation was that which ordered a quarterly inspection to be made, ostensibly to seek out reluctant whores, but undoubtedly to carry out medical inspections in search of the 'burning sickness'. In 1161 the penalty for being found with the disease was set at expulsion and a twenty-shilling fine, but sometime later when the real dangers of syphilis became obvious it was increased to a crushing 100 shillings.

Medical knowledge of the disease was still meagre at this time, but the 'phisitians' were immensely interested in it and would certainly have taken advantage of the epidemic of 1160 to try out various remedies. Vinegar and water, white wine, and even fresh animal's urine were recommended for bathing the infected parts. The more intelligent bawds and their girls probably tried these old leechdoms; they were well aware that diseased flesh was not good for business. Gonorrhoea seems to have been accepted as an occupational hazard, like all the other sores, itches and scabs endured in those insanitary times.

At least one English physician, the celebrated Gilbert Anglicus (*c.* 1190), may have recognized syphilis when he wrote in his *Compendium Medicine: 'in hoc genera causa est accessos ad mulierum ad quam accessit prius leprosis,'* ('the cause is copulation with a woman already infected with a leprosy'). 'Leprosy' was then a generic term for all pustular contagious diseases.

There were also Gilbert the Physician, Richard Anglicus and Michael the Scotsman (Scotus) diligently enquiring, and two highly esteemed Jewish physicians, Isaac of London (*c.* 1185) and Josce (Joseph) fil Medicus (*c.* 1190) contributing to research; the latter, as his name would imply, being the son of a physician.

One of the original items in the ordinance concerned the fees that court officials were allowed to charge; and others forbade the local officials to arrest anyone without leave of the court, or to allow them temporary freedom on bail, mainprise or against sureties. Besides usurping the authority of the court, such a practice helped to favour corruption and to 'weaken the ordinances'. It also deprived the court officials of some of their revenue and perquisites. It goes without saying that any fines levied on a brothelkeeper eventually came from the whores' pockets. That offences were concealed by venal officials is clear from the regulation which made such activities punishable by a spell in prison for the official concerned.

Any offence which involved a penalty of more than forty shillings was normally beyond the competence of the Court leet and had to be referred to the king's court. (However, in early times the Courts leet had been able to deal with crimes like murder and mayhem; only treason and religious offences were outside their jurisdiction. Treason was a matter for the king's judges; religious offences were dealt with by the bishop of the diocese concerned.) The powers of the Court leet must have been extended at some time after 1161 to accommodate those offences the penalties for which had been increased to one hundred shillings or more. Exactly when is unknown but it was most probably during the reign of Henry VI.

For the Great leets, a jury of twelve of the king's men were appointed not only to ensure that justice was done, but that it should be seen to be done. They were enjoined to give 'speedy judgements'. Quick decisions meant shorter interruptions in the serious business of whoredom. Nobody really wanted to lose revenue and perquisites, and despite the king's endeavours, justice was very much a business in those days. Moreover, as regards the stews, the noble 'farmer' had to recoup his outlay as quickly as possible and squeeze the greatest profits from his speculation. A king's caprice was like a lottery. The king gave; but the king could also take away.

The business of whoredom was based, then as now, on multiple corruption. When a king himself owned and condoned whorehouses, and lords and lord bishops were likewise heavily involved, it was not to be expected that the lesser – low-paid and sometimes unpaid – minions of the law should eschew corruption.

It would appear that there were originally eighteen licensed brothels on the Bankside, in 'great houses' according to the ordinance. How large they were we do not know, but they would not have been purpose-built. The brothels stood in their own large grounds; early maps show the houses along the Bankside with gardens stretching all the way back to Maiden Lane. If each had room for perhaps twenty women, the total is about three hundred and fifty prostitutes – clearly not nearly enough to cater for the demands of a city with a population then of at least thirty thousand and with hundreds of travellers daily passing through Southwark. There was also a male-female imbalance of 1:7 owing to the devastation and destruction by wars and pestilence. With such a plethora of women, small wonder that the unlicensed houses in Southwark multiplied. There must have been well over a thousand whores working in Southwark, which means that hundreds were operating outside the Bankside. Indeed the City of London's records disclose many clandestine brothels within the city itself, and outside its north-western perimeter.

It has been suggested that these 'stewehouses' were only bath-houses. Some may indeed have been bath-houses originally, but even then they were places of assignation and prostitution as well. The Roman *thermiae* (hot baths) became 'stewhouses', later euphemized into 'bagnios' but still keeping their sexual connotation. The Saxon word *stuves* is cognate with the Old Dutch *stoven*, and then the Norman-French *estuwes* or *estuves* (sometimes *estues*) which became 'stews' or 'stues' in English. These are literally the ovens which heated the water, as in the modern English 'stoves'. In Latin it is *stufas*, and this word is used in all the rubrics in the 1161 ordinance.

The Bankside houses were without any doubt brothels; this is made clear by the expression 'women who live by their bodies' and also by the word 'bordel' in the regulations. The word in Norman-French was originally *bordel des femmes louéés* (boarding house of women for hire) which is entirely unambiguous.

Perhaps the Church had thought that by providing and controlling these brothels they could limit the spread of sin and disease among worthy men. However, this essay into commerce was also highly profitable. It soon attracted the envy of the oligarchs of London, many of whom began to scheme how to join in.

It may seem very strange to us that a King who owned brothels in his French domains and had blithely licensed a row of Church brothels in his English capital city, should be able in 1173 to arrogate to himself the pious title 'By the Grace of God, Defender of the Faith', but seemingly at that time the stimulation of prostitution was no bar to the assumption of holy status.

The King drew vast revenues from rents of property within the English boroughs, of which there were about a hundred, London and Southwark being but two. During Henry's frequent absences abroad his affairs were administered by his Chief Justiciar, Ranulph de Glanvill. In 1181 Henry asked him to examine the legal status of the boroughs, and the Justiciar laid down the dictum that if any villein stayed peacefully in any privileged town for a year and a day 'he is thereby freed from his villeinage'. Southwark was such a privileged place or borough, and from time immemorial rights of asylum had pertained to certain churches there and in London. Now this right was confirmed into law. This freedom of asylum also encompassed the licensed brothels on the Bankside.

Henry II ruled for another eight years. He was an energetic and intelligent king, although occasionally give to bad judgments. As well as licensing the brothels and freeing the villeins, he began the conquest of Ireland and caused the murder of Becket. He died suddenly of an apoplexy, probably brought on by the news that his son John had rebelled against him. He died 'cursing the day he was born'.

NOTES

[1] L. J. Delaporte, *La Mesopotamie: les civilisations Babylonienne et Assyrienne*, pp. 95 ff.

[2] The case of Elizabeth Butler in the days of Edward IV is a clear example (see p. 97).

[3] Rule 29. The Latin rubric is more specific; it translates: 'Concerning a female custodian of a brothel having no husband [et non habentibus viros].'

[4] Henry Weber (ed.), *The Seven Sages: A Metrical Poem from the 13th Century*, p. 59.

V

A Plague of Plantagenets

Every English schoolboy knows that Richard I was tall, handsome, brave, and with a lion's heart, and spent his life fighting the Saracen infidels in the Crusades. He is told of his romance with the lovely Queen Berengaria (although not of his extremely ungentlemanly behaviour to her afterwards), and he thrills to the tale of Blondel's discovery of the incarcerated King. That he was a true scion of the noble Plantagenet house which was to plague the realm for centuries – faithless, cruel, belligerent and lecherous – is not taught to children. His one redeeming feature is perhaps that, unlike his forebears and his brother John, he was not avaricious for money's sake but for his endless campaigns of slaughter, especially after he took over the leadership of the Crusades from the unspeakable Frederick Barbarossa after he was drowned in Turkey in 1190.

It cannot be said that he was a bad ruler, because he hardly set foot in his English kingdom long enough to rule it. Nevertheless his influence was fell for the army of Englishmen whom he recruited for the Crusades who ended their days with their bodies mouldering by European roadsides or sweating their lives away as wretched slaves to the Turks. They left behind them thousands of widows and orphans who received neither succour nor thanks for the loss of their menfolk.

Richard's whoring and warring – he was once arrested in a Paris brothel and held by the *gendarmerie* – and in the last event, his ransom, bankrupted the kingdom and ruined his Jewish financiers. Meanwhile his brother John, his regent, milked the kingdom from pure avarice. Perhaps Richard's only remaining practical monument was his ordinance of 1189, *Of Necessary Chambers in Houses*, which required that privies, if constructed in stone, must be two feet six inches away from one's neighbour's; if lined with clay, three feet.[1] It is doubtful whether the 'gret Stueholders' on Bankside were in any way affected, for the Act referred only to London.

Richard's death in 1199 was a consequence of his restless, lecherous life. While he was dallying with some launderesses and neglecting the command of his soldiers, the French stormed the castle he was defending. In the *mêlée* the King was wounded. No physician was immediately available but eventually one 'Marchadeus the physician' was found. He, however, could not extract the javelin, and removed only the shaft, leaving the head embedded in the wound. It was only when 'like a bloody butcher'[2] he cut freely round the arm that he got the head out, but it was too late to save the King, who died in terrible agony, most probably of gangrene. The unlucky physician was savagely done to death a few days later for his pains.

Richard was succeeded by his brother John, who has the dubious distinction of being perhaps the worst king ever to afflict the English people. He was 'somewhat fat and of a sour and angry countenance . . . sometimes religious . . . sometimes scarce a Christian . . . [he was noted for] his insatiableness about money . . . [which] was gotten with much noise but spent in silence.'[3]

Hemingburghe,[4] after describing him as a continually angry tyrant, goes on to detail his unbelievably immoral behaviour, which included open carnal intercourse with the wives and daughters of his magnates, contemptuously disregarding the husbands and in fact deriding them in public by having their wives beget his bastards. At least six such children are recorded.

The most significant event of John's reign was forced on him by his angry and cuckolded barons, more concerned with the threat to their power and their lands than with the chastity or otherwise of their wives. Magna Carta has proved more vital to English democracy than any of its originators thought or intended.

About the only worthwhile action that King John took of his own accord was to speed up the construction of the stone bridge over the Thames which his father had started some thirty years previously. This bridge, opened in 1209, was welcomed by all travellers and merchants, and by the 'gret Stueholders of the Banke' as an unexpected bonus, since it facilitated access to their pleasure-houses.

A somewhat less useful, and more bizarre legacy was King John's re-introduction of the ancient Roman sport of bear-baiting. In an undated manuscript written from Ashby-de-la-Zouch in Leicestershire, it is stated: 'thyss straynge passtyme was introduced by some Italyans for his hyghnesse' amusement wherewyth hee and hys court were highly delyghted.'[5] The pastime was to remain very popular with kings and commoners on the Bankside for another four hundred years until Oliver Cromwell killed the bears.

King John died in 1216 and made way for his son Henry III, a hot-blooded and equally ill-tempered King of whom it was said: 'He was more desirous of money than of honour. . . . He was neither constant in his love nor in his hate . . . his most eminent virtue, rare in princes,

anfte fu te rofel, tout li fift pechoier
z tholom fiert lui, qui dvit fu du meftier
Li i efpies fu trenchans, z lanfte te ponner

4 One of the earliest illustrations of a brothel. From *The Romance of Alexander*, 14th century.

5 Prostitutes enticing a customer from a gymnasium into a brothel. By the Master of the Banderolles (1435-1480).

7 Interior of a brothel. By Virgil Solis (1514-1562).

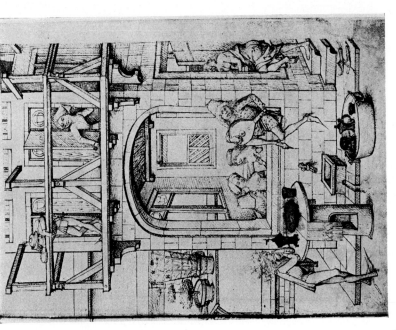

6 A medieval stewhouse. By the Master of the House Book.

was his continency.'[6]

Continent he certainly seems to have been. His lust for money seems to have superseded all other passions, and in avarice he was well matched by his Queen, Eleanor la Belle, who was equally un-loved by the citizenry.

Henry III, although constantly greedy for money, appears not to have bothered to augment his revenues by the well-known device of a *putage* or *putagium*, which was a tax on the whores themselves. This was already known in Europe as early as 1185 and as a *gabelle* (local tax) in Naples in 1283.[7] Strangely enough, not even his rapacious father had levied it. Perhaps the revenues raised from the *couillages* on desperately frustrated priests were thought sufficient.

Henry III was obsessed by a regard for cleanliness and sanitation to a degree unknown up to that time in royal circles (in contrast to John whose extravagance ran to having a bath once every three weeks), particularly in respect to defecatory matters.[8] He had a large number of privies, all of the greatest luxury, installed in his various palaces, and needless to say at the greatest expense. In 1249 he ordered a luxurious privy complete with a fireplace to be installed at Woodstock for the use of his Queen. It may be that this was the origin of the necessary ancillary equipment, described later[9] as *de rigueur* in noble households: 'see the hous of hesement be swete and clene and the privy borde covered with a grene cloth and a cysshyn [cushion], than see ther be blankad [blanket] doune [down] or coton for wiping.'

An event of a very different nature, which was to have reper-cussions in Southwark and on Bankside, was his transfer in 1267 of the Domus Conversarum (The House for Converted Jews), which had originally been established in 1213 by the Prior of Bermondsey Abbey in Southwark. Despite the cruel exactions and tortures suffered by the Jews, very few of them had apostasized and the number of inmates remained small. The economically-minded King decided to amal-gamate this business with that of the Mastership of the Rolls in New Street (the ancient name for Chancery Lane). Characteristically, he starved the organization of funds, so that those who had accepted conversion instead of death had to go begging for bread on London's streets until 1278 when Henry's successor gave to the Domus Con-versarum the rents of certain confiscated Jewish properties, some of which were on Bankside and clearly houses of prostitution; others were on the eastern side of Southwark High Street in an area known as 'le Bordych'.[10]

By this time municipal authorities overseas had realized that brothels were a very good business, especially as a municipal mon-opoly, as places where citizens could go and sin officially but free of

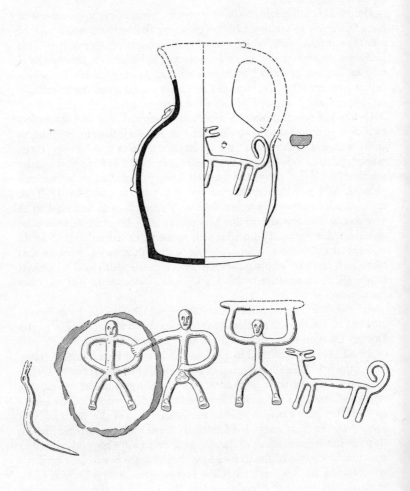

The London jug, c. 1250.

ecclesiastical consequences, while simultaneously augmenting the civic coffers – or, more accurately, lining the pockets of the city's rulers. Stern measures were taken to prevent private enterprises being established. The earliest-known municipal red-light district appears to be that of Avignon in 1234, in which the regulations required that the whores should not wear a veil, and also that if any whore (or Jew) touched any food on the market stalls they had to buy it or the food would be destroyed; other such districts were established in Toulouse and Montpellier. It was about this time too that brothels were required to have a red light outside so that they could be recognized.

It was a source of some chagrin that the Bishop of Winchester had this profitable monopoly in his Liberty. The London oligarchs constantly tried to secure jurisdiction over Southwark, usually on the grounds of security – that is, security for their properties across the river. There was a constant stream of City ordinances against free-lance brothelkeepers within its walls. To counter this menace an opportunity was taken about 1240 to 'assign' another area in 'Cokkes-lane outside Neugate', likewise in the extra-mural Liberty of Farring-don Without-the-Walls. Cocks Lane is recorded as early as 1200,[11] but exactly when it became 'assigned', and under what regulations, is not known.

There may, however, be a clue in a document of 1241[12] by which a certain Robert de Haverhill granted three shillings a year to the Canons of Holy Trinity, London, 'from land held of them in Cokkes-lane' from which the Canons were to pay two shillings a year to Roger de Turri. The important thing is that the document is also signed by 'Martin, Prior of St Marie, Southwark', i.e. St Marie Overie, which was one of the Bishop of Winchester's properties. It is known that the Prior of St Marie Overie owned properties in Chancery Lane and Fetter Lane which were let out to prostitutes, and this further information may perhaps clarify an otherwise puzzling point. It is difficult to imagine that the mayor and aldermen of London would appoint an assigned place without having some regulations for the conduct of the inhabitants. Yet no such regulations or ordinances are extant. It may therefore be that the bishop's regulations would apply to the bishop's properties, especially in another Liberty, for otherwise the law of London would have to apply. One may also note that in 1287[13] the Dean and Chapter of St Paul's Cathedral also held properties in 'Cockis lane', which were also let out to prostitutes.

In 1953 Mr Morton Green, a schoolmaster from Aylesbury, discovered between Mark Lane and Mincing Lane in the City a striking reminder of the uninhibited sexual morals of knights and citizens around the year 1250. This is a small jug about ten inches high, decorated on one side with a female figure with arms akimbo,

Figures on knights' jug found at Bruges.

bent to point to her vulva, which is clearly portrayed since her skirts are lifted high; she is linked to a male figure with one arm bent pointing to his penis. This jug is presently on loan to the London Museum.

In a very convincing article[14] Dr Gerald Dunning concludes that the figures represent a whore and her client on the Bankside. (While this is not to be discounted, the presence of brothels and whores in nearby Love Lane, Billingsgate, and Aldgate makes it equally possible that the jug derives from one of them.) No similar jug has been found elsewhere in England which must infer that it was made especially for a stewholder to entertain his customers with, or to regale them therefrom. The nearest approximations are the so-called 'Knights' Jugs' of English make, dating from the same period, one of which, in the museum at Bruges, shows a woman similarly stanced, parting her skirts widely and clearly revealing her vulva to a group of avidly gaping knights.

Henry III died in 1272 at the age of sixty-five of senile dementia, although another source[15] states that 'his insensate rages stemmed from syphilis . . . which he bequeathed to later generations of his family.' He was succeeded by his son, Edward I, nicknamed Longshanks because 'he was tall of stature . . . of a swarthy complexion but lean and of a comely favour.'[16]

He was a man of great valour and is regarded as one of England's great kings because of his martial prowess and military successes. Sexually, he was a man of a puritan disposition. He had the good fortune, too, to inherit a stable kingdom, although one historian[17] has noted that 'in merrie England of that day most of the population owned nothing but their bellies.'

True to the family tradition, he used every possible means to extract money, even resorting to the unheard-of expedient of compelling all freeholders with an estate of £20 a year to become knights. While this aroused the anger of the richest city magnates (who recognized it as another means of exaction) many men rushed to accept, as William Langland in his *Piers Plowman* acidly recalls: 'Barnes bastards han ben archidekenes and sopers and here sons, for seluer, han be knyghtes' (Baron's bastards became archdeacons and soap-sellers and their sons became knights). Langland goes on to say that even mechanics, artizans, bakers, woolcarders 'and cozening ribalds,' (cheating whoremongers) were also dubbed knights.

In 1275 comes the first reference in the City of London records to the notorious Gropecuntlane (although alleys with the same name are known in provincial cities and towns from the beginning of the century). It was an alley just off Cheapside, a continuation south-wards of the street later to be known as Old Jewry. Parallel to this alley was another called 'Bordhawe', later 'Burdellane' (Bordel or Brothell Lane), thus evidencing organized whoredom right in the centre of the City, despite many ordinances against it. Indeed in 1285,[18] within the framework of a street-cleaning ordinance, it was enacted 'that no putayne [whore] or comon bordelere [brothelkeeper] shall reside within the walls,' and later in the same year another ordinance, *Of Thieves and Whores*,[19] states that if such women are found in the City they 'shall be imprisoned forty days . . . and their limits assigned to them.' The places of assignment were either Bank-side or Cocks Lane by this time, but Bankside's pre-eminence was predicated in the next ordinance, *Of Boatmen*,[20] which forbade them to carry any man or woman, whether denizens or strangers, 'into the stewes except in the daytime', and they were to tie up at night on the City side. (This corresponds neatly with the Ordinance of 1161 for-bidding stewholders to own any kind of boat.)

The Bordych comes into history again briefly in 1281[21] when there was issued 'a licence . . . to Isaac, Jew of Suthwerk to sell his houses in Suthwerk but not to put them in mortmain.' Then in 1290, the year of the expulsion of the Jews from England, the property is granted to 'John and Matilda de Waltham . . . being a messuage now in the king's hands by the deth of Isaac de Suthwerk Jew of London, at a rent of one penny.' Isaac de London, Jew of Suthwerc, described also as 'Serviens Judaeorum', was a rich Jew who lived in Guildford in Surrey. His death was certainly not from natural causes. The trans-action was to remain on the books until it was clarified some fifty years later.

That the Bordych was in fact a brothel area is indicated by the presence on the site of a large pillory and cage in which unruly men and loose women would have been punished (such equipment would have been of no use in a timberyard). The fact that a king's Jew owned brothel property there raises the question as to whether this outpost contained a convenience for the use of young Jews, who were forbidden to enter any Christian whorehouse or even to touch a Christian woman. This would postulate the existence of Jewish prostitutes in defiance of the strict Rabbinical injunctions. These times, however, were fearful for Jews: imprisonment, torture and death were matters of daily life in this king's reign. Not all Jews and Jewesses could be as steadfast unto death for their religion as their co-religionists at Lincoln. Many must have apostasized[22] for want of any other means of securing their lives, and of securing thereafter a livelihood. Instead of being turned out to beg in the streets from unsympathetic Christians, they may have turned to whoredom; some may even have practised on Bankside once they were Christians.

Meanwhile the King was having trouble with his son Edward, the first to be known as Prince of Wales, because of his homosexual behaviour – although this is unproven – with the young Gascon, Piers Gaveston.

By the time he succeeded to the throne in 1307, Edward had other pursuits: 'he preferred to waste his time in the company of carters, boatmen, blacksmiths and diggers. . . . He was much given to the company of harlots . . . addicted to gambling at pitch-and-toss . . . and other improper occupations.'

Edward's compassionate nature may be seen from the fact that in 1321 he founded the Lock Hospital in Southwark (although it is thought to have existed as a chapel for some years previously) for the treatment of lepers. However, because of its proximity to the Bankside, it tended from early in its history to deal with sufferers from venereal leprosy. The term 'Lock Hospitals' later became synonymous with hospitals treating venereal diseases, until some forty years ago.

Medical knowledge of the diseases had advanced a little. About this time the English physician John of Gaddesdon (1280-1360)[23] gave some good advice to women on how to avoid venereal disease (and probably even conception). He advised that a woman who had just had coitus with a 'leprous man' could avoid infection if, immediately afterwards, she 'jumps, runs backwards down the stairs, induces sneezing by inhaling pepper, tickling the vaginal membranes with a feather dipped in vinegar so that the seed would flush out. Then she must wash her genitals with a decoction of roses and herbs boiled in vinegar.' Other physicians had different specifics, but quite a number now recognized that venereal disease was carried through copulation. For example Lanfrancus of Milan (1255-1315) stated that these ulcers arose from mixing with a 'filthy woman' who came already with the filthy disease; he advised washing in water and vinegar. Gerard de Berri (1298-1368) stated that the virile member suffers through copulation as a result of corrupt seminal fluid or a poisonous humour, and advises washing with mercury quenched in spittle.

In Edward II's time we begin to find the Bankside brothels being mentioned by name for the first time. One case was in the most curious circumstances. In 1321 the special papal agent sent by Pope Clement the Fifth to England in 1305, Cardinal William de Testa, bought for the Church's investment a brothel named *Aulus Comitis* (the nearest translation might be 'The Social Club').[24] It was bought cheaply because it was in a ruinous state and also because it was 'thought advantageous to our Lord the King'. He paid £300 in money of Bordeaux for the brothel and a further £200 for the surrounding land, plus twelve Requiem masses for the souls of the poor 'in the King's name'. Inasmuch as the Cardinal was administering the estates of the Archbishop of Canterbury, then the profligate Walter Reynolds who was also Bishop of Winchester, it is reasonable to suppose that this particular transaction concerned one of these houses.

In 1324 the King built himself a 'retreat'[25] on the Bankside called *La Roserie*, which was certainly used for debauchery and other similar pastimes. In 1361 this site was bought by John Trigg, 'Citizen and Fysshemongere', when it was described as 'a garden and ponds at the Stewes' and included the brothel known as *The Little Rose*. Moreover, next door to this residence was the brothel called *The Rose*, the provenance for which is very interesting, and is found in a Patent Roll of 1350.[26] It reads: 'Licence for the alienation in mortmain by John de Sancto Paulo King's Clerk of Westminster to the prioress and nuns of Stretforde-atte-Bowe of all his tenements and houses and shops . . . at les Stuves in Suthwerk . . . to have in satisfaction of 1 Mark of Ten pounds yeerlie of land and rent, which they held of the late king's licence to acquire and towards the support of a chaplain to celebrate divine service daily in the chapel built by the said John.'

John de Sancto Paulo was a converted Jew, who had taken this as his baptismal name and who had been made warden of the House of Converts. The above-mentioned property was part of some Jewish property which had been confiscated by Edward I when he expelled the Jews in 1290.

The first Bankside brothel to be mentioned is *The Bulhede*,[27] in a deed of 1306: 'Three messuages with the Bulhede subject to final accord between Miles and Joan Stapeltone and Stephen and Marie de Sarham.' In the same year the conveyance is recorded by Stephen de Sarham 'to Milonem [Miles] de Stapleton et Johannem [Joan] uxorem ejus [his wife]' of *The Rose*.

The same Stephen de Sarham also sold them the large estate which stood at Bank End (the beginning of Bankside on the east) including the brothel already known as *The Castell-uppon-the-Hoop*. Later several more brothels were to be built on this same piece of land. This curious name may even be due to a recollection of the existence in Roman times of a fort at this point. (There was a *Castle-upon-the-Hoop* in Friday Street in the City of London in 1425[28] which had a sign of a castle on an oval-shaped hoop, and it is thought that this indicated the site of a Roman or medieval fort.) To lend credence to this hypothesis, for many years before the brothel disappeared it was referred to as 'the Southwark Castle'.[29]

The atrocious murder of Edward II in Kerkelsey Castle in 1326 is already well known; a red-hot iron was thrust (through a horn, to prevent any external contusions) up his anus into his entrails. Despite his many faults he did not deserve such a fate, for he left his people in a much better condition than his father had. The allegations of sodomy would seem to have been invented later to justify his murder.

His son ascended the throne in 1327 as Edward III. One of his first actions was to grant a Charter giving the 'farm' (the right to control and exploit against payment of a fee) of the Guildable Manor of Southwark to the mayor and aldermen of the City of London. There was of course a very handsome cash consideration, but it was still a great bargain for the London oligarchs, and in addition gave them power to curb some of the hooliganism which erupted out of Southwark into the City. The measure of the impotence of royal law and order may be gauged when Edward III addressed his well-beloved citizens of London, saying *inter alia* that 'those who have committed manslaughters, robberies, and divers other felonies, [are] privily departing . . . after having committed such felonies, into the town of Southwark, where they cannot be attached by the ministers of the City, and there are openly received; and so for default of due punishment are emboldened to commit more such felonies. . . .'

Large gangs of hooligans – some numbering 200 or more – would burst over the bridge, robbing and beating up citizens, raping and looting, and then run back over the bridge to sanctuary. While the law-abiding burgesses of Southwark wished to have these ruffians restrained, they valued their own independence and resented being governed by the law of London. On the other hand only the City had the means and the men to maintain law and order. Nonetheless the malefactors could still find asylum in the Liberties of the Clink and Paris Gardens.

Nothing restrained the growth of the Bankside stews. By 1337 the nuns of Stratford already owned the whorehouse called *The Barge*, demonstrating that women of religion shared the attitude towards prostitution (and the profits therefrom) we have already observed in their male brethren of the Church.

At this point in time a small mystery appears. John Stow, in his *Surveigh* (1598), says that Edward III 'in his 19th year' (1345) and again in 1346 'confirmed the Ordinances of 1161'. Concanen and Morgan (1795) say that King Edward III also ordered 'that a distinctive badge or dress be worn by these women.' Moreover there is a paragraph in an ancient history[30] which avers that in the twenty-seventh year of Edward III (1354) the Parliament at Westminster enacted, at the instance of the Londoners, that 'no common Whore should waer anie Hood: except rayed or striped with diuers colours nor Furres, but garments reuersed the wrong side outwards . . . to set a deformed marke upon foulness to make it appear more odious.'

There is no trace of any such ordinances or acts; there is however an ordinance of the City of London of 1351,[31] *As to the Dress of Comon Women w'in the City, and as to the Sale of Fish*, which forbade those not of noble birth to wear costly clothes lined with fur. 'Lewd' or common women were to go 'openly with a hood of cloth of ray single [i.e. striped and unlined] and with vestments neither trimmed with fur nor lined . . . so that all folks shall know of what rank they are.'

The ordinance was aimed at all women who were not ladies, and would include almost every citizenness in London, respectable or not. Small wonder then that it was utterly ineffective, and although the masculine rulers of the City persisted in re-enacting this ordinance for many years, that itself is proof that the womenfolk of London refused to have their dress regulated by men.

In October 1345[32] that festering old sore, the Bordych, cropped up again when the king's yeoman, Henry Wishe, was granted 'a place in Suthwerk called le Borddich ten feet long and forty feet wide as well as part of the high strete whereon to make a gate.' This locates the Bordych immediately adjacent to the High Street. Two years later[33] the king's bailiff was ordered 'to retain in the king's hand . . . the plot of land called the Bordych . . . held in chief . . . by rendering one penny every Michaelmas'; but just a few months later[34] he was ordered 'to assign it as a dower to Kathleen, late wife of Henry Wysshe'.

Then on 7 May, 1349[35] the bailiff, Roger Daber, was peremptorily ordered 'not to intermeddle further' since it had been proved that all along the Bordych had been the property of the Prior of Bermondsey. Old Isaac de Suthwerk had outsmarted the king in the end.

The nature of a 'bordich' or bordel area is explained by Paul Dufour.[36] Abbots were compelled to concede an acre of land to every inhabitant who wished to set up a 'borde' or week-end cottage. Prostitutes who had been expelled from the adjacent city took refuge in these 'bordes', renting them from the owners when not in use. Eventually these lodgings of loose women became known as *bordels* in France and this name was brought to England by the Normans.

Fourteenth-century Southwark was both physically and morally dirty. The streets were unpaved and sewerless, and householders still 'did their easements in the streets'. The very names of the alleys give an accurate clue to their state: Dirty Lane, Foul Lane, Pyssynge Alley, Lowsie Mead and Dark Alley attest to the physical dirt; while Codpiece Lane, Sluts' Hole, Cuckold Court and Whores' Nest confirm the moral dirt. There were also Maiden (or Maid) Lane – in which there were certainly no maidens – and Love Lane – in which the only love available came at a price.[37]

These were coarse and lascivious times, headed by a profligate King and a heedless court. What Edward did not spend on his endless wars he spent on women and tournaments. At a time when almost every home in England mourned someone dead of the plague (the Black Death struck that year), he established the Order of the Garter on some senseless pretext at some equally senseless junketing.

William Langland, in *Piers Plowman*, indicates that frequenting the stews was a practice well known in his times : 'I schal fynde hem fode that feythfullech lybben, saf Jak the jogeleur and Ionette of the Stvyes and Danyel the dice player and Denote the Bawd.' ('I shall find food for those that live faithfully, but not for Jack the trickster and Janet of the Stewes and Daniel the gambler and Denote the procuress.')

Elsewhere he refers to Bankside in the couplet: 'he Sleuth [sloth] wedded on Wanhope [despair] a wenche of the stewes,' and he describes the activities of such folk as 'Pernel of Flanders'. Pernel, a bastardized form of Petronella, the Dutch form of *peronelle* (Old French for a hussy), and its variations Parnel, Pernel and Prunella, were all names favoured by prostitutes. Indeed as early as 1290[38] there is mention of a whore with the apposite name of Parnell Portjoie (Parnel the carrier of pleasure) accompanied by her equally suitably-named ponce, Nicholas Pluckrose.

Incidentally, *Piers Plowman* takes a swipe at the scandal of brothel-keepers becoming rich enough to become jurors and thereby pervert the course of justice, when he finishes the couplet by saying that Wanhope's father was a 'juryman that never swore trew'. This particular scandal was to be ventilated many times during the centuries. He also gives a passing mention to that other red-light district in a reference to 'Claryce of Cokkeslane'.

Unfortunately there are no contemporary descriptions of the Bank-

side whorehouses. From records, however, we know that they were
detached houses standing in their own gardens which to the south
bordered on the Bishop's Great Park, from which they were divided
only by a lane, ditched on both sides with running water, called
variously Maid or Maiden Lane. This lane ran more or less parallel
to the river until it turned south-west to meet the Gravel or Gravill
Lane which divided the Clink Liberty from that of Old Paris
Gardens. The houses would have differed little from ordinary houses
of the period except that with the passing years they would have often
been rebuilt and embellished to include new refinements; certainly
some would have been enlarged to cope with expanding business and
provide rooms for more women. Some would even have had some
elements of luxury, such as reception rooms, although refreshment
rooms and bars would still have been forbidden. There still seem to
have been only eighteen brothels, all clustered towards the eastern
end of Bankside, sometimes known as Bank End.

The dreadful scourge of the Black Death in 1348 struck Southwark
very hard. Even the newly-appointed Chancellor, Thomas Bradwine,
died in the palace of the Bishop of Rochester just a few hundred yards
away from the Bankside; clearly the plague-bearing rats and their
fleas had no respect for the cloth.

There is no evidence that the Bankside brothels were closed down
during the pestilence, although men were warned that *in peste venus
pestem provocat* (during the plague copulation with whores increases
the danger of infection) and indeed a contemporary chronicler,
Knighton, reports that the brothels may well have profited because
all officials had fled and the population was imbued with a fatalistic
spirit – 'live for today because tomorrow we'll be dead' – and this
encouraged a fantastic promiscuity.

Neither bishops nor bailiffs were troubled about the death of
harlots; in fact the Bishop of Winchester did very well financially
from the fines levied on the estates of dead persons – in a year this
revenue had swelled tenfold. To this must be added the *heriots* of
cattle and livestock which the heirs were compelled to hand over to
their landlord, the Church. This greed later caused a glut and a consequent fall in prices. Rents fell because thousands of peasants had
died and there were none to take their places. The direct result of the
economic dislocation was to be Wat Tyler's revolt some thirty years
later.

Things were still going smoothly on Bankside, however. In 1361 [39]
the King granted a licence to William de Edyndon to make an
exchange 'in lieu of a messuage in Lestues in Suthwerk which he lately
had . . . of the bishop of Winchester, [the bishop] having found that it
will be more advantageous that the messuage . . . of the value of nine

shillings yearly, should remain annexed to the manoir.'

In November 1362[40] the King granted a pardon to 'the prioress and nuns of Stratford-atte-Boghe of the £4 10s. 4d. required of them for the king's use . . . out of the lands at les Stewes which John de Sancto Paulo late keeper of the House of Converts granted them to find [from the revenue] some works of piety.' This makes it clear that the nuns used the sums earned from prostitution to further their own charitable works. The brothels operating at this time on this estate were *The Bell, The Barge, The Rose* and (very probably) *The Unicorne.*

To show that every care was taken to safeguard these properties against Acts of God, the King ordered in 1364[41] that 'the bankes near the Stewes opposite the Manor House of John de Mowbray shall be repaired,' and he also liked to keep up appearances, as witness his urgent instruction in 1370[42] for Southwark to be cleaned up and the pavements restored 'because of the manie prelates earls barons and magnates' who were to pass through the borough to attend the funeral of Queen Philippa.

There is a most peculiar case in the records of the City of London[43] for 25 March, 1365, concerning a 'bawd of the Stewes' named Thomas Rose, who had an indentured servant named Thomas Bunny. When Rose sold his brothel to a woman named Joan Hunt, he also sold Bunny as a servant. According to Bunny's later complaint to the mayor, she 'set him to al maner of grievous work suche as carrying water in tynes [tuns]'. In the course of his labours Bunny fell and sustained a bad injury, but Joan Hunt continued to work him hard and when he faltered 'incited her paramour Bernard to beat and ill-treat Bunny'. Bunny then became seriously ill and she turned him 'oute of the brothel . . . into the streete' and later, when he wanted to return to work, she 'was unwilling to reform her ways and make amends to him: he prayed a remedy from the Court.' Although the mayor's decision was to exonerate Bunny so that neither Joan nor her executors should have any further claim on him, the case shows that a man could literally be sold into servitude.

Bunny was probably an ostler in terms of the ordinance of 1161 and it is strange that he should have had to appeal to the City of London mayor's court; presumably the Court leet in Southwark was not competent to deal with such a case. It also demonstrates that despite the rule forbidding women to own brothels in the stews, Joan Hunt had been able to buy one and run it without any let or hindrance. Furthermore, it demonstrates that a whoremistress might keep a paramour, while a whore was strictly forbidden to do so in terms of the same ordinance.

By now the King, worn out by his excesses, was beginning to go senile. His mistress, the power-crazy Lady Alice Perrers (Chaucer's 'Lady Meed'), was in effective control of the kingdom. Somehow Edward bestirred himself in July 1376[44] to grant his son Thomas de Woodstock 'tenements at Lestues late of Richard Lyons now in the king's hand.' Unfortunately the names of these tenements are not known but it can be taken as certain that some of them were brothels and that the royal family had by no means lost interest in this particular part of their kingdom.

It is just possible that we have here the earliest record of the brothel *ad leonem*, the literal meaning of which is 'to Lyon's place' or 'at Lyon's place'. It is a peculiar name, being the only one without the prefix 'le' borne by all the other brothels and inns. In this way the owner's name may have become immortalized.

Nemesis was now overtaking Edward. A contemporary chronicler reports: 'He fell into a weakness . . . not unusual in old men and far more difficult to cure because of old men's chilliness . . . he fell into this disorder because of his lust for that wanton hussy Alice Perrers.' The disease was most likely an enlarged prostate infected with gonorrhoea contracted in a lifetime of lechery.

When he died in 1377 he failed for a million florins, thereby ruining the two greatest European bankers of his time. He left the exchequer bare, a kingdom torn by factious nobles, and a young son who now ascended the throne as Richard II. The land was swarming with poor and starving ex-soldiers from the ceaseless wars – many were heroes of the famous victory at Crecy. There were thousands of distressed and evicted peasants, ruined smallholders and petty traders. The country was ripe for revolution and an unfrocked priest named John Ball of York was already fomenting trouble.

When an unknown tiler of Maidstone struck and killed one of the hated tax-gatherers in 1381 and became the leader of a rebellion that almost overturned the kingdom, the Bankside stews were affected almost immediately. Wat Tyler rallied round him a large and disciplined army of Kentish men, stopped to release John Ball from Maidstone jail, and marched to London. The rebels swore loyalty to the young King because they expected help against the rapacious extortioners around him; they also demanded release from serfdom, a demand which unnerved the barons and rich burgesses. Their first victims were lawyers, whom they regarded as their worst enemies: 'from the half-pledged pleader to the aged justices with all the jurors . . . all such must be slayne before they could enjoy freedom.' Their slogan was 'With King Richard and the True Commons' and of all they demanded 'With whom haldes you?'

The rebels were welcomed into Southwark with open arms and 'that same day being Corpus Christi in the morning these comons of

Kent despoyled a house near London Bridge which was in the hands
of Froes of Flaunders who farmed out the sayd house from the Mayor
of London.'[45] This is the only indication that William Walworth,
then mayor of London, was a brothel-owner, and the first that these
brothels on Bankside were farmed out to Flemish bawds. Later when
Walworth stabbed Wat Tyler to death, he surely had in mind less his
loyalty to the King than the fact that Tyler had burnt down his
whorehouses and released the whores from bondage. Walworth was
knighted on the spot for this gallant deed. Wat Tyler's head and
those of dozens of his confederates meanwhile adorned the Great
Gate of London Bridge, while thousands of his supporters were
murdered the length and breadth of the country. The first attempt
to remove the degradation of serfdom from the British people was
drowned in blood. The whorehouses were quickly rebuilt and back in
business.

The reference to the Flemish women needs some explanation.
There had been Flemish mercenaries in William the Conqueror's
army and Flemish merchants and artisans in England for generations.
Many of these had amassed great riches and honours. Flemish
moneylenders were also well known and continually unpopular.
There is no doubt that the Flemish traders also did a little white-
slaving of women and girls into the English brothels.

Dutch men and women were known as excellent business people
and managers, and the Dutch whorehouses were numerous, well-
appointed and well-patronized in addition to being very efficiently
run. They undoubtedly brought with them to the Bankside expertise
and new ideas and perhaps even certain elements of hygiene and
sanitation. These Flemish bawds were frequently a target for abuse
or attack; nonetheless they became an institution which lasted until
the brothels on Bankside were closed down. Among their patrons,
however, their popularity is indicated by the use of the Dutch name
Petronella by thousands of whores who wished it to be known that
they were both fashionable and expert in their craft.

That these brothels were flourishing may be seen from the royal
ordinance (issued by the mayor of London) of 1383[46] for the punishment of bawds and strumpets, and their banishment (if found in
London) to the old ghetto of Bankside or the new one in Cokkeslane.
They were to have their heads shaven, and then be 'carted' in a wagon
with a red-and-white striped awning – the whores wearing matching
red-and-white striped caps, and holding a peeled white rod in their
hands. Then, accompanied by 'minstrels', they were taken to the
nearest prison, put in the 'thew' (a sort of pillory), whipped, and then
escorted to the nearest City gate and roughly thrust outside, and forbidden to enter the City again. Those who had originated in the Bank-

side were duly returned thither. The ineffectuality of all this punishment is evident in the ordinances themselves, which provide for repeated offences and increased penalties.

By now many respectable burgesses of Southwark resented deeply the existence of these brothels and the disorders which they brought upon their 'village', especially in their High Street. In 1390 they successfully petitioned the King,[47] who responded 'in accordance with the supplications of the Commons of the borough of Southwark no brothels to be allowed there except in the places already ordained.'

Such 'successes' were purely relative; for three years later the mayor of London had to issue another ordinance *Concerning Street Walkers by Nyght and Women of Ill-repute.*[48] This forbade anyone who was not of proven good repute, or his servants, to go about the streets after 9 p.m. without a light (aliens by 8 p.m.). It went on to describe how 'broils and affrays' caused innocent men to be murdered because they consorted with 'common harlots, at taverns, brewhouses of huksters and other places of ill-fame . . . and more especially through Flemish women who profess and follow such shameful and dolorous life. . . . [All prostitutes were] to keepe themselves to the places thereunto assigned . . . the stews on the other side of the Thames and Cokkeslane.'

The energetic nuns of Stratford enter history again in 1397 when they sold to Ralf Ride (or Rede) 'one of the three messuages . . . being le Rose betwene le Barge on the west and another tenement on the east.'[49]

The Rose was one of Sir William Walworth's brothels that Wat Tyler had destroyed in 1381, so this confirms that the two brothels were still in business and, moreover, helps to pinpoint their location. The third one, 'the Belle in the bishopps lordship at the Stuves', had already been noted as early as 1390.[50]

The state of the nation remained unchanged. A Commission to Parliament reported that 'malefactors and rapers of women grow ever more violent . . . more rife . . . in almooste every part of the kingdom.'[51] This was due to the complete mismanagement of the national affairs by the King's guardians, compounded by their corruption and extortions. Then suddenly one day in 1389 the young man walked into his Privy Council and asked them 'What age am I?'; to which they replied 'Twenty years!' Whereupon he answered 'Then I am of full age to govern my House, my servants and my realm!'

Sadly, he did not prove to be a very successful monarch, and he seems to have gone to pieces after the death of his Queen, Anne of Bohemia, as most of his subsequent actions seem quite unbalanced. His downfall came in 1399 at the hands of his cousin Henry of Lancaster, who deposed him and had him murdered in Pontefract

Castle in 1400.

NOTES

[1] H. T. Riley (ed.), *Liber Albus*, 'De Cameris Necessariis in Domibus', B. III/II, p. 280.

[2] Bishop W. Stubbs (ed.), *Chronica de Roger de Hovenden*.

[3] Sir Richard Baker, op. cit.

[4] R. C. Hamilton (ed.), *Chronica... Hemingburghe*, op. cit., Vol. I, p. 247. 'Sub anno 1215. . . . Rex iste Johannes suam semper continuando tyrranidem . . . as irecundiam provocate . . . in libidem . . . et incredibili luxu femineo fretus magnatum omnium uxores et dominas concupivit, deridendo maritas eorum post perpetrata flagitia.'

[5] Edward Walford, *London Old and New*, Vol. VI, p. 53.

[6] Sir Richard Baker, op. cit.

[7] Domino du Cange, *Glossorium*. See under *gabelle: putagium.*

[8] L. F. Salzmann, *Building in England to 1540.*

[9] Jan van Wynkyn de Woorde, *Boke of Keruynge* (The Manual of Carving), c. 1400. See *The Babees Boke* (ed. E. Rickert), E.E.T.S. Orig. Ser. 32, 1868. A 'blanket' here means a white woollen cloth of fleece, 'coton' is cotton flock. The reference to down brings to mind Rabelais's disquisition on the most suitable feathers to use for the purpose. He chose those of the goose.

[10] Probably derived from Anglo-Saxon *bord-wic*, basically a place where wood or timber was kept, but see also p. 73.

[11] E. Ekwall, op. cit.

[12] *Ancient Deeds*, A. 1661, 25 Henry III (1241), p. 193.

[13] MS. Dean and Chapter of St Paul's, A. Box 23, 404 (1287).

[14] Gerald C. Dunning, *A Mediaeval Jug found in London, decorated with human and animal figures.*

[15] James Rae, *Deaths of the Kings of England.*

[16] Ranulph Higden, *Polychronicon*, op. cit.

[17] G. M. Trevelyan, *History of England.*

[18] H. T. Riley (ed.), *Liber Albus*, 'De Vicis et Venellis Mundandis' (Of the Cleansing of Streets and Lanes), B. III, Part II, Edward I, p. 239.

[19] Ibid., 'De Larouns et Putayns', B. III, Part II, Edward I, p. 246.

[20] Ibid., 'De Batelariis', B. III, Part II, Edward I, p. 242.

[21] *Calendar of Patent Rolls* (C.P.R.), 10 Edward I (1281), p. 4, membrane 22, 22 Nov.

[22] In 1305 the number of converts in the Domus was 23 men and 28 women,

all of whom were reduced to begging for bread although allegedly resident in the refuge.

23 John of Gaddesdon (1280-1360), *Rosa Anglica*, Lib. II, para. vii, 'De Lepra' (Of Contagious Diseases).

24 Thomas Rymer (ed.), *Foedera*, Vol. II, fol. 880, 14 Edward II (1321), 'Super Venditione Domus facta G. Cardinale quae Lupanar Vilium Mulierum existebat' (Concerning the Purchase by Cardinal William of a Brothel for Vile Women).

25 *Issue Roll*, 34 Edward III (1361), 210, mem. 12, cited by H. Colvin in *The King's Works*, Vol. I, p. 508.

26 *C.P.R.*, 24 Edward III (1350), Part I, p. 468, 6 Feb.

27 *C.P.R.*, 34 Edward I (1306), 'Surrey', pp. 227-9.

28 *Wills in the Court of Hustings (C.W.H.)*, 5 Henry VI (1427), p. 442, Roll 155(73) under the date 20 July, 1425: 'William Chichele devises le Castell on the hoop . . . formerly le Burhgate.'

29 W. Rendle, *Inns of Old Southwark*, p. 62.

30 Samuel Danyell, *Collection of the Historie of England* (1618), section 'Life and Raigne of Edward III, anno regni 27', p. 205.

31 *Letter Books of the City of London (C.L.B.)*, Book F, p. 208.

32 *C.P.R.*, 18 Edward III (1345), Part II, p. 562, 26 Oct.

33 *Calendar of Close Rolls (C.C.R.)*, 21 Edward III (1347), p. 340, mem. 11.

34 *C.C.R.*, 21 Edward III (1347), p. 343, mem. 11, 22 Nov.

35 *C.C.R.*, 23 Edward III (1349), Part I, p. 24, 7 May.

36 Paul Dufour, op. cit., Paris edition, 1854.

37 It is from this time that the word 'strumpet' (from the Latin *stupro*: filth) is found in writing; it must, of course, have been used in common speech long before 1348.

38 *Rolls of Gaol Delivery*, 18 Edward I (1290), Public Record Office.

39 *C.P.R.*, 35 Edward III (1361), Part II, p. 24, mem. 21, 5 June.

40 *C.P.R.*, 36 Edward III (1362), Part II, p. 257, 5 Nov.

41 *C.P.R.*, 37 Edward III (1363), Part I, p. 359, mem. 37d, 3 Feb.

42 *C.P.R.*, 43 Edward III (1370), Part II, p. 341, mem. 2, 10 Jan.

43 *Calendar of Plea and Memorial Rolls (C.P.M.R.)*, 40 Edward III (1366), Roll A. 11, p. 54.

44 *C.P.R.*, 50 Edward III (1376), Part I, p. 297, 11 July.

45 Henrie Knighton, 'The Anonimalle Chronicle', in *Chronicon*, pp. 140-1, fol. 344 verso.

46 H. T. Riley (ed.), *Liber Albus*, 'Of the Punishment of Courtesans and Bawds', B. III, Part IV, 7 Richard II (1384), p. 395, fol. 239b.

47 *Rotuli Parliamentorum*, 14 Richard II (1390), p. 282, item 32.

48 *C.L.B.*, Book H, 17 Richard II (1393), p. 402, fol. 287, 17 Nov.

49 G.L.C. reference documents for L.C.C. *Survey*, 'Southwark, Bankside'.

50 *C.C.R.*, 14 Richard II (1390), p. 280, 20 May, 1389.

51 William of Malmesburie, *Eulagium Historiarum*, iii, 357, *tempo* 6 Richard II, cited in *Statutes of Parliament*, cap. VI.

VI

'All Harlottys and Horrys
and Bawdys that Procures'

Despite the wars and revolts and pestilences of the previous century, the England of 1400 was a much richer country, even though the poverty of the peasantry and the artisans was still appalling. And because of the turmoil and the death of so many of their menfolk, the position of women had seriously deteriorated, their destitution leading to an increase in prostitution to an extent not before experienced.

The thriftless and licentious way of life of the Plantagenet kings and their courtiers and prelates is aptly summed up in a contemporary mystery play, *The Judgement*,[1] which also infers some class distinction even between whores: 'And ye Ianettys of the Stewys and lychoures [lechers] on lofte [on high]. . . . All ye, all harlottys and horrys and bawdys that procures, to bryng theym to my lures, Welcom to my see.' The speaker is Satan, inviting them all, from the lowest Janet of the Stewes to the royal and noble lechers on high, to come to hell. In passing, it shows that Janet was a generic name for low-class whores.

English manners were generally free and easy in Chaucer's time – 1340-1400 – and the populace had become more mobile. The roads were atrocious but the inns were always full, and while there were a few private rooms for the wealthy travellers, the ordinary people slept in beds made up in recesses rather like horses' stables. While most pranced naked on the rushes which covered the floors, all were careful to wear a nightcap or kerchief round their heads. The high-born Knight de la Tour Landry felt constrained to grumble at the English women, complaining that 'there is maner nowe amonge servinge women of lowe estate, the which is comen [into the towns] . . . her colers [collars] hanging down in the middle of her backe . . . her heles . . . doubed inth filth and it [her gown] is sengille [fastened with a single button] abowte her breast . . . and in somer it were beter away for flies hideth them thereinne.'[2]

Perhaps a better example of the accepted coarseness of contemporary manners and speech is set out in Chaucer's 'The Miller's Tale'.

An adulterous young wife, surprised when disporting herself with one lover by yet another lovesick swain, flings up the window in haste to offer him a kiss:

> Dark was the nyght as pitch, as black as coal
> and at the window oute, shee put her hole.
> And Absalom, so fortune framed thys farce
> offered his mouth and kiss't her naked arse
> ecstatically, before he knew of this. . . .
> He knew quite well a woman has no beard,
> yet something rough and hairy had appeared.

Fourteenth-century Englishmen were well known for their bad language; indeed many of today's expletives or 'obscenities' were then in current use. From the beginning of the century we have evidence in print of their generality.

For example, a man who was sexually impotent was described (*c.* 1300) as 'cunte-beten'. Twenty-five years later lusty girls were being advised, 'geve thi cunte to cunning and crave afftir wedding',[3] while the author of *Sir Tristram*,[4] describing another girl, wrote, 'her queynte aboven her kne naked, the knyghts knew'.

As a further comment upon the free and easy habits of the English women of 1325, providing evidence of a word still current today, is this line from the ballad 'In May hit murgeth' (In the Merry Month of May): 'Wymmon, war thei with the swyke that feir ant freoly is to fyke', which may be translated: 'They were deceitful women who would fuck freely and fairly with anybody.'[5]

One of today's popular expletives was widely used. *The Menagier de Paris* (*c.* 1393) observes that it was long the custom for servants to use the word *sanglant* (bloody) in such phrases as *de malis sanglant fievres* (a bloody awful cold) and *de male sanglante journee* (a bloody rotten day).[6]

In the dictionary known as the *Promptorum Parvulorum* (*c.* 1340)[7] there is a reference to a 'pyssynge vessell or pispot'. The popular word for a penis was a 'yard' (which was not a measure of length). In a medical work of 1379 it is explained that 'the urine passyth oute by the yerde'. A very popular term of abuse, used by kings and commoners alike, was 'fitz a putain' (son of a whore).

Cotgrave's dictionary[8] informs us that a *cul* is 'an arse or a bumme or tayle or Nockandrewe', and also provides the interesting information that the phrase *jouer a pique en cul* means 'to thrust out an harlott', just as if it were an ordinary phrase in daily use. Cotgrave also sheds light on a more sinister contemporary custom in an explanation of the word 'gayole-prison'. This, he says, is linked with the word 'gibbet' or hanging post. It was doubtless a comfort to the malefactor about to be hanged to know that the status of the noble exercising *haute justice*[9] on him could be ascertained by the fact that a Count was allowed to use a gibbet with six pillars; a Baron, four pillars; a Castellain, three pillars; but a simple Justiciar had to be content with only two pillars. Whether the Bishop of Winchester fell into the first or the last category is unknown – to the malefactor the end result was the same.

In 1382 a Parliament sitting in Cambridge passed the first 'Sanitation Act'. It was a great improvement in principle although its practical application was very slow. There was still very little comfort in most dwellings. For the comfortable bourgeois, oiled silk might do for windows and perhaps oiled linen in his bedroom; but a determined housebreaker could quite literally bash his way through the thin walls of most houses. Only towards the end of the century did the upper classes have separate chambers. These were richly furnished, often with materials pillaged from the French during the many campaigns, and there were to be found furs, feather beds, household utensils, tablecloths and necklaces, cups of gold and silver, linen, sheets and many other luxuries. English ladies were also to flaunt themselves in the fine clothes of the French.

In the urban houses of the poor, however, the family still shared with the domestic animals and poultry. Every night a dozen persons of all ages and both sexes could be found sleeping on the floor. In such conditions it was obviously hard to foster a respect for morality, clean language or indeed for life and property.

The rushes on the floor would frequently be rotten and fleas, lice and rats would be equally part of the household, a prime cause of disease and of the life-long plagues of itches, sores and eczemas.

In the rural areas too, immorality was rife, since the dwellings were even more primitive than in the towns. In addition there were certain other hazards, including the feudal lord's right of *Jus Cunni* (the right to have the defloration of any bride). Up until the end of the fourteenth century the lord of the manor could claim dues and fines from serfs, one of which, the *leyrwite*,[10] was for unauthorized lechery. It was exacted from girls who had been incontinent or had lost their virginity, and was also payable by unmarried women who had become pregnant. Since the resulting children joined the manorial (slave) stock, the lords thereby derived extra revenue, extra property and new concubines.[11]

To escape from such vile conditions, women and girls ran away to the towns, where jobs were few and prostitution the easiest – often the only – way out of their miseries. But in the towns there was also great unrest, for everyone preyed on the poor. Chaucer witnesses that 'brewsteres and bakeres and butchers and cookes . . . mooste harm worken to the pore people that piecemeal buyen.'

The consequent pressures eventually had another corollary, as Chaucer once again noted, when in 1376, after the Black Death, a Statute was passed to freeze wages. The outcome was inevitable: 'Suddenly they [the workmen] flee away and disperse from their own district . . . and the great part become thieves.'

In such circumstances there was a never-ending flow of 'living furniture' for the Bankside brothels; from the miserable hovels in every part of the country came the Janets and Pernels of the Stewes to serve in the public and – now mushrooming – private brothels.

The clergy played their part. It was not unknown for a girl to be cajoled or 'cozened' by the chaplain while attending church service, and then sold or impressed into the stews.[12] Many more were forced into becoming priests' concubines.

In Southwark – as elsewhere in London – the streets were danger-ous by day and by night. By day the narrow lanes, barely wide enough to take two horses abreast and deep in mud and filth, were made more hazardous by lazy servant maids emptying chamberpots of excrement into the centre gulley to save the fatigue of running up and down the narrow staircases. At night men lurked in the unlit streets, ready to murder, rob or rape the unwary.

In the midst of all this gloom there were bright gleams, for human-ity marches ever forwards. One advancing field was medical research. The English surgeon, John Arderne (1307-1392), a protegé of John of Gaunt, had made a detailed study of the 'inward heat and excoria-tion of the urethra' and had produced a palliative ointment.[13] (He is one of the first known members of the Barber-Surgeons' Guild, which he joined in 1370; a fraternity of surgeons, however, had been in existence long before.) As early as 1280 the Jewish physician Elias le Mire was practising in Southwark, and he must have numbered many a whore and bawd among his patients. His contemporary, Arnold de Villanova, trained like Elias in Salerno, advised that 'overmuche carnall copulacyon . . . febleth moche the syghte.'[14] He also suggested that 'immediately after carnall copulacyon one should not letten bloude bicause of duble weaknynge of nature,' but ended on an en-couraging note by observing that 'in ver [Spring] . . . doth more encrease humours and therfor in this season moderate use of carnall copulacyon . . . is convenient.'[15]

Perhaps this percipient doctor had diagnosed that sexual frustra-tion was the cause of psychological disorders. He had already recom-mended that monks should cohabit with whores as a cure for 'insanity', and he spotlighted the dubious continency of contemporary nuns by giving a prescription for them to maintain (and indeed, he claimed, restore) their virginity: 'If a woman drinks two minas of water, in which a blacksmith has quenched his iron pincers, three times a day, she will be permanently sterile.' Doubtless the Bankside quacks read all this avidly.

As to venereal disease, at least one doctor, Valesco de Tarentum, writing about 1400, had observed that: 'ulcers and infections of the penis . . . through coitus with an unhealthy infected woman . . . [are] most often found in young people because they have much sexual connection with women who have diseases in their genital organs . . . which is catching and so the penis is infected.'[16]

From an anonymous MS. of the fifteenth century comes a valiant attempt at a cure: 'For sore pyntylles: take lynschede [linseed] and stampe smal, & then temper itte wyth swete mylke and then sethe [boil] theme together and then thereof make a plaster and ley to and anoynte itte with the joste of morell [juice of the Wood Nightshade] till he be whole.'[17]

According to John Wycliffe,[18] many monks and friars pretended to know medicine in order to seduce women and girls. Beneath the rubric *Under Colour of Physic they Commit Adultery*, he explains: 'If they are subtle in physic and knowing a woman's privities' they tell them that in the absence of their husbands they will be ill or even die unless they accept the monk's help. In this way '*they* defoulen on the wymmen'. 'When Lords [husbands] are away from home in wars or in justice or in parliament or in other lordships and when merchants do be in the country and when plowmen be all day long in the fields, then these pharisees [lecherous ones] run fast to their wives under cover of holiness and fornicate with them.'

During all this time that grand old edifice, London Bridge, was playing its noble, but impartial part for the benefit of the Bankside Stewes. An ancient MS.[19] of the time of King Edward I states that in 1281 the number of people who dwelt on the bridge was 'innumerable', while in 1358[20] we know that there were some 138 shopkeepers and residents.

The traffic was heavy both day and night, with impatient horsemen, rude waggoners and laden porters, all impeded by hundreds of pedestrians, onlookers, customers and tourists, creating a tumult. To which were added the harlots who importuned the passing men by clutching at their gowns and harnesses and increased the general cacophony by their come-hither cries or screams of abuse at retreating, unwilling clients. They also lurked in the numerous niches, some of which were used as urinals, and there was even as early as 1377 a large public 'prevey' [privy][21] (although whether this catered for women is questionable) in a state of disrepair.

NOTES

1 *The Towneley Mystery Plays* (ed. G. English), E.E.T.S. Extra No. LXXI, p. 378.

2 *Book of the Knight de la Tour Landry* (ed. T. Wright), E.E.T.S. Orig. Ser. 33, Chap. XXI, p. 31.

3 H. Kurath and S. Kuhn, *Middle-English Dictionary*.

4 Thomas the Rhymer, *Sir Tristram* (ed. J. A. Murray), E.E.T.S. Orig. Ser. No. 61.

5 Kurath and Kuhn, op. cit., see under '*fyken*'.

6 *Le Menagier de Paris* (*c.* 1393), in Sir Humphrey Gilbert, *Queen Elizabeth's Academie* (ed. F. J. Furnivall), E.E.T.S. Extra No. VIII, p. 150.

7 *Promptorum Parvulorum sive Clericosum Dictionarus Anglo-Laterans* (ed. E. L. Mayhew), E.E.T.S. Extra No. CII.

8 Randle Cotgrave, *French-English Dictionary*.

9 Ibid.

10 William Hale Hale, *Series of Precedents and Proceedings in Criminal Cases; Extracts from the Act Books 1473-1640 of the Ecclesiastical Courts in the Diocese of London.*

11 See an article by A. T. Bannister in the *English Historical Review*, No. 44, 1929.

12 William Hale Hale, op. cit.

13 John of Gaunt, described elsewhere as a '*magnus fornicator*', must have afforded Arderne a great deal of practical experience, for he was riddled with pox.

14 Arnoldus de Villanova (1240-1311), 'Breviarii Additiones' in *Regimen Sanitas Selerni,* Lib. I, cap. 5, col. 1338.

15 Ibid., Lib. I, cap. 18, col. 1096.

16 Valascus de Taranta (Valesco de Tarentum), *Philonium* (1418), Lib. VI, cap. 6, cited in F. Buret, op. cit., Vol. II, p. 28.

17 J. O. Halliwell, *Dictionary of Archaic and Provincial Words*, under reference 'Pintle – Penis – Mentula'.

18 John Wycliffe, 'Of the Leaven of Pharisees', in *English Works* (ed. F. D. Matten), E.E.T.S. Orig. Ser. 74, p. 10.

19 *C.P.R.*, 9 Edward I (1281), p. 422, 8 Jan.

20 Charles Welch, *History of Tower Bridge*, p. 258, citing the Bridge House Records for 1358.

21 *C.P.R.*, 50 Edward III (1377), Roll A. 22, p. 237, 3 Feb.; and *C.L.B.*, Book H, 6 Richard II (1382), p. 212, fol. 162b, 18 Feb.

VII

'Lewd men and women of Euill Life
Dwellinge in the Stewes'

With the dawn of the new century most English men and women were entitled to expect better things to come. In the event it was to bring upon them more war and rapine, more burdens, oppressions, revolts and even a civil war of sorts, and consequently more misery and destitution amongst the commons, and even more resort to prostitution by the womenfolk.

During this century the Bankside Stewes appear to have enjoyed their greatest prosperity, and for the first time we have some descriptions of the places and houses and the individuals who ran them from records still extant.

Soon after his accession, Henry IV turned his attention to Southwark. In 1402 he ordered his 'Bayliffe' to *Remove Nuisances from Southwerk'* with an appendant clause *'cum in statuto Cantebrigg'* (meaning the Liberty within the control of the Archbishop of Canterbury).[1] In particular the streets were to be cleansed of the rotting intestines of animals and similar offensive matter such as excrement (*'fimis intestibus et aliis sordidus amovena'*). Since there were other rotten things in the borough of Southwark in 1406[2] he granted some extended powers to the mayor and aldermen of the City of London whereby they were enabled to arrest malefactors in Southwark but try them in the City at Newgate.

The angry burghers of Southwark naturally protested at this, because as denizens of the Shire of Surrey they could not be put under the jurisdiction of the hated authorities of London. However the King had other things on his mind, and also in his blood, for no action was taken and the King died in 1413, 'in a syphilitic condition' characterized by large leprous-like pustules on his face and hands.[3] He was in good royal company for in 1414 King Ladislas of Poland 'contracted on his genital parts a disease attributed to a poison deposited by a Cortezan of La Perouse, of which he died.'[4]

1413 was the year of accession of Bluff King Hal (Henry V) the future victor of Agincourt. It also marked the start of the deliberations of the Great Council of Constance, which was to draw no less than 50,000 ecclesiastical participants before it ended in 1416, who, it is said, had to be content with only 1,500 whores.

Henry V, although constantly involved in waging war, found time to sponsor two ordinances in 1417 dealing with his subjects' sexual proclivities. The first, on 20 April,[5] entitled *Ordinaunce pour Remover les estues*, directed the mayor and aldermen of the City of London to the many grievances and abominations, damages and disturbances, murders and larcenies 'in the City and in Southwark . . . through lewd men and women of evil life . . . in the Stews belonging to men and women in the City and Suburbes . . . [who have been] subtiley drawn by false imagining . . . as well as others of little money . . . by those who keep these stews.'

On the same day[6] it was found necessary to make another ordinance which cast a cold light on the activities of the supposedly respectable rulers of London, stating *inter alia* '. . . that from henceforth no Alderman nor Substantial Commoner shall have [as tenants] anyone charged or indited [as being of an] evill and vicious life.'

Knowing that many of these whorehouses were owned or run by respectable City merchants and guildsmen, and in an attempt to end the scandal and persuade honest burghers away from this distasteful profession, the good Alderman Robert Chichele, a great philanthropist and benefactor, donated a large sum of money into a fund designed to compensate such citizens, in accordance with a City ordinance that 'no man or woman in the City of London or the Suburbes . . . should keep any stews in the City or Suburbes . . . [except] for his own seemliness to have . . . in his own house an honest stew [a stove to heat water].' Regrettably, the worthy Alderman's efforts were unsuccessful, since to the end of their existence the records show numerous cases of ownership of Southwark brothels by citizens.

It is an interesting sidelight on the endeavours of the same paragon of virtue, Robert Chichele, who was later to become mayor, to discover that he was directly concerned in a Bankside property himself, as witness the 'INDENTURE of demise by Joan Sarson . . . of land, a house and gardens at "lestywes" from Maiden Lane . . . which they had by enfeoffment of Robert Chichele, Citizen and Grocer of London, and others . . . at a quitrent of 12d.'[7]

If the historian Holinshed is to be believed, Henry V was not a 'wanton' profligate king, and he died of cancer of the bowel. Two other historians, however, one a Frenchman and the other a Scotsman,[8] are on record that 'the malady which the said king had from his life unto death was a conflagration in the margin of the anus . . . known as the "sacred disease" or Saint Anthony's Fire.' Saint

Anthony's Fire was syphilis;[9] in which case King Hal seems to have 'quenched his wantonness' somewhat too late.

His infant son succeeded him as Henry VI in 1422 and alone of the Plantagenets he appears to have lived as a decent man – or at least as decently as those barbarous times would allow. The disease, which he had doubtless inherited from his father, was to plague him all his life and later to send him into periods of imbecility. It is in his lifetime that the Bankside's activities are illuminated for posterity.

The young King had his first encounter with sex when he was sent to Paris in 1431 at the tender age of ten and confronted at the Porte de Saint-Denis by a fountain in which three nude *filles de joie* swam around for his special delectation. Whether he was then taken for a conducted tour of his family's property in the Parisian whores' quarter is not recorded, but there is documentation of the colourful street names then employed there.[10]

There were, for instance, rue Grattecon (Gropecunt Lane); rue Poilecon (Hairycunt Lane); rue Tirevulve (Pullcunt Lane); rue Puits d'Amour (Whores' Holes Lane); and rue de le Con reerie (Yawning or Gaping Cunt Lane). Dufour describes this as 'a hideous sobriquet', but the contemporary English equivalent was 'Sluice Cunt' and it was not then regarded as particularly hideous.

Dufour also mentions a property in the rue Tirevulve which was called *L'Ecu de Bourgogne* (The Escutcheon of Burgundy), once owned by William the Conqueror, 'of which the kings of England had the quitrent'.

Such names were undoubtedly given to similar infamous lanes in Southwark, and were to be found in brothel-quarters all over the world, proving *inter alia* that such phrases and descriptions are consonant with the speech of prostitutes in all languages.

Up to that time the King's Marshal in Paris had been allowed to take from arrested whores, as an extra 'perk', their clothes and jewels, but 'King Henry VI who was then the master of Paris enjoined that hereafter the marshal shall not take . . . to his profit . . . the cinctures [rich girdles], jewels, habits, raiment or other adornments belonging to the wenches and other dissolute amorous women.'[11]

Another French author,[12] again referring to the notorious 'Rue Baillehoe next to the church of Sainte Merry' says that it had become an object of great scandal to the faithful because of the shockingly obscene scenes there and that 'Henry VI, King of England . . . taking into consideration also that he owned many other licensed properties in the neighbourhood, ordered these aforementioned women of evil life to go back to the Cour Robert, wherein they had previously lived for many years, and abandon the Rue Baillehoe . . . but the Canons of the Church of Ste Merry, who owned these brothels, tried to oppose the carrying out of the King's ordinance.'

It must be observed that even this pious young King was not averse to owning the whorehouses, but only anxious to shift any nuisances elsewhere. Prostitution was acceptable in principle, but in the next manor. In the same way and on the same principle the mayor and aldermen of the City of London proposed to drive their own whores and whorehouses over to the other side of the river, while still retaining ownership of the brothels.

From this reign we have evidence that the Courts leet of the Bishop of Winchester's Liberty were meeting regularly and administering the regulations laid down in the ordinance of 1161.

The Bodleian MS. e MUS 229 gives details of eight Great leets between 1446 and 1459. All of them tightened up in one way or another the rules governing the conduct of the officials, as well as changing some of the punishments for offenders. At the Great leet of 7 October, 1446 it is interesting to note that all sorts of actions (plaints) were admitted for pleading and answering 'accordynge unto the custumes of the cite of London . . . and adiuged [adjudged]' by those laws. This must mean that at some time in the interval the City of London had been given certain powers even over the Clink Liberty and the Bishop's own ancient rights.

At the Great leets held in 1450, 1451, 1452 and 1454 the bailiffs were forbidden to arrest or attach anyone without a warrant, at anyone's suit (except that of the king or the lord of the manor), in the 'said fraunchise', unless they were found in an actual breach of the law; and in no case were they to search without the constable also being present.

At the session in 1452 it was enacted that the brothelkeeper was not in future to employ as an ostler any man who 'before thys tyme hath ben a soldiour . . . beyonde the sea', the penalty now being 100s. And at the session in 1455 it was enacted that no constable or any other official should keep any woman at table 'at mete or drynke', the penalty being a forty-shilling fine. Fraternizing between constables and courtesans was clearly very prevalent for such a heavy fine to be levied, and it had obviously led to a slackening of the officials' vigilance.

The jury – the 'twelve king's men' – convened for the Great leet could order an arrest, but in making the arrest the bailiff had to be accompanied by one of the constables, and he had to show the jury 'the bille oute of the court of al the names that be presented accordynge to the mater'; that is, the court's orders for all defendants to appear. If the offenders 'bee not redy to pay their amercyments [fines]' the bailiff was to pay twopence to one of the constables to 'brynge hym into prysonne'. On the other hand, if the bailiff himself breached the ordinance he had to pay into the court twenty shillings for each breach.

At the Great leet held on 11 October, 1458, class distinctions were clearly to be upheld: 'that noo mannes wif dwellynge within the lord-ship shal be brought to prysonne for scoolding, like as comon women ben.' But even for this offence the constable was instructed to make a proper and formal presentation to the jury who would then 'enquer' into the details of the scold's activities and decide her punishment.

Perhaps the most important enactment at this session was that in the future, on every leet day, all matters between plaintiffs and defendants had to be tried by the 'veredictes of xij [12] men by wagyng . . . or abydynge in law' and moreover must be 'fully deter-mined and fynnisshed without longer delays.'

The last record in the MS. is dated 10 April, 1459 and it was enacted that day that present and future bailiffs were to take no more than sixpence for signing a warrant for any tenant of the lordship; and that the steward of the court (or his deputy) was not to take more than eightpence for entering a plea for any tenant, nor was he to 'take from them any token'. However it was lawful for the bailiff to allow bail to any tenant or resident in the lordship who had been arrested, provided they gave him 'sufficient sieurtie unto the nexte court daye'.

Another reminder that the ancient rules were unenforceable is the new rule that no matter how many times a tenant of the lordship had been presented (charged), 'he shal take but xij*d* thogh they be never presented so often, lyke as the olde custume of the manoir hath ben her beforen.'

Clearly the ancient rule had been that twelve pence was only pay-able once, but venal officials had made it a regular charge, and this had become so rife that the Great leet now tried to put matters right. The old customs were again invoked against corrupt officials to compel them to 'syne [sign] and execut all maner of warrantys and writtys [writs] takyng their fees therefor as of old tyme hath been custumed . . . of the manoir.' Finally, every tenant or resident of the manor who was 'standynge under arest atte the sute of any man by the space of three wekes afore the greet leet or at the said leet day' must be given his summons to attend three full days beforehand, again 'accordynge to the old usage'.

The very fact that all these enactments had to be regularly reviewed demonstrates that the incidence of corruption had increased greatly in the intervening centuries, but now, in the time of this rather more decent king, some attempt was being made to ease the burden on those unlucky enough to be found in breach of the regulations, and to ensure that all revenues went to the lord of the manor and not into the pockets of his minions. It was a well-meant gesture fated to be

ignored or abused, for it would have been a very audacious whore or
bawd who would challenge the all-powerful bailiff, or even the lowly
constable.

There is a reference to another Great leet held in the reign of the
next king – Edward IV – but there are no details. The ordinary
Courts leet met quite frequently, about every month or six weeks, and
dealt summarily with minor offences such as tippling, sale of forbidden victuals, harbouring strange (unregistered) women, cases of
affrays and being drunk and disorderly, and so on. The records are
sparse, but the few that exist testify to the same range of petty
offences time and time again.

However, in the same reign a much more serious type of skul-
duggery was prevalent, and was exposed in a Parliamentary enactment entitled *They that dwell at the Stews in Southwark shall not be
empanelled in Juries*. They were also forbidden to keep any tavern
but in the Stewes. This ordinance of 1433[13] referred in the preamble
to the great mischiefs which had been done by evil people 'without
conscience, dwellynge in the suspecte and wycked place callid the
Stews in the burgh of Suthwarke' and called attention to the great
poverty and 'right dissolute govenment' which had enabled some
people within a few years to 'come sodenlye to grett rychesse', by
keeping brothels and harbouring common women, murderers, thieves
and criminals. With these riches they had bought up a great deal of
land and property all over Southwark (and even in the City of
London!) with a huge annual return. This wealth had enabled them
to buy, in particular, freehold properties, thus enabling them to be
sworn in as jurors at inquests on felonies, at courts involving trials,
and even at royal assizes before the king's judges. Hence, often by
perjured or fabricated evidence, they could secure the release of their
friends and fellow criminals, so that many murderers and robbers had
got away 'and lett unpunnysshed'. Moreover, these same people were
running inns, taverns and brothels in the High Street, 'in lyke wise
as they deden at the Stewys'.

This is one of the earliest recorded instances of the 'packed' jury.
It was also a veiled protest at the fact that the Southwark swindlers
were being allowed to do what the 'respectable' city burgesses had
been getting away with for many years.

Henceforward, nobody who dwelt in or held property in the
Stewes was to be allowed to hold property or keep inns or taverns elsewhere in Southwark. In this way they were prevented from acquiring
the privileges accruing to honest property-owners or honest tavern-
keepers, including the right to be jurymen or to hold any other quasi-
judicial office in the borough.

In the event this ordinance was to be as ineffectual as all the previous ordinances concerning the 'governance' of the Stewes and of the brothels outside the Stewes, although doubtless for a short period the king's bailiffs and constables were a little more circumspect.

We have referred to the City authorities as 'oligarchs'. They were in fact not elected councillors or aldermen by any democratic process by the citizens. Rather they were 'sadde and discrete men', chosen by the various guilds and livery companies, and there were periods when one or other livery company predominated, so that its members or nominees ran the City. At one period the Fishmongers were so powerful that they effectively ruled the City and chose the mayor for years on end. At other periods it was the Goldsmiths, and of course very often the all-powerful Mercers. So that when the City 'farmed' Southwark, it was in the interests and to the profit of these oligarchs.

Henry VI was an ineffectual ruler. His uncles who administered the kingdom were not much better. The 'Good Duke' Humphrey, as the King's 'Protector', was a well-meaning man and a completely inept politician. His second uncle, the gallant general, John Duke of Bedford, was, among his other activities, the Firmarius (a sort of Warden or High Constable) of the Liberty of Paris Gardens, adjacent to the Stewes. Fugitives from Bankside and elsewhere could find refuge there for a small pecuniary consideration, provided they caused no disturbance.

The third uncle was Henry Beaufort, illegitimate son of John of Gaunt, and a cardinal. He was described as the richest man in England, 'greedy of wealth and power, a large creditor . . . and a defrauder of the impoverished crown'.[14] One must add, too, the profits from a string of whorehouses bequeathed to him by his father and those from a most profitable moneylending business.

Beaufort, who was also Bishop of Winchester, died in 1447 and he left £400 to be distributed to poor prisoners in several prisons, including 'those confined within my Mansion of Southwark'. This was Winchester Palace, and is not only the earliest reference to a prison in the premises, but is undoubtedly the first reference to the Clink prison.

In this period there are references to a number of Bankside brothels by name. One, called *The Greyhonde*, stood in 1377 in Horseshoe Yard. In 1409 there is mention of an inn called *The Horseshoe* when on 10 June 'John Hill, ffysshemongere' released to George Syckes and William Schuborne 'five gardens at the Stews, three of whiche are now converted into one great garden'. In 1416[15] Henry V granted 'lands and tenements at Le Stewes . . .'. The previous owner was John Frigg who had leased it to one Walter Stephen as 'a tenement and a wharf adjoining the stews'.[16] *The Horseshoe* was in fact a very large estate, and through it ran Horseshoe Alley (from Bankside to Maiden Lane), which existed until 1973.

In 1425 *The Horseshoe's* neighbours on the east side were *The Herte* and *The Bulhede. The Hert* or *Hart* is first mentioned in 1353 when Sir Thomas Ughtred sold it to John de Halis. De Halis divided it into halves in 1360. The eastern half was *The Hart*, which he sold to William de Neuport. By 1425 it belonged to one Brenchesley; in 1428 it belonged to Thomas Palmer, and by 1432 it belonged to one Hough.

De Halis had sold the western half, then called *The Bulhede*, to Robert de Thames in 1360. He sold it to William le Ferrour in 1390, who in turn divided it into two halves. There is a deed dated 27 August, 1425 showing that *The Bulhede* was then the property of John Cosyn, 'parchementemakere of London', Robert Holande, 'shermen', and Robert Wolde, 'goldsmythe of London'. These partners granted to John and Margery Lethenard of Southwark '. . . tenements in les Stewes . . . betwene the . . . hostell callid the Bulhede on the east and the . . . hostell of Thomas Palmer on the west callid leHerte.' The brothel in the middle was called *The Crane*. The above references enable us to pinpoint the locations of all three whore-houses.

In 1417 the brothel *The Rose* is noted as the property of Roger Wylford, who then sold it to William Flete, and in 1427 the famous brothel then known as *The Castell vpon the Hoope* is mentioned; it was later to be known as *le Castell.*

Another document from this period (1429) describes an incident that demonstrates the militancy of the Bankside women when their anger was aroused.[17] 'Betwene Estren & Whtsontyde a fals Breton mardred a wydewe in here bedd,' after he had procured some alms from her. He sought sanctuary by clutching the altar in St George's Church close by Bankside. Having agreed, by ancient custom, to forswear the realm, he was escorted out of the sanctuary by the constable and his assistants to be sent down to the coast to take the first vessel leaving England's shores. But '. . . the women of that same parysch where he hadd done that curseyd dede, comen oute with stones and canell dong [excrement from the sewer ditches] and ther maden an ende of hym in the hyghe strete . . . notwythstandynge the Conestable and othere menne also . . . there was a grete companye of theym and they hadde no mercie no pytte.'

About this period – at least on the Continent – there was the pleasant custom of greeting great dignitaries with a reception committee composed of the 'daughters of the city', scantily clad and willing to accommodate the male visitors. In some cases, the city's brothels were made free to the visitors, at the expense of the munici-

9 Prostitutes and clients round a table. By an unknown Flemish artist, 16th century.

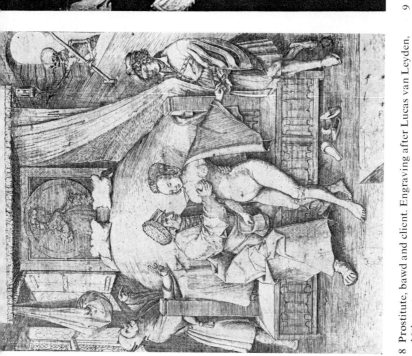

8 Prostitute, bawd and client. Engraving after Lucas van Leyden, 16th century.

10 Coronation procession of Edward VI, 1547. The Bankside is clearly visible on the far side of the Thames. 18th century engraving after the original painting (now destroyed).

pality. Doubtless similar facilities were laid on from time to time in London, when the services of the Southwark and Cokkeslane daughters would be utilized. There is no record of any such practice although there were many such grand occasions. Possibly the sums of money disbursed were put down to some other expenses, such as catering or board and lodging. Indeed the brothels would almost certainly have been utilized to accommodate the huge entourages of plenipotentiaries from Italy, Spain and France, who would have expected such conveniences from their English hosts, in reciprocation for the facilities rendered to English V.I.P.s abroad. Certainly in Berne, Ulm and Frankfurt,[18] at this period, such diversions were almost *de rigueur.*

In 1436 King Henry's Parliament received an urgent appeal 'agaynst myslivers dwellynge in that suspect and wycked place called ye Stewes.'[19] It seems that some had had the temerity to set up in the 'hie streete of the seid burgh stewhouses and houses of bordell.' The petitioners explained that '. . . wher through [whereby] many Wemen ben ravysshed and broght to euill lyvynge, neighbours and straungers ofte tymes robbed and murdred . . . and also there been certayn aliens callid Fflemmynges . . . as well ffrensshmen and Piccardes . . .' who were being harboured in these evil houses.

Once again it was ordained that brothels must be confined to the place 'callid the comon stewes'.

In April 1439 a case was heard before the City Chamberlain[20] which reveals the *modus operandi* of the contemporary bawds, as well as shedding a little light on their clients. A bawd named Margaret had procured a young girl named Isabel Lane 'for certayne Lombards and other menne unknown, which Isabel was deflowered against her will . . . for money paid to the said Margaret.' Then this Margaret 'took the said Isabel to the Comon Stewes on the Bank of the Thames in Surrey against her will for immoral purposes with a certain gentleman on four occasions against her will.'

Another case on the same day in the same court mentions a young girl who had been procured for a 'certain important Lombard [as well as for a] verie prodigall Venetian'.

Another method of recruiting is exposed in the sad case of one Elizabeth Boteler (Butler),[21] who made a petition to the Bishop of Durham complaining that while in a friend's house in London she had been cozened by one Thomas Boyd, 'innholder at the Stews side', to go with him to his premises on Bankside on the promise of higher wages and excellent working conditions. However, when she got there she found she was in a brothel and '. . . hee would have compelled me to do suche thyngs and service as other hys servants done there'. Being a god-fearing woman she had resisted all his threats and blandishments.

Boyd had brought her before the Court leet of the Bishop of Winchester, secured judgement against her for a sum far beyond her means and kept her in prison for three weeks. Somehow she had managed to get this petition to the other bishop, who presumably intervened. The result, tantalizingly, is unknown, but it would be good to learn that Elizabeth's virtue was kept inact.

Then quite suddenly in 1450 all the pent-up misery and frustration of the commons of England burst; after several small disturbances and a Lollard revolt in 1414, their anger boiled over into a major rebellion. The even tenor of the lives of the Southwark burgesses was rudely upset when Jak-amend-all (otherwise the Capteyn or Jack Cade) irrupted into the borough with his armed men of Kent. Cade had the support of the commons of Southwark and London, and the wealthy burgesses feared for their lives and property. Not all of them, however. One very important individual in Southwark, Richard Poynings, owner of the brothel[22] *The Crosse Keyes* in the High Street, became Cade's sword-bearer. (Another rich Southwark landowner, Sir John Fastolfe, was less courageous: he left until the rebellion was over.)

Cade's army consisted in the main of well-armed and disciplined veterans of Henry V's wars, as well as soldiers discharged by Duke John of Bedford after the loss of the French possessions. They maintained good order and confined their activities to decapitating a few of their worst enemies, sacking the Southwark prisons and releasing the prisoners. They looted the Bishop of Winchester's palace and released the prisoners in the Clink. Cade also (as Wat Tyler had done before him) broke down the Bankside brothels.

In the end the rebellion was broken, Cade and his leaders were executed and their heads stuck on spikes over the Great Gate over London Bridge. However, the wealthier supporters of the rebellion had to be treated with kid gloves, and Poynings (whose name suggests very ancient Saxon forebears) and certain other powerful Southwark magnates were excused with fines. The King probably needed Poynings's influence to keep order in the still turbulent borough.

Cade's rebellion was in fact the prelude to the Wars of the Roses. In 1453 Henry VI was stricken with another attack of imbecility; there was confusion for several years before he was superseded by Edward IV and finally despatched in the Tower on 21 May, 1461.

The last reference to Southwark in this unhappy monarch's reign was during his residence in Coventry in 1460. On 3 June of that year he had set up a commission of twenty respectable citizens of London and Southwark because Southwark was infested with prostitutes, many homicides and plunderings had occurred, and it had been at last realized that although '. . . the ministers and officers of the church have cited [these disorders] to the correction of their souls according to canonical sanctions, . . . they continue to sin because the church cannot compel them to appear for their crimes by ecclesiastical censure only.'[23]

The commissioners were instructed to remove all prostitutes and others dwelling in the borough, and if necessary to imprison them, as well as any who were to appear 'by the certification of the officers of . . . William bishop of Winchester, who refused submission to ecclesiastical correction.'

The impotence of the ministers and officers of the Church was scarcely surprising since the corruption and sexual licence of that body had bred such scepticism and contempt that even the constant threats of Hell and Damnation no longer deterred those who sought some little sexual pleasure in this world.

In February 1461 the Londoners acclaimed Edward IV as their King and three months later at the Battle of Tewkesbury the Yorkists consolidated their victory. With the arrival of Edward IV we are back on familiar territory as far as royal virtue is concerned.

He was tall and handsome, and described by Sir Thomas More as 'of a goodly personage . . . of visage lovely, of body mighty, strong and clean made, howbeit in his latter days . . . somewhat corpulent . . . he was in youth greatly given to wantonness.'[24] This last is an understatement, corrected by Dominic Mancini[25] who observes that 'he was licentious in the extreme and most insolent to numerous women, for after he had seduced them and was weary of dalliance, he gave them up much against their will, to other courtiers. He possessed without discrimination the married and the unmarried, the noble and the lowly, but he took none by force. He overcame all by money and promises but having conquered them he dismissed them.' Even the sober *Cambridge Mediaeval History* is in agreement: 'He was cruel, faithless and treacherous upon occasion: an indolent yet masterful voluptuary, his pleasant address made him personally popular.'[26]

Edward not only cultivated the wealth of the great London magnates but also utilized to the full the bodies of their wives and daughters.

As is to be expected, under the benevolent despotism of an unashamed sexual profligate the whorehouses on Bankside flourished without interference, although faint evidence that the old 1161 rules still existed comes from a City record of November 1475[27] 'that the keepers of the Stewes should not harbour men or women at night, under penalty.'

At this time *The Hart* was in the possession of the churchwardens of the parish of St Margaret's, in which all the Bankside brothels lay.

The Bulhede between 1475 and the end of the century is described as 'John Colyns tenement' and Colyns's kinsman Robert held *The Rose*, which later reverted to John's son, Thomas.

In September 1478 John Bannastre succeeded his father as owner of 'the gret Garden lying in the marshe at le stewes'. This land, later to be known as Banaster's Gardens or the Great Pike Gardens, lies a little to the west of Bankside. It was later to come into possession of the landowner John Merston, who owned the adjacent brothel *The Cardinal's Hatte*.

Now there is recorded a curious case of brothel-swapping. On the 'laste daye of Septembre Anno Regni vii of Edward IV' (1468),[28] John, the Prior of Merton, secured *The Cardinalles Hatte* in the parish of St Margaret's, in exchange for the inn (brothel) called *le Popes Hed*[29] in the Borough High Street, which belonged to the Hospital of St Thomas, whose Master was William Cross. The Prior was to pay an annual rent of 'decem solidi' (ten shillings).[30]

The document discloses that *The Cardinalles Hatte*, situated 'on banco T[amesi]mio' (on the bank of the Thames), had been in existence since the thirty-third year of King Edward III (1360). As in 1321, with Cardinal William de Testa's purchase of a brothel for the financial advantage of the Church, this transaction also was completed because 'it was advantageous' to the Church's investment, if not to the Glory of God. One wonders whether, as a result of Cardinal William de Testa's financial acumen, the brothel was then named after him when it had been restored from its ruined condition.

In 1451 the stewhouse called *The Belle* is mentioned in conjunction with a 'bruehous called le Dolfin'. (As far as can be ascertained *The Dolphin*, in the Clink Liberty, was in what is now Clink Street, where there was also an inn called *The Bell*.) But *The Belle* here mentioned is almost certainly the one referred to in 1390 as [32] '. . . the bell is in the Bishops lordeship at the Stuves' and the companion to *The Barge* and *The Cock*.

In 1466 *The Barge*[33] is flourishing, as also are *The Pecock*[34] (which may have been in Maiden Lane just at the back of the others), and *The Bernacle-on-the-Hope*. This latter establishment does not appear again, but from its appellation 'on the hope' it is most likely to have been in Deadman's Place next to *The Castle* at Bank End, or at the corner of Maiden Lane.

The 'hope' or 'hoop' was a piece of dry land in the midst of a fen[35] and here refers to the stream which ran along the middle of Deadman's Place into the river; it was a very considerable stream crossed by many small bridges, and is so shown in many contemporary maps. In 1437[36] there is mentioned 'a tenement or inne called the Helme upon the hoope in St Margaret's parish', but its location is not clear,

other than that it was on the stream side next to the Bankside. This
too may have been adjacent to the 'hoop' in Deadman's Place.

In 1454 one Thomas Slyfield [37] 'demises all his lands etc. in South-
wark in the parish of St Margaret enfeoffed from Thomas Palmer.'
Palmer was the owner of *The Hert* on Bankside. Part of the parish of
St Margaret's was in the Clink Liberty.

It will be recalled that one of the rules laid down in 1161 was that
there must be on inspection at regular intervals by the constables to
seek out *inter alia* unwilling and unlicensed prostitutes and any signs
of the *morbus indecens* or the *nephandam infirmitatem*.

In Dr F. Buret's *Syphilis in the Middle Ages* there is quoted a
scabrous and horrifying account of such an inspection in a French
brothel in this period (*c.* 1450). Inspections in the licensed Bankside
stewhouses must have been very similar, as undoubtedly French
experience would have been utilized there. The original, in old
French, is given in the notes at the end of this chapter; this is a rough
translation:

> In sublimate, a dangerous and poisonous corrosive dangerous to
> the touch, and at the centre of the rapid flow; in blood which is
> put by the side of stoves to dry out the cloths when the moon is
> full, of which one towel is black and the other greener than
> chives; in chancres and figs [venereal sores] and in the filthy tubs
> in which nurses wring out the blood from the towels; in the little
> baths in which prostitutes wash their private parts. [38]

This is obviously part of a first-hand description of an inspection
and an account of the rudimentary methods of hygiene in use in the
middle of the fifteenth century. It is also indicative of the 'evidence'
held ready for the inspectors under the terms of the ancient statutes.

There were the sanitary towels for the menstrual flow ('when the
moon is full'), some of which, however, were stained with a greenish
discharge which was clearly pathological. (Dr Buret surmises this to
be a reference to gonorrhoea.) There were also great tubs of water,
now dirty, into which corrosive sublimate (of sulphur or mercury) had
been added as a cleaning agent, too dangerous to be handled by the
inspector, although in these tubs the 'nurses' (probably maids or
washerwomen, but perhaps also midwives) would wring out these
cloths. Finally there were some small tubs used by the girls to wash
their genitals after intercourse. (It is possible that this is the earliest
reference to a *bidet*, which is not mentioned again in France till about
1700.) In England at this time they were still 'pyssynge hard into
chamberpots' and would continue to do so till about 1690.

Such scenes would certainly have been witnessed by inquisitive physicians trying to find out about the origins of the venereal diseases and seeking cures for them. They would also have made physical examinations which by their nature would have been perfunctory and unhygienic, and just as likely to spread any disease as to cure it. But their researches were certainly of some value when the worst venereal plague in history struck Europe half a century later.

If the temporal rulers were sexually lax, the activities of the highest ecclesiastical authorities were even more shameful. For example, Pope Sixtus IV (*c.* 1471) – who allegedly caught syphilis from one of his many mistresses – became the first pope to issue licences to prostitutes and to levy a tax on their earnings, augmenting vastly the papal revenues in the process. Indeed the Roman Curia partly financed the building of St Peter's by this tax and the sale of licences. His successor, Pope Leo X, is said to have made some twenty-two thousand gold ducats through the sale of licences, four times as much as he made by selling indulgences in Germany.

At this time the Church was assisting the spread of vice in all directions, not least in the great increase in prostitution, despite daily fulminations from on high against the sins of lechery and fornication. The rule of celibacy which had been imposed on priests contributed its share, bringing into being the racket known as *cullagium* or 'couillage', which was especially rife during the fourteenth and fifteenth centuries.

The origin of the word itself is explicitly coarse, as may be expected from a time when spades were called spades. It stems from the Old Norman-French word *couille*, which was translated[39] as 'a man's yerde [penis] but less properly a codd or ballock'. This then became in English *cullions* (testicles), and is linked with the Old French *coite*, which meant copulation in its most vulgar sense (as we should say 'fucking' today). The *Grande Larousse* gives a later derivation: '*couillage – concubinage (vieux mot)*'.

The practice had other manifestations, one of which was the institution of *focarii* or priests's 'hearth girls'. We have already noted Henry I's deception of the bishops in 1129 when he promised to ban the *focarii* but instead 'depressed his subjects' by instituting a lucrative system of licences which became known as *couillages*.

Henry's successors continued this system of licensing and it was still being recorded in the reign of Henry V in his French possessions.[40] King John hit upon the brilliant idea of raising even more money by taxing the *focarii* themselves – an idea supported by the Emperor Otho. Even after John had been interdicted by Pope Innocent III in 1208, the unrepentant King 'discerning quasi-conjugal relations to be the tenderest spot . . . and the readiest means to extort money . . . caused all the women [the *focarii*] to be seized and forced the unfortunate churchmen to buy back their partners at exorbitant prices.'

The result was that both types of extortion – from priests and their women – became established and were so great a source of revenue that many bishops condoned the practice, despite the denunciation of 'this disgraceful traffic by which such prelates regularly sell permission to sin' by the Lateran Council in 1215. Couillage continued unabated, so much so that in 1338 Pope Benedict III allowed absolution and dispensation for a 'concubinary priest', rating it at less than half a florin.

The French and German bishops went one better: they collected the *cullagium* from *all* priests, informing them that they would have to pay whether or not they wished to be celibate.

The prevalence of this practice in England is attested by John Wycliffe,[41] who pointed out that there would be no cure for lechery 'yif men wolen paie rente bi yeere and dwelle stil ther-inne also longe as hym list' (as long as men were willing to pay a yearly fee and let the women stay). He went on to say that some prelates gave leave to their priests to dwell in sin 'fro seven yere to seven yer' if they paid twenty shillings a year 'or more or lesse' – apparently one could bargain for a long-term lease – and that 'summe byschoppes getith in a yer two thousand marks or pundis.'

It is inconceivable that the Bishop of Winchester or his minions would have overlooked such extra revenue from their properties on Bankside, and indeed with such free dispensations priests readily frequented the stews – although it is but fair to say that there is no record in England of the Roman practice whereby prelates shared a number of brothel-girls on a profit-sharing basis, as described in a contemporary ballad:[42]

> Th'Italian Stewes (to make the Pope good cheer)
> payd twentie thousand Duckets in a yeere.
> Besides they give a Priest (t'amend his fee)
> the profit of a whore, or two or three . . .
> Methinkes it must be a bad Divinitie
> that with the Stewes hath such affinitie.

The collection of couillage went on in England till the dissolution of the monasteries by Henry VIII;[43] it continued unchecked in Roman Catholic lands. The Synod of Cambrai in 1565 enacted that priests consorting with loose women should be punished at the discretion of Church officials, which left the door as wide open as before.

The growth of prostitution was also stimulated by the more idiotic gyrations of the Church's policy towards marriage. We learn that sexual intercourse between married couples was illegal on Sundays,

Wednesdays and Fridays, forty days before Easter and forty days before Christmas, not to omit the three days before attending Communion. Abstinence had also to be practised from conception until forty days after a child's birth. Only normal sexual positions were allowed, aberrations such as rear penetration, '*mores canes*' (as dogs do it), were reprehensible.

If married couples did indeed obey such ludicrous rules, no wonder that frustrated men resorted to the stews, while the ranks of prostitutes were swelled by a like number of deprived women. There are many references in medieval literature to houses of resort in which the wives of respectable citizens could be found in part-time (and often unpaid) prostitution.

Not surprisingly, the commons had little respect for the clergy. In the Ecclesiastical Court of the London Diocese[44] in 1491 one Thomas Nashe 'cried out in English "what be you all but horis harlottes and bawdes?" ' while a few years later Michel Monford, indicted for swearing, blaspheming and refusing to pay his tithes, shouted (when asked why he never came to church): 'To hear thy prechynge? Itt is nott worthe a turde!' As a final side-glance on the extra-curricular activities of some churchmen, from the same source comes the record that in December 1490, 'Henry Whitehorne [a chaplain] . . . procured and solicited young girls and the servants of various men, to entice them to the crime of fornication. He took these girls, and the said Margaret, over to the Stewsside, where as their bawd, he sold their services.'

As Mr Monford demonstrated above, the language used by the commonalty was direct; in the stews, of course, it was habitually foul. The names of some of the alleys have already been noted but it is apposite to dwell briefly on some of the speech patterns and terminology current at this time. Certain basic words have been in use since at least 800. In Thomas Wright's invaluable *Vocabulary of Anglo-Saxon English*, under the heading 'Archbishop Alfric's Vocabulary', occur 'Mamilla: a tit' and 'Papilla – titskycel [nipple].' About 900 appear the terms 'Turdus: a scric' and 'Virilia: tha werlican [penis].' Fifty years later, under the rubric '*de membris hominem*' (of human genitalia), there are some slight changes and additions:

Mamilla: tittas
Virilis: pintell
Anus: baectharm
hic pirtomen: an ars-hole
hic wlva: ae cuntte
hic veretrum: pyntylles

and as a complete non-sequitur, 'hec anus: a nolde wyff'.

Between 1000 and 1450 there were a great many innovations in common speech, but sexual descriptions remained remarkably constant, as witness those listed under the rubric 'Nomina reprehensibilis mulierum' (nasty names for women):

> Hec meretrix: Strumpytt
> hec tabernaria [a frequenter of inns] : ibidem [the same]
> hoc elena: strumpytt, meretrix[45]
> hec pronuba: Bawdstrott
> hec concubina: leman

while under the nasty names for men appear:

> hic Leno: baustrott [bawd]
> hic Adultter: spowsbrekere
> hic pelingus: hor-coppe [bastard][46]
> hic Scurra: a harlot.

There are other words, today regarded as vulgar, which then were in current use. For instance, in the religious play *The Castell of Perseverance* (1425),[47] there is the phrase 'all myn Enmyte is nott worth a fart: I schyte and schake al in my schete.' In the same year another glossary[48] reports that a large penis was called a Priapus because it was 'a pyntyll the size of a rinorceros'.

Sexual matters were openly reported in matter-of-fact terms. Take for example the delightful mid-fourteenth-century ballad entitled *A talke of x wyffys*.[49] These ten ladies are sitting outside an inn relating to each other their husbands' shortcomings in a rather delicate area. Their heart-rending experiences are worth a slight digression in our narrative.

The first wife says that she knows her husband's 'fide-cock' (penis) 'well and fyne' because it is but 'the lengthe of a snayle and getteth ever worse everie daye'. She daily prays to God 'to gyve hym evyll hale' (to give him bad luck) because his 'yard' is so small that he must be using it elsewhere.

The second complains that she is much worse served, because when she measured her husband 'when he was in hys most pryde' (at his best) in the morning, it was only three inches long; and she remarks, reasonably, 'Howe shulde I be served with thatte?' But the third wife is in an even worse plight and 'fulle of woe', for when she opens her husband's breeches 'hys pyntyll pepyth oute be-foren lyke a warbrede' (it peeps out before him like a maggot).

The next grumble comes from the fourth wife who says: 'Owre

syre fyde-cocke ffayne would I skyfte: He ys longe and hee ys smalle,
and yet hath the fydefalle' (she would like to throw away her
husband's plug because although it waxes and wanes, it still droops)
and it is useless to her because 'the leste fynger on my honde, is more
thanne hee whenne hee doth stande'.

The fifth wife complains that her husband's 'tarse' is like a deer in
rut, only once a year, and even then, if he is not careful he misses his
aim like an unskilled archer.

The sixth wife's complaint is more poignant because although her
husband's ware 'was of a good a-syze'

> he is whyte as ony mylke
> he is softe as ony sylke
> yett sertis, hee may nott ryse.
> I lyrke hym upp with my honde
> and pray hym that he wold stond,
> and yett he lyeth styll.

The seventh wife, to prepare the ladies for her own sorry story, calls
for more wine to raise their flagging spirits, remarking that in all
England and Wales there is nothing comparable with her trouble,
for 'whan oure syre comys in, and lookes affter that sorry pynne, that
shulde be hanging between his legges' he is just like a lark 'brooding
upon two addled egges'.

The eighth wife can get very little satisfaction because 'whenne
the ffrost freezes, oure syre's tarse lesys [shrinks] and all-way goes
a-way'.

The ninth wife holds up a foot rule to illustrate her point, for she
has to admit that while her husband has a pintill of a 'fayre length,
he beares a sory strengthe'; 'I bow hym, I bend hym, I stryke hym, the
Devill mot him serve! [the devil must be looking after him]. He bee
hotte, hee be colde, tho' I turne hym two-folde [twist it double] yett
hee may nott serve.'

The tenth wife has the last word, remarking that she is so disgusted
with her husband's apparatus that 'of all nothings it was noughte' so
that if she tried to sell it, it wouldn't be worth a No!

Such salacious ballads were common, as were also riddles with
double entendres, which were by no means the prerogative of the
noble or learned. One example must suffice.[50]

> Thus my riddle doth begin:
> a mayde woulde have a thinge to putte in
> and with her hande she brought it to:
> it was so meek, it would not do,

and at length she used it so
that to the hole she made it go.
When it had done as she coulde wish
Ah!Ha! quoth she, I'm gladde of this.

The title of the riddle was *A Mayde wente to thredd a nedle.*

While maids and madams thrived, King Edward's life was coming to its end. Although only in his early forties, his gormandizing, drinking and wenching had wasted his strength. He died of a fever in 1483 and was succeeded by his young son, Edward V.

This unlucky boy was to be murdered within a few weeks by his uncle, Richard Duke of Gloucester, but curiously enough there was time to issue an ordinance in his name on 1 May, 1483. *Contra Meretrices Vagrant Circa Civitates*[51] ordered the Lord Mayor and aldermen to arrest 'all suche Strumpettes & mysguyded and idill women, aswell dwellynge as resortynge to the said Cittee . . . or Suburbes . . . [to] depart and withdrawe theym selfes and in noo wyse be so hardy as to come agen'. These idle and misguided women were to be bundled over the water to the Bankside Stewes, in order to ensure that others eschewed the horrible sin of lechery.

With the death of Edward V and the usurpation of Richard III it went hard for Edward IV's favourites, especially his 'merry love', Jane Shore. 'Crumplin' Dick', as the new King was known in Yorkshire on account of his hunchback, seems to have favoured her for himself but she went back into the arms of her old lover, Lord Hastings. Richard revenged himself by having Hastings murdered and eventually caused her 'as a comon harlott to be putt to opyn penaunce'. (Despite all her hardships she outlasted all her enemies, for she died in 1527 in the reign of Henry VIII.)

Ten years later a Welsh lordling, described in Richard III's Proclamation of 23 June, 1485 as 'Henrie Tidder . . . of bastard blood [and of] . . . insatiable covetise', defeated Richard on Bosworth Field and ascended the throne as Henry VII.

The land was in a parlous state. Plagues and the thirty-year-long civil war had taken their toll. There was in consequence more robbery and murder than ever before, 'worke undone at home and loiterers linger on the streets and lurk in alehouses along the high waies.' These 'vacabunds' wandered into the towns in search of work or bread, the women to swell the ranks of prostitutes. From this period comes the nursery rhyme, 'Hark! Hark, the dogs do bark, the beggars are coming to town'.

The early Tudor poet John Skelton described the dress and behaviour of the poor harlots of this time, in his poem 'Eleanour Rummynge':[52]

Some wenches come unlaced
some huswyves come unbraced
with theyre naked pappes
that flyppes and flappes
it wigges and wagges
like tawny saffron bagges.

Before we embark on their history under the Tudors, let us enumerate the licensed brothels on the Bankside as they stood at the end of the fifteenth century, as pieced together from the scanty records. From Bank End on the east, going westward along the river bank:

le Castell-uppon-the-Hoope (The Castle)
le Gonne (The Gun)
le Antylopp (The Antilope, The Antelope)
le Swanne (The Swan)
le Bulhede (The Bull Head, The Bull)
le Herte (The Hart)
le Olyfaunt (The Oliphant, The Elephant)
ad Leonem (At the Lion, The Lyon, The Lion and Ram)
le Hertished (The Hartshead, le Hartyshorne)
le Beere (The Bear, perhaps The Beer[house])
le Rose (The Rose)
le Barge (The Barge)
le Belle (The Bell, The Bell Inn)
le Vnycorne (The Unycorne, The Unicorn)
le Boreshed (The Boar's Head, The Boar)
le Crosse Keyes (The Crossed Keys)
le fflower delyce (The Flower de Luce, The Fleur de Lys)
le Cardinalshatte (The Cardynall Hatt, The Cardinal's Hat,
The Cardinal's Cap).

Whether these were the names they bore in 1161 is not known. Nor is it known when they were first 'christened', although since Roman times whorehouses have always had distinctive names. They may originally have had Latin names like *Aulus Comitis*. As we have seen, *The Bulhede, The Rose* and *The Castell-uppon-the-hoope* are mentioned in 1306. Given the conservatism of the times and of the ecclesiastical authorities it is reasonable to suppose that the names changed rarely, if ever, with the exception of those that would have been anachronistic, such as *The Gonne, The Fleur de Lys*, or *The Cardinal's Hat*.

From time to time other brothels are named in the records but these would have been unlicensed. These are *The Ship* or *Galleon*,

The James,[53] *The Lyly, The Thatched House,* and (perhaps) *The Popeshed* or *Pope's Head.* In the sleazy alleys off the Bankside and later along the High Street, there were many more. A number would have been known to the constables only 'by their owner's name'. One such owner was honoured by a mention in Fabyan's *Great Chronicle* for 1494: 'and uppon the secunde days of julii was sett uppon the Pyllory a Bawd of the Stewys namyd Thomas Toogood the whyche beffore the mayor was provid gylty that he entysid ii [two] women dwellynge at the Quene Hythe to become hys servauntys and to have menne in comon wythyn hys howse.'

The Toogood family will be found later, still carrying on the same profession on Bankside, quite undeterred by small setbacks such as this. The occurrence brings to mind some lines in the 'Interlude' entitled *Hyckescorner*[54] current at this time wherein one of the characters, Pity, says 'Now-a-dayes in England Bawds be destroyers of many young women and full lewd councill they give unto them . . . Mayors on sin doeth no correction.' This mayor was an exception.

The principal character, Hickscorner, described as a libertine and a scoffer, gives us the earliest description of the *modus operandi* of a brothel at this time:

> Marry, I kept a fair shop of bawdry,
> I had three wenches that were full praty,
> Jane true and thriftless, and wanton Sybil,
> If you ride her a journey she will make you weary
> For she is trusty at need.
> If ye will hire her for your pleasure,
> I warrant, tire her ye shall never,
> She is so sure in deed.
> Ride, an you will, ten times a-day
> I warrant you she will never say nay. . . .[55]

The other whores were Kate and Bess (four, not three as he had boasted).

This same play also enlightens us as to the names of two of the oldest and obviously most popular (or most notorious, for this is a Morality Play) brothels. The character now speaking is Imagination:

> . . . and of the stews I am made controller
> of all the houses of lechery.
> There shall be no man play doccy [doxy] there
> at the Bell, Hartshorn, ne elsewhere
> without they have leave of me.[56]

But at the end of the fifteenth century the Bankside Stewes were to receive a catastrophic blow from which they would take half a century to recover. This was the epidemic of a 'new' venereal disease – as yet unnamed, but later to be known as 'syphilis' – which raged throughout Europe from 1496 and reached England through Bristol in 1498 from Bordeaux, and was for this reason originally known as *morbus burdigalensis*.[57]

NOTES

1   *Rotuli Parliamentorum*, 4 Henry IV (1402), Part III.

2   Ibid., 7 Henry IV (1406), Part III.

3   James Rae, op. cit., quoting from Thomas Gascoigne's *Chronicle* for 1413.

4   Ottakar Horneck von Steiermark, *Reimchronik*, 1743. A rhyming chronicle of Austria in the Middle Ages, quoted by F. Buret, op. cit., Vol. II, p. 59, as *'le Chronique d'Hornek'*.

5   *C.L.B.*, Book I, 5 Henry V (1417), fol. 193b, p. 178, 20 April.

6   *C.L.B.*, Book I, 5 Henry V (1417), fol. 194, pp. 178-9, 20 April.

7   *Ancient Deeds*, Vol. II, C. 5214, 11 Henry V (1433), 20 Feb.

8   F. Buret, op. cit., Vol. II, p. 98, quoting (a) Enguerrand de Monstrelet, *Chroniques*, Pavia, 1595, Vol. I, cap. lxv, fol. 325, (an English translation was made in 1849 by Thomas Johnes); and (b) Johan de Fordun, *Scoti Chronicum sive Scotiae Historiae*. (An English edition of this work was issued by W. F. Speke in 1871.)

9   James Rae, op. cit., p. 59, states: 'it was syphilis with a phagodaemous ulceration'.

10 Paul Dufour, op. cit.

11 Paul Dufour, op. cit., p. 469.

12 M. Rabutaux, *De la Prostitution en Europe depuis l'antiquité jusque'a le fin de l'xvi siècle*, p. 47.

13 *Rotuli Parliamentorum*, 11 Henry VI (1433), No. I, p. 447.

14 *Shorter Cambridge Mediaeval History*, Cambridge University Press, Cambridge, 1955, Vol. II, p. 998.

15 *Ancient Deeds*, Vol. III, D. 508.

16 *Records of the Worshipful Company of Cordwainers*.

17 Harley MS. 565 (1428-9), British Museum, p. 117.

18 H. H. Ploss and M. Bartels, *Woman*, Vol. II, p. 100.

19 *Rotuli Parliamentorum*, 15 Henry VI (1436).

20 *Calendar of Plea and Memoranda Rolls (C.P.M.R.)*, Roll A. 66, p. 17.

21 W. Rendle, op. cit., p. 330, quoting 'P.R.O. *tempo* Edward IV (1461-1483)'.

22 Samuel Pepys, in his *Diary*, states that *The Crosse Keyes* was a brothel.

23 *C.P.R.*, 38 Henry VI (1460), Part II, p. 610, mem. 131, 3 June.

24 Sir Thomas More, *History of Richard III*.

25 Dominic Mancini, *Ad Angelum Catonem de occupatione Anglie per Riccardium Tercium. 1461* (translated by C. A. Armstrong as *The Usurpation of Richard III*).

26 *Shorter Cambridge Mediaeval History*, Vol. II, p. 1061.

27 *C.L.B.*, Book L, 15 Edward IV (1475), p. 136, fol. 114.

28 Stow MS. 942, British Museum, fol. 313b.

29 John Aubrey states that there was a brothel on Bankside called *The Pope's Head*, but there is no trace of it in any other document. (See O. L. Dick (ed.), *Aubrey's Life and Times*.)

30 After the Reformation this *Pope's Head* was known as *The King's Head*. It was destroyed by fire in 1676; underneath were found the remains of a building dating from Roman times.

31 *C.C.R.*, 29 Henry VI (1451), Vol. I, p. 255, 'sold to Philip Malpas, Merchant'.

32 *C.C.R.*, 14 Richard II (1390), p. 280.

33 *Ancient Deeds*, Vol. II, B. 3294, 18 Edward IV (1479), 2 May, 'conveyed by William Hille to John Merston'.

34 *C.C.R.*, 11 Edward IV (1466), Vol. II, p. 208, item 771, 18 Oct.

35 E. Ekwall, *Dictionary of English Place Names*, p. 249: '*hop, hope, hoop* – O.E. a piece of enclosed land in the midst of a fen'; or 'dry land in a fen'.

36 *C.C.R.*, 15 Henry VI (1437), Vol. III, p. 130, 10 July.

37 *C.C.R.*, 32 Henry VI (1454), p. 498, 15 May.

38 En sublime, dangereux a toucher
et au nombril d'une coulette vive,
En sang, qu'on mect en poylettes secher
chez les barbiere, quand plein lune arrive,
Dont l'ung est noire, l'autre plus vert que cive:
En chancre et fix et en ces ords cuveaulx
ou nourrices essanguent leurs drappeaulx:
En petite baings de filles amoureuses. . . .

39 Randle Cotgrave, *French-English Dictionary*, op. cit.

40 Sir John Hardy, *Norman Rolls*, Vol. II.

41 John Wycliffe, 'Synne Rentes', in *English Works*, op. cit., pp. 35, 62 and 213.

42 F. J. Furnivall (ed.), *Ballads from MSS.* quotes this ballad, 'The Image of Ipocrasie', from the Landsdown MS. (*c.* 1533), fol. 29, lines 794 ff.

43 Ibid., p. 72. Furnivall cites the Reports of G. Waring to Thomas Cromwell with details and lists of 'Names of suche Persones as be permitted to live in adulterie . . . for money'.

44 William Hale Hale, *Series of Precedents and Proceedings in Criminal Cases . . . of the Ecclesiastical Courts of the Diocese of London.* Cases Nos. 26, 39, 87 and 278.

45 Note the curious use of the name Helen for a whore, perhaps a reflection of the monastic association of whoredom with Helen of Troy.

46 London Cockneys still use the expression 'a whore's cop' as a term of abuse, or to describe an unwanted pregnancy or a bastard.

47 *The Macro Plays* (ed. F. J. Furnivall), E.E.T.S. Extra No. IX, p. 143, line 2210.

48 *Catholicon – Anglicon* (ed. S. J. H. Herrtage), E.E.T.S. Orig. Ser. 75.

49 The Porkington MS. 10, *A Talk of Ten Wives on their Husbands' Ware* (1460-5), fol. 56 verso.

50 F. J. Furnivall (ed.), *Love Poems and Humorous Ones*, Vol. II, p. 21, item 19.

51 *C.L.B.,* Book L, 1 Edward V (1483), fol. 189b, p. 206, 'Against Vagrant Whores in the City and Southwark'.

52 John Skelton, 'Eleanour Rummynge', in *'Magnyfycence' and Other Poems* (ed. R. L. Ramsey), E.E.T.S. Extra No. XCVIII, p. 99.

53 Details copied on a lease dated 'Februarie ye last 1621' sent by Mr Martin Yalden, now in the G.L.C. Records Room: '. . . an INDENTURE dated the laste day of February, 12 Henry VII (1497), between Thomas Langdon, Bishop and Richard Webster for thirty years at £4 13s. 4d. half yearly ". . . and a voyd ground . . . on ye wharf upon ye east partie of the tenement called the James of Robert Rake".'

54 *Hyckescorner* (Hicks' Corner), 'enprynted by me Wynkyn de Worde'; see W. C. Hazlitt (ed.), *Old English Plays*, Vol. I, p. 174.

55 Ibid., p. 165.

56 Ibid., p. 188.

57 David Riesman, *Syphilis*, p. 285.

VIII

'The Perylous Infirmitie of the Brennynge'

It is almost impossible to appreciate the immensity of the shock which the onset of this new and unstoppable strain of the 'perylous infirmitie of the brennynge' caused in Europe and England. The detailed history of its ravages may be read elsewhere; it suffices to give here a brief résumé.

The disease was thought to have been brought to Europe from America by Columbus's sailors. The first treatise on it is dated as early as 1496 and was written by Grünpeck of Augsburg, although a similar disease was diagnosed much earlier and may have been that known as 'ape-galle', described in a MS. dated about 1390[1] as the 'Brennynge of the Pyntyl' (the burning of the penis), or even the *nephandam infirmitatem* of the ordinance of 1161.

The disease was named 'syphilis' after a character named Syphilus in a poem on the subject by Girolamo Fracastoro, who in 1521 had investigated a 'scabby itch' pointed out to him by his barber.

The physicians in fact knew nothing about this disease. Many at first refused to treat it at all in sick prostitutes, which gave rise to the saying that 'Venus ill had to be taken care of by Venus well'. Fernelius (1496-1558) was the first to give a true picture of the disease as a contagious disorder.

No nation wanted to be saddled with the odium of its origin, but at first it was called the *morbus gallicus* (the French disease) because it had been spread by the French army in Italy; although Doctor Widman of Tübingen[2] actually recorded as early as 1457 that it was known as the French disease.

Wherever men and women were herded together in dirty and insanitary places, this contagion was bound to spread. The whorehouses and their inhabitants became one of the prime objects of public odium, although conditions there probably weren't much worse than elsewhere. Erasmus, who was in England at about this time, expressed disgust at the stench in English houses arising from the filth embedded in the decaying rushes on the floor.

Henry VII, that 'mooste Cristen and mooste Excellent Prince' as he was to be styled, led a relatively chaste life, his only sexual digression being his lifelong mistress Mary Boleyn.

He was not very well disposed towards whores or whoredom. As early as 1487 he had ordained that no whores should be allowed to follow his armies. He must have known of the ravages of the disease in 1503 since Sir Nicholas Nicolas states[3] 'Henry VII's wife had a young servant for whom twenty shillings was paid . . . to a surgeon which healed him of the French pox.' When the disease continued to spread, he reacted with a characteristic efficiency. Fabyan[4] records, under the twenty-first year of Henry VII (August 1505–August 1506): 'THIS YERE the stewis or comon bordell beyond the watyr ffor what happ or concyderacion the certaynte I knowe nott, was ffor a seson Inhybyt and closed upp But it was not long or they were sett opyn agayn allbe it the ffame went that where beffore were occupyed xviij [18] howses ffrom hens fforth shuld be occupyd but xij [12].'

The original directive has not been found but there is no doubt that these brothels were closed down by the King because of the unexpectedly rapid spread of syphilis. He was following administrative practice abroad in clamping down quickly on the brothels. That the Bankside whores were more scared than can be imagined from this distance in time, and that they in fact expected the closure to be permanent is clear from the contemporary ballad *Cock Lorells Bote,*[5] in which appear the following lines:

> Syr, this pardon is newe founde
> by syde of London brydge on a holy grounde
> late called the Stewes Banke.
> Ye knowe wel alle that there was
> some relygyous women in that place
> to whom menne offered many a franke,
> and bycause they were so kynd and liberall
> a mervyllous aventure there is be-fal. . . .
> There came such a wynde fro wynchester[6]
> that blewe these women over the ryver,
> in where, as I wyll tell you.
> Some at St. Katheryns strake a-grounde
> and manie in holborne were founde:
> Some at Saynt Gyles, I trow,
> also in ave maria aly and at westminster,
> and some in shordyche drew theder
> wyth grete lamentacyon.
> And by cause they have lost that fayre place,
> they wyll bylde at colman hedge in space

a nother noble mansyon.

The wind from Winchester (the Bishop's Liberty of the Clink) was the ill-wind which brought the disease and the closing of their business premises. The whores then crossed the river to St Katherine's parish (just east of the Tower of London) then, as now, outside the bounds of the City of London. Some settled in St Giles in Holborn, some near the King's Palace at Westminster. Others went to Shoreditch, which was outside the City walls but within easy reach of Bishopsgate. None of these places was far enough away to prevent the women returning to Bankside when the scare was over, but it is clear from the narrative that when the King closed down the Bankside brothels they thought it was 'for keeps'. All the areas above-mentioned were known as red-light districts by then, so that many of the women would have stayed on to ply their trade in a different milieu, never returning to the Bankside.

Within a few months, twelve of the Bankside brothels were allowed to reopen; there were obviously only enough women considered disease-free to staff that number. By good chance a piece of first-hand contemporary evidence has been saved about these twelve whore-houses, in the record of the Southwark Court leet for the twenty-first year of King Henry VII.[7]

They seem only to have been closed down for a very few months, for the records start with the fines levied on the stewholders from 13 October, 1505. Ten brothels are listed, and the owners or managers are all charged with staying open on feast days and harbouring women at table and board 'contrary to the customs of the manoir'. Their fines were as follows:

le Castell	John Grey	fined	8 d.
le Antylopp	Davyd Arnold	„	8 d.
le Hert	Margery Curson	„	8 d.
le Olyphaunt	Edward Wharton	„	8 d.
ad Leonem	Richard Gardiner	„	8 d.[8]
le Hertyshorne	Margaret Toogood	„	4 d.
le Vnycorne	John Sandes	„	4 d.
le Boreshed	William Aldersley	„	4 d.
le Crosse Keyes	Anna Ratclyffe	„	4 d.
le fflower delyce	Joan ffreeman	„	4 d.

In June 1506 *le Barge* reopened, run by Robert à Murray, who was then fined 12d. The twelfth house, *le Beere*, reopened on 29 August, 1506 under the management of Eleanor Kent, who was fined 4d.

The only one of the whoremasters about whom there is any

additional information is John Sandes, who is elsewhere described as a 'Cooper' and a member of the City Guild of that trade.

All of them appear more or less regularly during the remainder of the sessions, with some curious interchanging of the owners or managers which demonstrates that a small clique of people ran all the brothels and may infer a sort of brothelkeepers' Mafia. Margery Curson appears at all the sessions in respect of *le Herte*, but John Sandes is also found in charge of *le Castell*. John Gray is found sometimes at *le Olyphaunt* but so too are Edward Wharton and the Scotsman, Robert à Murray. Margaret Toogood (who is perhaps the widow or daughter of the unlucky Thomas of 1494) stays at *The Hertyshorne* for only a few weeks, thereafter it is run variously by William Baylley, Joan Gardiner (or Gardyner) or Edward Wharton. It is sometimes called *le Hertyshed*, so it can only be supposed that the tired and overworked clerk of the court lapsed occasionally. He probably wrote the records up afterwards from memory.

'At the sign of the Lion' (*ad Leonem*) has no less than five managers during the year. Joan Gardiner replaces Richard Gardiner; she in turn is replaced by Joan Tydman, who stays two weeks, then John Taylloure, who stays three weeks and Ludovic Gwynne who lasts only one week.

At *le Boreshed* William Aldersley gives way after a few months to Agnes Gardiner who then makes way for Annian Gardiner. Joan ffreeman takes over *le Crosse Keyes* from Anna Ratclyffe for the latter part of the year, while her place at the *fflower de lyce* is taken over by Katerin Mosse. David Arnold relinquishes the ancient *Antyllop* after some months to John Gray, who hands it over to Robert à Murray for a month, but by the end of the year John Preston is in charge.

The Gardiner family are so prominent that the conclusion is inevitable that they were a gang of brotheleers, as also the brothers David and Robert à Murray. All seem to have been people of some substance and some of them seem to have been elected as constables on occasion, as witness the sessions of the court called for the 'View of Frankpledge', wherein citizens stood surety for each other's behaviour.

From this one may gauge something of their standing in the community. John Sandes, John Gray, Robert à Murray, Joan Gardiner and William Aldersley all stand in for six and eightpence each; but at an earlier 'View of Frankpledge' John Gray, Davyd Arnold, Margery Curson and Edward Wharton stand in for forty pence each, Richard Gardiner for twenty pence, John Sandes for twelve pence and finally Joan ffreeman for four pence.

From time to time some of these otherwise sober citizens fall from grace and are fined twopence for being 'common tipulatores' (tipplers of ale), serving and selling illicitly measures of ale for which they are not licensed. It is instructive to note that these are breaches of an ordinance passed in 1161, which is still being utilized, although the breaches are now akin to parking fines, since they are so frequent and regular.

Of them all, John Sandes seems to have been the ringleader: *The Castell* and *The Unicorne* were amongst the very largest properties on the Bankside.

These brothels then were the twelve survivors of Henry's purge. Of the other six listed originally, there is no evidence that they were ever re-licensed, but they were certainly back in business soon afterwards, probably as fake inns or taverns and certainly as brothels.

Cock Lorells Bote also contains another useful piece of information. It goes on:

> . . . and frances flaperache, of Stewys capteyn late,
> with gylys vniuste mayer of newgate
> and lewes vnlusty the lesynge monger,
> here also baud baudyn boller
> and hys brother, copyn coler.

The expression 'capteyn of the Stewes' seems to have been a popular nickname for the bailiff of the Liberty of the Clink – it occurs again in the next reign in a fulmination against one Henry Frances who was appointed as 'Bayliffe of the Clincke and Capteyn of the Stewes and all the whores', by Archbishop Stephen Gardiner. (Indeed, were it not that this ballad is so much earlier in date, it would have been tempting to regard the verses as applying to Henry Frances and his collaborators.) The word 'flaperache' is probably a synonym for a procurer or pander. The exactions of the unjust (corrupt) Giles, Keeper of Newgate Prison; the miserable Lewis the Liar or rumourmonger; as well as Baldwin the drunken bawd and his brother, the wrathful pimp, show the chain of command.

Any woman found suffering from syphilis by the bailiff or his constables was fined one hundred shillings and expelled from the Bankside. It is possible that she also had to attend the nearby Lock hospital which by now was certainly dealing with venereal diseases as best it might. On the Continent the punishment was more dire. In France some women were executed for carrying on business in defiance of the ordinance; in other cases bawds and procuresses were soldered into an iron collar, whipped through the streets, fined heavily and then banished in perpetuity from their homes.

It is thus rather surprising that Henry VII allowed these brothels

to reopen so quickly; in other countries the brothels were closed for
years. He was not, of course – unlike his illustrious contemporary
Pope Sixtus IV or his successor Innocent VII – suffering from a
similar complaint himself and was perhaps more constrained by his
mania for money than any hygienic considerations. Henry VII seems
to have been a curious mixture in character. He was not known to
have been at all sexually profligate; yet there is an anecdote recounted
by Sabatier[9] that the kings of England and their nobles all had their
private brothels and that in the reign of Henry VII there was a room
in his palace with the label over the door 'Room of the King's Whores'
(*Chambre des filles de joie du Roi*). Such a chamber, however, was
most probably kept for the entertainment of the king's foreign guests;
it is very unlikely that Henry VII ever used it. (This story has been
repeated several times with reference to Henry VIII, but in the
original it is clearly Henry VII.)

Sabatier also details some of the methods used by the beadles and
constables to extort money from their victims. They would warn the
bawd and independent girls that those against whom complaints had
been lodged would be arrested. This was merely another way of saying that unless a 'sweetener' was paid, they would suffer. Probably
some dozens would be arrested and those who had money would be
released while the others, both guilty and innocent, would sit in
prison until money was found. Those who were diseased would be
sent to hospital.

Undoubtedly the epidemic had the effect of making the authorities
tighten up the sanitary regulations. There are accounts from this time
of, for example, the high standards of the brothels in Venice, whose
courtesans were celebrated for their elegance and manners, fine dress
and excellent organization. Clean whores were also a tourist trap and
assuredly some of these foreign refinements would have percolated
through to backward Albion.

The brothel mentioned in the list above as *le Castell* is that formerly known as *The Castle-upon-the-Hoope*, which had stood at the
corner of Bank End for centuries. In 1479 the owner was John Eierby,
Citizen and Fysshemonger of London. Dying in 1500,[10] he left the
estate 'with four cottages and a wharff' to his wife Elizabeth, with the
proviso that after her death they were to be sold and the proceeds
devoted 'to deedes of almes and werkes of charitie'. Nevertheless the
property had quickly passed into the hands of John Sandes and it is
very unlikely that any of his revenues found their way into charitable
deeds – unless he thought it an act of charity to take girls and women
into his brothels to give them food and a gainful occupation.

A genuine act of philanthropy did occur in 1504 when John Littel-
baker[11] died and left some stews-side houses to the Tallow Chandlers'

Company of the City of London. These included *The Olyphaunt* and *The Crane* next-door; he also assigned to 'Agnes Heuman and John Croche my servants to have and enjoy my therde tenement called at the signe of "the Barge" . . . and after the death of Agnes my wife . . . to them that longest livieth.' All three were brothels and, with the exception of *The Crane*, were to remain so for many years afterwards, all then being in the possession of the Tallow Chandlers' Company. *The Crane* was later known as The Soaphouse[12] and was then either a soap manufactory or a warehouse.

The first mention of *The Lyon*[13] or *le Lyon* was in 1492-3; in 1505 it was described as *ad leonem* (at the sign of the Lion); but on 28 March, 1505 John Russell conveyed to Roger Fitz, 'the Lyon and the Ram . . . beynge at the Stewes w'in the Manor of Southwark' and under this name it continues to appear for many years. The Fitz family became very considerable property-owners in the district.

John Skelton[14] says that when the brothels were reopened many people 'renneth straighte to the Stues' and it is probably no coincidence that in 1506, at the command of the Lord Mayor, 'a large Cage was set up on London Bridge in whiche scoldes and prostitutes were displayed'. This supplemented the much more ancient 'caidge'[15] which had belonged 'to the office of the Bailiff of two-thirds of Southwark . . . from time immemorial.'

The immense profitability of the reopened Stewes is apparent from the records of a case of high treason against a certain Captain Canby, a servant of Lord Dudley, in the last year of Henry's reign. This man literally terrorized the authorities of London, using Dudley's fearsome influence, and by wholesale bribery and threats and even mayhem made a great fortune, which Fabyan says 'by reason of a Stewe that he kept by the water-side'.[16]

Henry VII died in 1509. He passed on a great fortune and a solvent kingdom to his son, and in his will[17] he left two thousand pounds to charity. One thousand five hundred pounds was to be distributed amongst the very poor, the lame and the blind, the bedridden and 'mooste nedy ffolkes', of which some three hundred pounds was to be given to the 'miserable Prisoners remaynyng in anie Prison within our said Citie or the Suburbes . . .condemned for debt . . . or remayne in prison oonly for lack of payment of their fees'.

The Clink Prison of the Bishop of Winchester is so named for the first time when his son, faithfully carrying out his father's wishes immediately, issued a warrant from the Tower of London on 15 May, 1509 confirming Dr Bekenshaw's distribution 'atte the Clynke' during April of five sums of money aggregating £313.

The young and handsome prince ascended the English throne in May 1509 under the style and title of Henry VIII, and this son of an obscure Welsh princeling now assumed all the rights and privileges of royalty as if he and his forbears had indeed been of royal blood. (His very remote ancestress Nest ap Twdr had indeed been a mistress to the first Henry, and was called – amongst other things – the Mother of Kings; but that was more than four hundred years earlier.) Before the end of the century he, his son, and his two daughters were to transform the destiny of the English people. They were to chart a new religious course, to lay the foundations of English capitalism and initiate its great expansion and (quite unwittingly) to invigorate the growth of English democracy. However, before continuing this pane-gyric, it is sobering to remember that if Pope Clement VII had allowed Henry a divorce (he could not do so because he was a Medici and could not afford to antagonize the Emperor Charles V whose favour he relied on to regain the Medici throne of Florence), and if the young prince had not contracted syphilis, England and the English people might today be Catholics, whorehouses might be licensed still, and English democracy might never have developed as it did. Every English man and most English women should be thank-ful for a weak Pope and a little spirochaete, for the former because his action made the King throw off the papal yoke and for the latter because it changed the chaste and energetic young prince into a vengeful bigot and a sexual profligate.

From whom Henry caught the disease is a matter of conjecture. Katherine of Aragon, whom he married in 1509 and who bore him at least seven children – of whom only Mary survived – may have been syphilitic;[18] or he may have been infected by one of the light ladies laid on for his convenience at the famous Field of the Cloth of Gold somewhat later.

The new King was at first occupied with matters of state and the suppression of internal unrest and was soon to be bedevilled with religious politics. Nonetheless he was keeping an eye on whoredom and as early as 1513 issued a Proclamation forbidding *Brothel keeping in the Host*, and for the first time inflicting upon English women the horrible punishment of branding with hot irons on the face, for whoredom with his soldiers.

Among the other troubles the King had inherited was a people still restless under the twin afflictions of dire poverty and the demands of war. Starving and destitute men and women thronged to the large centres, only to be press-ganged into the army, or to swell the hordes of prostitutes.

In July 1519 the King ordered Cardinal Wolsey to purge London and Southwark of such vagabonds and loose women. The reports to the Cardinal from the City officials charged with this task shed some light on the brothelkeepers of Bankside and their clients. Fifty-four

persons were taken at the 'Stewhouses within the Liberty of the
Bishop of Winchester in the Clink . . . [including] John Willyams,
footman to the Kynge: [and others] at the signes of the Castle, the
Bull, the Hart, the Olyphaunt, the Vnycorne, the Beare' Head and
other houses designated by the names of their owners.'[19] These latter
were Christopher Good, Henry Herring (or Hemyng), Barthlimaeus
Atkynson, John Bartone, Rolyng Whyte, John Kerbyrd, Robert
Cathard, Robert Doggyng, John Brank, Robert Byglay, William
Erswyth and John Aston. Most of the persons picked up were men,
but four prostitutes are also mentioned by name. Of the owners
Atkynson and Barton appear on the roll of the Court leet of 1505 in
the View of Frankpledge but not as offenders.

A number of changes and omissions may be noted. The ancient
Bulhede is now *The Bull*, and a new name appears, *The Beare's Head*
(although this may well be the old *le Beere*). The omissions are even
more intriguing. *The Cardinal's Hatte*, *The Crosse Keyes*, *The
fflower de lyce* and *The Rose* were still operating – presumably under
private management – so that it must be assumed that they had been
tipped off beforehand and had made sure that 'noo suspicyous evyll
wommen and vacabundes' were defiling their premises.

Included in the round-up were Will Borage, Yeoman of the King's
Guard, Davyd Glynne, 'Scholer and King's Servant', and other loyal
minions of His Majesty. Interestingly, Frenchmen were found in
brothels run by Frenchmen and Germans (or Dutchmen) in those of
their compatriots.

This purge seems to have been as ineffectual as any of the previous
ones, for ten years later Richard Fox, then Bishop of Winchester,
reported to the Cardinal that there was little crime in his diocese
except in Southwark, where miscreants were 'dysynge and cardynge
tell past mydnyght & there one pycketh an others pursse . . . and doth
resort theym in and owt at a backe dore'.

The Cardinal's delicate nostrils were also offended by the physical
stink in Southwark, and he always carried a pomander or spice-ball
'whyche hee was wont to hold to hys nose when he passed through
an unwashen crowde'. The moral stench would have been less trouble-
some to this proud prelate, whose illegitimate daughter was Abbess of
Salisbury,[20] and whose exploits were delightfully discussed in a contemporary ballad:[21]

Jef. 'He hath no wyf, but Whoares that bee hys lovers. . . .'
Wat. 'Hath he children by hys Whoares also?'
Jef. 'Ye! and that ful prowdly they go: Namely one whom I do
knowe which hath of the churches goodes clerly more than ten
thowsand pownds yerly and yett is nott content, I trowe! His name is

Master Winter. . . .'

This bastard son held four archdeaconries, a deanery, five prebends and two rectories, and Wolsey was still seeking more for him when he fell.

Wolsey's own popularity may be gauged by a further remark in the same ballad: 'This butcherly sloutche [before whom] ladies must croutche as it were unto an Emproure.'

At this time, as we have noted earlier, it was the custom to have, in the houses of the great, chambers for embroidresses and needle-women, and very often this title (like that of the *lotrices* [laundresses] in an earlier age) was a synonym for women to be used for the sexual gratification of noble visitors.[22] Cardinal Wolsey is supposed to have had such chambers in his palace at Hampton Court, over the door of which was written in Latin 'The house of the whores of my Lord the Cardinal'.[23]

A confirmation that there were, despite the rash of freelance brothels now in Southwark, still only twelve that were licensed, comes from a record dated February 1524:[24]

Certificate of John Skragges, John Kyngsmyll, Will. Chamber and John Horwood, Commissioners of the list of Inhabitants in South-wark chargeable with the first year's payments:
Parish of Ste. Margarets [upwards of 54 names, part of one membrane being lost].

    4 Scots   )
   12 Bawds of the Bank)   Total 71
   35 Parysshe Garden)

In the twenty-fifth year of Henry's reign, 1535, Parliament enacted the first *Acte for the punnyshement of the Vice of Buggerie*,[25] thereby making into a felony with a death sentence what had been for centuries an ecclesiastical offence. This ordinance was enacted thrice in his reign. One of the known victims was Lord Hungerford of Heitesburie, who was a friend of Thomas Cromwell.[26]

Also in 1535 the King directed that 'brothels to be as far as possible publicly and entirely suppressed . . . [being for] unclean persons unfit to associate with honest men.'[27] But 'as far as possible' was still not very far, for in 1537 there is a sharp reminder of the continuing profit-ability of brotheleering when a rogue named Robert Allen was brought to justice. Allen had started life as an ostler in a City tavern but had been charged with theft and grievous bodily harm, spent a term in the Marshalsea prison for debt, and then had managed to acquire and run a Bankside brothel for seven years 'for theeves and masterless men,' thereby acquiring so much money that he had bought property which brought him in forty pounds a year. Had he been content to leave it at that, he would have still been in business, but for some reason he robbed and assaulted a Mrs Harrison (there was a brothelkeeper named Harrison in the 1519 raid who had twice been convicted as a common tippler). For this crime Allen was hanged.[28]

By this time the King had seemingly decided on a full-scale campaign against vice. He had already in 1536[29] enacted that 'noone shall keep houses for dicing or unlawful games' (although in 1537 he granted his faithful minion William Baselee [Baseley], sometime Bailiff of Southwark, the right to install bowling alleys in the Manor House in Paris Garden nearby). Incidentally Baselee controlled 'alle that hys [the King's] tenements sometymes called the Rose sett upon the Stewes Bank . . . as farre backe . . .unto Mayden Lane . . .' which was still the property of the nuns of Stratford at Bow, but shortly to be confiscated.

At this time too, the bear-baiting and bull-baiting rings were flourishing side by side with the whorehouses. There is still extant a rough sketch (dated to 1537)[30] which shows *The Barge* and the lands of the nuns next to a square marked *The Rose*, *The Barge* being on the western side; hence it seems that the nuns still owned *The Barge* property as well, and this is supported by an Ancient Deed[31] of 1 June, 1539 when Sir Ralph Sadelyer (or Sadler) released to Henry Polsted 'all property formerly in the possession of the late prioress.'

In 1540 the Bishop of Winchester demised the Bear Gardens to William Payn, including several messuages 'all stewe houses on the Bankside'. The names of these brothels were not mentioned, but they would almost certainly have been *The Bell* and *The Barge*.

A plan dated 1542 in the Public Record Office shows a great part of the High Street and environs immediately south of London Bridge. It is the earliest known. It shows the boundary post on both sides of the High Street marked 'here endeth the mayer and begynneth the kynges', meaning the boundary of the City of London's jurisdiction and the commencement of the King's Guildable Manor. It shows the locations of the Marshalsea prison as well as the well-known brothels *The Blue Maid* (or *Blue Mead*), *The Half-Moon* and *The Mermaid*. The latter was still existing as an inn-cum-brothel after 1690. St Thomas's hospital and some of the ancient inns are also shown.

The plan shows very clearly 'foulle lane', which was the start of the 'way to the bancke', but ends at this point. It would have been useful to have had the extension showing the location of the Bankside brothels. It does, however, mark 'The Sink', and the pillory and cage on the island site in the middle of the highway. The Sink, located next to the market place, must originally have been where the market refuse was sluiced down, but over the centuries had become the focal point for a number of low-class whores. The historian of Southwark, Dr William Rendle, remarks that even in his day (*c.* 1880) it was 'a sink of iniquity'.

On the east side of the High Street just south of the bridge is depicted a very large pillory, which occupies the site of the ancient Bordych. Of special interest are the 'stulpes' or posts marking the entrance to Old London Bridge.

There are extant many ancient deeds [32] of this time showing much buying and selling of tenements and messuages and gardens on the 'stewes-side'. One such [33] harks back to a very ancient edifice, when on 16 January, 1542 the King authorized Admiral Lord Russell 'to grant a house called the prior of St Swithins House . . . which belonged to St Saviour's Winchester, to Nicholas Bishop of Rochester'.

One of the earliest and most enduring sports on Bankside must have been 'whorebashing'; this unsavoury pastime was still recorded in Smollett's time. There is a reference to a Tudor version in March 1543 [34] when some hooligans were presented because '. . . that nyght they used [stone bows] rowynge on the Thamys, and Thomas Clare told Milsent Arundel howe they shott at the queenes on the Bancke.' Although the use of such bows (for casting stones) had also been forbidden by the King's ordinance, the miscreants may have thought that when whores were targets, it was permissible. Their punishment is not recorded.

The internal situation of the country was by now causing the King great concern. The Reverend Symon Fysshe [35] had appealed to him to do something, because the poor in the realm were lamenting their miserable poverty 'and were oppressed with muche greater rentes than hath of ancient tyme been payed for the same groundes'. He pointed to the terrible effects of such grinding poverty: 'Who is shee that wil set her handes to worke to get three pence a daye, and may have at least twenty pence a daye to slepe an houre with a frere [friar] or a moncke or a preste? What is hee that wolde laboure for a grote a day and may have at least twelve pence a day to bee a Baude to a prest or a moncke or a frere? . . . Howe many men marry priests' ladies just to get a livinge by it?'

The King's reaction was swift, but at a tangent to the problem; in May 1545 he ordered all vagabonds to the galleys, [36] using the pretext which had by now become somewhat shopworn, that young men were beguiled and undone 'with the detestable vices and fashions commonly used at the Bancke and suchlike naughtie places . . .which they haunt . . . and lie nightly . . .for the satisfying of their vile wretched and filthie purposes.' His real intention became clear when the ordinance informed the vagabonds that they were to be press-ganged into his ships for the war he intended 'against his enemies before the first of June next coming.' In September,[37] when his army was in Boulogne, he ordered the commander 'to rydde alle harlottes and comen women out of Bullen . . . and send away all sicke and maimed.' This was but the prelude.

On 13 April, 1546 he dropped his bombshell, dramatically described by Fabyan and Wriothesley in almost identical terms:[38] 'THYS YERE at Eastre the Stewes was putte downe by the Kynges Proclamacyon made ther' with a Trumpett and an harolde-atte-armes'.

The Proclamation, No. 265,[39] addressed to the Lord Mayor and Sheriffs of the City of London, commences: 'THE KING's Most Excellent Majesty, considering how by toleration of suche miserable and dissolute persons . . . have been suffered to dwell . . . in open places called the Stewes and there, without punishment or correction, exercise their abominable and detestable sin, there hath of late increased and grown suche enormities' as to invite the vengeance of Almighty God but also to cause great annoyance to the 'common wealth' by enticing the youth to fleshly lusts. The brothelkeepers and the women must therefore, before the Easter coming, 'depart . . . incontinently to their natural countries with their bags and baggage.'

This infers that these stews were still manned and managed by foreigners, although the phrase might also refer to anyone not a Londoner. It would certainly affect the many Dutch and Flemish Madams and whores. This use of the phrase 'bags and baggage' brings a familiar, homely touch to the proceedings, reminiscent of many a Victorian *pater familias*.

The proclamation then imparts the first official indication that these whorehouses were painted white: 'All householders, as under the name of Bawds, have kept the notable and marked houses and known hostelries [that is] suche householders as do inhabit the houses whited and painted with signs on the front for a token of the said house, shall void with bag and baggage.' The original ordinance of 1161 made no such stipulation, but it is most likely to have been incorporated in the Statutes of the eighteenth year of Edward the Fourth (1479).[40] However, in the Harley MS. 1877, fol. 3, item 2, in the British Museum is found the brief jotting: 'It apperith in a proclymacyon temp.Edward 6 that the Stewes were whited on the owt side and signes painted upon them.'

The ordinance of 1161 stipulated that the whores should be known for what they were: now it was the turn of the brothels. Signs painted on a flat white surface could be clearly seen from across the river by potential City customers (who did not need this extra information anyway) and they helped to distinguish the brothels from the ordinary inns and taverns, whose signs swung out at right-angles. At this time too, most inns had lattice windows with red curtains, as another distinguishing mark, although the distinction between inn and brothel was a very fine one. The most important difference was that a licensed brothel was forbidden to sell food and drink, or harbour any man or woman other than those inhabiting or frequenting for the purpose of fornication. It is tolerably certain that the same man often owned both the licensed inn and the nearby licensed brothel. That this was so is made clear in the proclamation which now forbids 'anyone whomsoever' had supplied any kind of victual not only to 'forbear their victualling', but to forbear receiving any guests or strangers in their house to eat or drink until they had received clearance from the Privy Council and had also 'bound themselves not to allow any misorder in their houses.'

To make sure of his intention the King further decreed that 'no owner nor mean tenant of any such whited houses where . . . the lewd persons have had resort and used for their most detestable life do [after Easter] . . . presume to let any of these houses . . . in the street called the Stewes,' nor were they to give any new leases until the Privy Council's permission had been secured and sureties given that the new lessees would be of good character.

Finally, in order that 'all resort to the stews-side should be eschewed', there was to be no more bear-baiting in any place on that side of London Bridge, and those who kept 'beares and dogges' were not to use them for sport. (Kings, of course, can make exceptions to their own laws. Some six months later Henry granted one of his Yeomen of the King's Bears[41] a licence to 'make pastime with the king's beares at the accustomed place called the stewes . . . notwithstanding the Proclamation'.)

Henry's aim in banning bear-baiting was to prevent insurrection by outlawing assemblies of those thought to be hostile towards him. In the event he had left it too late, for he was dead and buried the next year. Within a short time the brothels were to be back in business and the anticipated rebellion broke out under the leadership of Robert Kett in 1549.

Henry's real reasons for suppressing the brothels may never be known. It is hardly likely that it was done through Protestant or Puritan conviction, for Henry was neither – he was a lapsed Catholic. Although many aspects of Lutheranism suited him, and Protestant support helped him in his campaign against the Pope, the Lutheran attitude to sex and whoring could not yet have won him over to this extent.

He was far from being a sexual puritan, as his extra-marital love life attests. Indeed Archbishop Stephen Gardiner, also Bishop of

Winchester, is reported to have been a pander to the King, offering him the delights of the best 'Winchester Geese', as the Bankside whores were nicknamed, as well as sharing them with him upon occasion. Gardiner it was who had appointed Henry Frances to the 'Capteynship of the Stewes and all the Whores therein'.[42]

John Donne,[43] that reformed rake who became Dean of St Paul's, suggests that it was 'Katherine, for the Court's sake [who] put down the stews' but it is highly unlikely that Henry would have heeded the advice of the placid Katherine Parr, or indeed anyone's advice. Yet another view[44] would have it that Henry considered it convenient to close the brothels to comply with the wish of some zealous reformers and thus gain their support, but the protagonist is careful to add the sagacious rider 'and finding them [the stews] not productive to the public treasury.'

Perhaps a more convincing explanation is that advanced syphilis had begun to unhinge his mind. He was seeking to vent his own sexual sufferings on all around him. Before he died Henry was very ill 'of a lingering fever' which caused the mental and moral degeneration manifested in his treatment of his wives. His violent rages were also part of this degeneration, and the leg sores and painful discharging sinus were making him even more choleric than usual. Dr Rae supports this view[45] and says that Henry exhibited the symptoms of syphilitic periostitis (inflammation of the membrane covering the bone), as well as a syphilitic ulcer on the leg, and signs of visceral syphilis. All this may give some explanation of the degeneration of a young, handsome prince of great promise into a violent, brutal, ill-balanced tyrant. He died in a stupor at the early age of fifty-six.

Whatever the cause, the outcome was that the Bankside whores were hounded out of their age-old sanctuary by the King's command, at least until things had quietened down a little. Things were never to be the same again, not least because the King's seizure of the Church lands meant that these properties could now be developed by private enterprise. The property-developers came in with a rush and within a hundred years had transformed all of Southwark into something very different. Whoredom too was to undergo a great transformation and likewise a fantastic increase. King Henry's harolde had blown his trumpett in vain !

NOTES

1 See William Becket, 'On the Antiquity of Venereal Diseases', *Transactions of the Philosophical Society*, December 1717.

2 F. Buret, op. cit., Vol. II, p. 32.

3 Sir Nicholas Nicolas (ed.), *Privy Purse Expenses of Elizabeth of York, 1503*, p. 104.

4 Robert Fabyan, *Chronica Major* (ed. A. H. Thomas and I. D. Thornby), 'sub Anno xxi Henricus VII [1504]'. N. B. Fabyan's dating is faulty; 21 Henry VII is 1505-1506.

5 E. F. Rimbault (ed.), *Cock Lorells Bote*, published *c.* 1510 by Wynkyn de Woorde.

6 This may indicate that the temporary closure of the Stewes was on an instruction from the Bishop of Winchester or his bailiff, and not a royal ordinance. Neither Fabyan nor Wriothesley state specifically that it was a royal *fiat*. Fabyan says: 'ffor what happ or concyderacyon . . . I know nott.' The stronger possibility, however, it that it was a royal instruction.

7 *Ecclesiastical Commission 1/85 i*, 21 Henry VII (1505-1506), Hampshire Records Office, Winchester.

8 See pp. 119 and 152. On 28 March, 1505 John Russel had conveyed the lease to Roger Fitz. Hence Gardiner was either tenant or manager at this time. Later the Fitz family bought the freehold and the property remained in the family for many years.

9 A. Sabatier, *Histoire de la legislation sur les femmes Publiques et les lieux de Debauche*, p. 239.

10 *Wills in the Prerogative Court of Canterbury*, Register 12 Moone, Vol. X, p. 193.

11 Ibid., 19 Henry VII (1503-1504), Register 10 Holgrave, Vol. XI, p. 337.

12 M. F. Monier-Williams, *Records of the Tallow Chandlers' Company*, Vol. I, Appendix C. 26.

13 *C.C.R.*, 7 Henry VII (1492), p. 353.

14 John Skelton, 'Magnyfycence' in *Magnyfycence and Other Poems*, op. cit., line 1226.

15 *Calendar of Inquests Post-Mortem*, Misc. Vol. VI (1392-1399), p. 188.

16 Robert Fabyan, *Chronica Major*, op. cit., p. 349.

17 Thomas Astle, *The Will of Henry VII*, p. 9, item 154.

18 McLaren Yearsley, in *le Roy est Mort*, states that her portrait in Winchester Cathedral 'is obviously that of a congenital syphilitic'.

19 *Calendar of Letters and Papers (L & P)*, 11 Henry VIII (1520), Vol. III, pp. 127 ff.

20 F. J. Furnivall (ed.), *Ballads from MSS.*, p. 73.

21 'A Satire against Wolsey', ibid.

22 William Alexander, *History of Women*, Vol. I, p. 12.

23 Ibid.

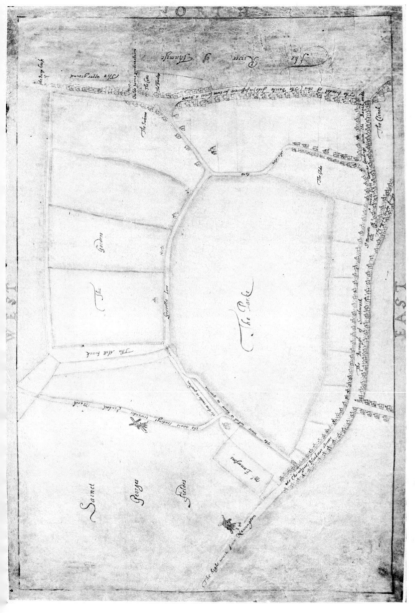

11 Map of Southwark made in 1618 by Ralf Rathbone. The Bankside is on the right.

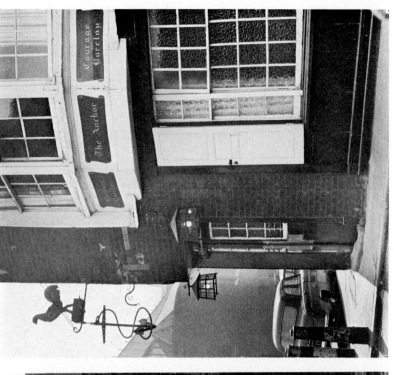

12, 13 The modern Bankside. *The Cardinal's Cap*, No. 49 (left), with its adjacent narrow alley, and *The Anchor*, No. 1 (right), on the site of the ancient *Castle-upon-the-Hoope*.

24 *L & P*, 15 Henry VIII (1524), Vol. IV, p. 53, item 136: ' "The Subsidy"; estreats of the Subsidy leviable on the King's Household'.

25 *Statutes of the Realm*, 25 Henry VIII (1534), p. 441, 1 March.

26 Raphael Holinshed, *Chronicles of England Ireland and Scotland* (1586), Vol. III, p. 952: '1540 . . . the eight and twentieth of julie . . . the lord Hungerford of Heitesburie . . . he suffered [beheading] for buggerie.'

27 Concanen and Morgan, op. cit. They give no reference.

28 *L & P*, 28 Henry VIII (1537), Add. Vol. I, p. 440, item 1290, 'The Demeanour of Robert Allen'.

29 *Rotuli Parliamentorum*, 27 Henry VIII (1536), Vol. 22, p. 559, item viii.

30 In the G.L.C. Records Room.

31 *Ancient Deeds*, Vol. V, No. 12173.

32 *Calendar of State Papers (Domestic) (C.S.P.D.)*, Vol. 17, 28 Parl., cap. 43, p. 14.

33 *L & P*, 33 Henry VIII (1542), item 700.

34 *L & P*, 34 Henry VIII (1543), Part I, p. 185, 28 March.

35 Symon Fysshe, *A Supplycacyon for the Beggers* (ed. J. M. Cowper), E.E.T.S. Extra No. XIII.

36 Royal Proclamation No. 250, 26 May, 1545.

37 *Acts of the Privy Council*, Henry VIII, 1545, p. 249, 'from Wyndessor'.

38 Robert Fabyan, *Chronica Major*, op. cit., sub anno 1546; Charles Wriothesley, *A Chronicle of England During the Reign of the Tudors* (ed. W. D. Hamilton), Vol. I, p. 163.

39 Steele MS. 288, Society of Antiquaries of London.

40 *C.P.R.*, 1 Edward VI (1547-1548), p. 249, refers to this earlier ordinance.

41 *L & P*, 37 Henry VIII (1546), Vol. 21, p. 88, item 199, regarding 'Thomas Fluddie, Yeoman'.

42 'Reminiscences of Archdeacon John Louth of Nottingham', in J. G. Nichols (ed.), *Narratives of the Days of the Reformation*, Camden Society No. 77, p. 48.

43 John Donne, 'Epigram on Mathew Raderus', line 57, in *Poems*, 1650.

44 William Blair, *Prostitutes Reclaimed*, p. 70.

45 James Rae, op. cit., p. 74.

IX

'It is made but a laughing matter
and a trifle'

In January 1547 England had a new king, the youthful Edward VI. For a while the land was to enjoy some relaxation from the pressures it had suffered under his father; many restrictions, and consequently many fears, were removed through the more tolerant attitude of his new ministers, although the oppression of the peasantry went on as before.

While his first Parliament dutifully confirmed his father's laws, by the time of Edward's second Parliament there were signs of a more merciful approach towards sexual sins and sinners. For example, the death penalty for sodomy was re-enacted but the victim's goods and estates, formerly confiscated, would now revert to the widow or heirs.[1] Parliament could not restore the decapitated head to its body, but at least the sacred rights of property were safeguarded.

The Bankside Stewes had been formally abolished but they were not forgotten. That whoredom still flourished is evidenced by Latimer in one of his interminable sermons before – and to – the young King in 1549 when he harangued the assembled court with the words:[2] 'My lordes, you have put down the Stewes, but I pray you, whow is the matter amended? What avayleth that you have but changed the place and not taken the whoredom away? . . . There is nowe in London [more] than ever was on the Bancke.' It was now considered but a laughing matter and a trifle that there were privileged places for whoredom: 'The Lord Mayor hath nothing to do there: the sheriffs they cannot meddle with it: and the Quest [the Ward Inquests] they do not enquire of it.' 'I would wish that adultery be punished with death' was his stern recommendation.

The now unlicensed whorehouses were stealthily creeping back into business, awaiting the assuredly better times to come; although the King's first charter of 1550 granting the Lord Mayor and Sheriffs of the City the power to 'farm' the Borough of Southwark may have caused them a momentary shiver. For a payment of £647 2s. 1d. the City had gained thereby an extension of its juridical powers, but the

130

King had cannily excepted the Liberties of the Clink and Old Paris Garden.

When this became clear the sigh of relief that went up from the Bankside whoremasters and their girls must have been palpable; not to mention that from the many substantial 'sadde and discrete menne' – the burgesses of the City of London and Southwark, who still owned these houses and still derived great revenues from them, and from the owners of the gambling-joints which were now springing up in neighbouring Paris Garden.

The Harley MS. 1877, as we have observed, has a brief note of a 'proclymacyon tempo Edward 6', but no record of this survives. It may have been merely a re-enactment of Henry VIII's proclamation; or it may have been an extension of the ancient ordinance of 1161; or perhaps the Elizabethan compiler of the MS. jotted it down as a matter of interest.

In the charter of 1550 the King also devised to the City of London his parks and messuages in Southwark, including *The Antilope* and 'the house or tenement called the swanne and messuages called . . . the Mermaid, the Rose, the Lokke, the Whyt Harte, the Crown, the Blue Mead and tenpence-halfpenny rent.' Some of these were well-known brothels; *The Mermaid* and *The Blue Maid*, situated in or near Maiden Lane, reappear as brothels shortly afterwards. Whether *The Antilope* and *The Swanne* were those on Bankside is uncertain; both names were popular and were borne by many taverns. Since most contemporary documents are unclear on site details, it cannot be excluded that these were the two of the same names on Bankside. *The Lokke* was the small lazar house which had been founded in the time of Edward II and which by now was undoubtedly treating 'persons infected with the French pox'.[3]

In 1553 the King presented to the City his great palace of Bride-well, next to Fleet Street, as a place of succour for the indigent. Very shortly afterwards it was changed to a 'house of correccion' for scolds, loose women, vagrants and disorderly people, 'there to be kept with thin diet onely sufficing to sustayne them in helthe and [they] shalbe set to work . . . at occupationes they shal be founde fitt for.'

The King's intentions had been kindly but the Bridewell became a prison and a fearsome hell-hole, dispensing a variety of horrible punishments, not the least of which was frequent whipping. Very many of the Bankside's inhabitants were to be exiled to this grim place in the course of the next two centuries. The Southwark prostitutes had much to fear now that the City had control. The Court of Aldermen did not waste any time; by September 1552 the newly appointed Alderman for the 'Bridge Ward Without' was 'takyng order for the suppressynge of euill rule, bordell howses and other vyces and offences.' And he was operating under the law of the City, which meant shaving the head, whipping at the cart-arse while half naked, standing in the pillory or cage, ducking in stinking water, and then incarceration in either the Clink or the even more vile Bridewell.

Such punishments should in theory have made even the most hardened sinner or 'mysliver' reflect and repent, but it is a measure of the tenacity of the prostitutes, and an indication that there was no other alternative source of livelihood open to the great majority of them, that by and large these brutalities failed to stop them. Brutality bred hardened (and not so dumb) hostility; what was already coarse became even coarser, both in life and in language. The insanitary behaviour of the Bankside's inhabitants has already been remarked upon. It left little to the imagination, albeit that in many respects it did not much differ from that of their more respectable neighbours. The same may be observed of their language.

According to John Awdeley[4] the following words were current amongst whores and the lower-classes at this time. *Nygle* meant 'to fuck' and *wappynge*, 'fucking'. A whore was called *a Mauks*, and *bychery* meant whoring. Lewdness was then *lecherous loyterynge*, which by contrast is a most charming, even poetical, phrase for use in such circles.

A better clue to the common speech is found in the remarkable Latin-English cribs into the vulgar or colloquial tongue called *Vulgaria*, used in the Tudor grammar schools. The pupils were drawn from the rising middle class because up until then 'the understand-ynge of latyn was almost contemned of the gentylman',[5] the nobility's attitude being that 'the study of letters should be left to sons of rustics'. The children were taken into the school at the age of seven and crammed for nine years for university entrance, because all the subjects for entry were presented in Latin. The method was to present Latin 'precepts' with an English translation, which had to be learned by rote. In the circumstances the range of words and phrases in the *Vulgaria* is, to say the least, quite remarkable for its sophistication in certain unexpected areas, especially as regards sex instruction, the more so in that, in the words of Udall, the Master of Eton, these generally unruly youngsters were 'dirty ill-mannered young gawks'.

The best-known *Vulgaria* are those of John Stanbridge[6] and Robert Whittinton, both published originally in 1519 by Wynkyn de Woorde, and, most famous of all, that of William Horman,[7] which was also published in 1519.

Stanbridge commences on page six with useful personal data:

hic podex   an ars hole
Hic urine   pysse

Hic penis   a mannes yerde
hic vulva   locus ubi puer concipitur

(Stanbridge seems to have lost his nerve at this point, probably from *pudeur*, and gives the procrastinating answer that it is the place where children are conceived.)

On the page devoted to 'The Contents of a Room' the essential information comprises *inter alia*:

a pyspot	matula
a sege	latrina
a tourde	stercus
a farte	fedo
a stynke	feteo
shyte	cumo
pysse	mingo

On page seventeen are such painful admissions as 'I am almoost beshitten' as well as the warning 'Thou stinkest', together with the serious charge ' *"concubit cum pellice tota nocte"*: "he lay with an harlot al nyghte".' Page twenty introduces the innocent schoolboy to the adult concept: ' *"alter supponit uxorem suam"*: "he is a kokolde".'

Robert Whittinton (or Whittington) has a somewhat more adult approach, giving good advice mixed with horrible warnings of the harsh realities of Tudor life. For example: 'Vpon London Brydge I saw iij or iiij mennes heddes stand vpon poles'; 'Vpon Ludgate ye fore quarter of a man is set vpon a pole'; 'Vpon the other syde hangith ye hawnce [haunch] of a man with ye legge'.

William Horman's book is much more compendious and it would surely have been impossible for anyone to memorize even a quarter of its contents. It is divided into categories touching upon every aspect of life. It very soon gets down to fundamentals. On page fifty-seven useful advice is given about venereal disease: 'the ffrenche pokkes is a perylous and wonderfull sykenes for it infecteth onlie with touch-ynge.'

It is in the section headed *'de Vitiis et Improbes moribus'* (Concerning Evil Life and Manners) that these sophisticated seven-year-olds are introduced to sex. Horman's style is refreshingly blunt:

mulier portentosae libidinis	An excedynge stronge hore;
multas foemenas incestavit	He hath deflowered manie women;
meretricatu producit vitam	Shee liveth by baudry;

and (in English only to save space):

Grete drynkynge of wyne maketh one redy to lechery;
Comen women with oft misusynge of theyre bodie, be made
barren;
Whoris caste awey theyr children;
He gropeth uncleanlie children and maydens;
My doughter was intysed of hym to do lechery;
All thy conversacyon is amonge brotells and drudges.

Page 119 gives useful phrases for use once the child is in the brothel:
'Thou art a strong harlott', and as a conversational opening gambit,
'Shee is baude to an hoore'. The next page gives the child a forestaste
of adult life to come with the following erudite apophthegms: 'Unclene women of theyr bodies, dwells afore haunt of ynnys [inns] for
the more lucur [to earn more money];' 'Shee is a woman well borne
and of great kynne [of noble family] but a strong hoore;' and 'Hee
kepyth other mennes wyves.'

There are also observations about fashions and morals: 'Kerchiefs
of raynes [stripes] and shyrtes be instrumentys of pryde and lechery';
and 'Unclene lyvynge women shewe oute theyr brestis.' The chapter
concludes with the unforgettable truism 'Some loves theyre lemman
beter than theyre true wyfe.'

With all this very valuable information impressed on their fresh
young minds these young gentlemen were obviously well equipped to
face any sexual hazard with an appropriate phrase. But what is of the
greatest interest to this narrative is that they were expected *as a
matter of course* to consort with prostitutes and to be familiar with
brothels such as those on the Bankside. There, however, the conversa-
tion would be much more colourful and certainly not conducted in
Latin.

Under Edward, the bear-baiting and bull-baitings were back again,
although the King himself seems not to have been greatly interested.
But he was just as fearful as his father about public gatherings being
used for plots, as is shown by a proclamation made in 1553-4, once
again against vagabonds[8] but casting the net much wider, 'forbicause
Divers Printers Bokeselers and plaiers of enterludes [actors]' were
preaching sedition 'among the kings maiesties lovynge and faythfull
subjectes'.

In contrast to the lives of the emerging middle class, the plight of
the poor was still desperate. William Harrison,[9] writing about 1570,
describes their condition: 'Our fathers, yea ourselves also, have lien
full oft upon straw pallets on rough mats covered onlie with a sheet
under coverlets made of dagswain . . . and a good round log under
their heads . . . [if] our fathers had within seven years after marriage
purchased a matteres [mattress] or flockebed and thereto a sacke of

chaffe to rest his head upon, he thought himselfe as well lodged as the lord of the towne.'

He then attacks the 'greedie guttes' who used their wealth to entertain lavishly and wastefully, but denied even the scraps from their tables to the poor, saying, ' . . . they will most uncharitably and unchristianly rebuke them, chide them, rattle them, yea and threat them, that the poor, being checkt of them that should chearish them, are driven to despair.'

Phillip Stubbes, writing in 1583,[10] graphically portrays the conditions in London itself: 'Whereas the poore lye in the streats uppon pallets of straw (and well if they have that too) or els in the mire and dirt as is commonlie seene, having neither house to put in the heads, covering to keep them from the cold nor yet to hide their shame withall, nor penny to buy them sustenance . . . but are permitted to dye in the streats like dogges or beasts . . . [if they are unlucky enough to have caught the plague] strait way thei throw them out of their dores . . . and then laid down either in the streets or else conveied to some olde house in the fieldes . . . where for want of due sustentation they end their dayes most miserably.'

He concludes his observations by saying that if he had not seen all this for himself he would not have believed that heathen Turks could have behaved so.

A property developer named Henry Polsted, who had already secured a large tract of land on Bankside including both *The Rose* and *The Unicorn* from Henry VIII, was in 1550 granted by Edward VI the right to pases on to his son Thomas, Citizen and Taylour of London,[11] 'his messuages at le Banke formerly called le Steweside', for which small service the King received £7 6s. 8d. This is the first indication that the old name of Bankside had been restored subsequent to the banning of the brothels.

In 1552 Henry Polsted divided up this property amongst a number of lessees. John Allen got 'the Beare Yarde with the Beerehows'; Leonard Willis got 'The Rose Garden'; and John Davison got both *The Rose* and *The Unicorn*. This was the original property of the nuns of Stratford-atte-bogh which Sir Ralf Sadler had received from King Henry VIII in 1539 after the confiscation, and which Polsted had bought from him shortly afterwards. It then comprised '12 messuages, 16 gardens and four acres of land including the Bear Garden'. Part of this estate included the King's Pike Garden, which still contained some of the original fishponds.

A fascinating reminder of the smelly nature of the neighbourhood comes from a record[12] concerning the acquisition of some property in Paris Garden by one Stephen Merdeman. This is undoubtedly a case wherein an ancient 'gong-farmer' (dung remover) had adopted (or perhaps had been dubbed with) the patronymic suitable to his occupation. Dung-shifting was a very profitable business, so there was no shame – perhaps even a *cachet* – in being recognized as the 'merde man' for Paris Garden.

From Edward's reign we have the first contemporary illustration of the row of Bankside whorehouses, in a painting of his Coronation procession on 19 February, 1547. The original was displayed in the Great Dining Room in Viscount Montague's mansion at Cowdray in Sussex and was destroyed when the building was burnt down in 1793, but fortunately some time before that an engraving had been made by Basire for the Society of Antiquaries. The engraving is in the Print Room of the British Museum.

The southern panorama is clear, with Old London Bridge on the far left, and the Bankside and its embankment clearly delineated. On the left is Winchester House, next to which is a smaller building which is most probably the Clink prison. Next, occluding the entrance to Deadman's Place, is a building which must have been *The James*. Then there are depicted some eighteen or nineteen houses in the plain ungabled pre-Tudor style. Two sets of stairs are shown, one at Bank End and the other about half-way along the bank. This is most probably Goat Stairs, the origin of whose name is unknown but which was most likely to have been the name of an adjacent alley or tavern.

With the accession of Edward VI, Protestantism became the established religious dogma in the land. The reign was long enough to entrench the tradition against legalized prostitution and licensed brothels which characterizes England and other Protestant countries, in contrast with the acceptance and toleration of such 'sinful' manifestations in Roman Catholic lands to this day.

The one positive step taken by the Protestants – allowing priests to marry – did stop the scandal of priestly fornication as well as other sexual divagations. By his seizure of the Church lands Henry VIII also made an end of the Church's profits from prostitution and brothels.

Unfortunately for the English people, the young King died in July 1553 of the legacy left him by his father, a combination of congenital syphilis and tuberculosis. He was succeeded by his sister Mary.

The political and religious events of her reign have been discussed exhaustively by historians; so far as concerns this history, the first thing that her first Parliament did was to abrogate all the laws of Henry VIII. This included lifting the ban on the Bankside Stewes. Their troubles were not quite over, though, because of the tremendous complexity of trying to sort out the ownership of confiscated Church lands, which had already been sold to many rich and powerful landlords and property speculators.

Those still in business were now under 'private enterprise' and it seems that they remained so, for according to Harrison (who was writing about 1572):[14] 'The Stewes and publicke bordell howses are abolished and so continue untill the tyme of Quene Marie, in whose daies some of the Clergie made laboure to have them restored againe: and were very likely to have gained their sute if shee had lived a while longer. Suche trees. Suche frute. For the Stewes, saith one of them in a Sermon at Paules Cross, are so necessary in a comon welthe as a jaxe [a lavatory] in a mannes howse.'

The bishop who preached from St Paul's Cross was very likely Stephen Gardiner, who had been rusticated during Edward's reign but was now restored to power, and had even been appointed Lord Chancellor. He certainly knew of the physical and financial benefits of his own stews on Bankside and could also testify to the quality of at least some of his Winchester Geese. He was not a unique case; there is plenty of testimony to the worldly ways of bishops. That doughty old Scot, Schir Davyd Lyndesay of the Mount, had observed in 1535[15] that 'bischopps . . . may fuck their fill and be vnmarit [unmarried]', and in 1542 that sturdy Puritan Henrie Brinckelowe[16] was fulminating against Stephen Gardiner openly keeping other men's wives, and suggesting that 'if all the byssopp of Ingland were hanged whiche kepe harlots and whorys, we shuld have fewer pompeos bysshops.'

The level of the general morality in high places during Mary's reign may be gauged from the fact that one of the most prominent clergymen in the land was Hugh Weston, who in 1553 was installed as Dean of Westminster, but whose sexual life was an open scandal, so much so that he was stated to have many times been bitten by the Winchester Geese of the Bankside Stewes (to 'be bitten' by one of these whores was to have one of the venereal diseases) and himself to be much practised in the art of passing his experiences on to others.[17] It became so outrageous that he had to be removed from office in August 1557 by Cardinal Pole.

In 1558 Mary died. Her father (or perhaps her mother)[18] had left her the legacy of congenital syphilis, which had undoubtedly played a large part in her psychological make-up. The most striking physical manifestation was her rhinitis about which her husband, Philip of Spain, had complained in a letter couched in very frank terms: 'there was a disgusting smell from her nose'. Her physical disabilities, coupled with the arrogance she had inherited from her mother, undoubtedly played a part in her religious bigotry which brought death to so many Englishmen. Her death averted a complete disaster for the nation, and a fervent sigh of relief went up (at least from all Protestants) when her sister Elizabeth ascended the throne.

For the sinful elements inhabiting Bankside, the rejoicing was tempered with some apprehension since Mary had tolerated the brothels, while Protestantism and prostitution (at least in theory) were uneasy bedfellows. They would not have forgotten Bishop Latimer's last sermon before Edward VI in 1550 and the implicit threat in his words:[19] 'I would wish that adultery be punished with death . . . for there never was more lechery in England than is at this day . . . it is made but a laughing matter and a trifle.'

William Harrison[20] some thirty years later was more specific in his proposed measures. His rantings have some value inasmuch as they disclose what sort of punishments were already being meted out to these women.

> Harlots and their mates, by carting ducking and dooing of open penaunce (in sheetes in churches and in market steeds [places]) are often put to rebuke . . . howbeit this is counted with some either as no punishment at all to speake of, or of smalle regarded by the offendors . . . I wolde have some sharper law . . . For what great smart is it to be turned oute of an hotte sheete into a cold, or after a little washing in the water [a ducking] to let lose again unto their former trades? Howbeit the dragging of some of them over the Thames betwene Lambeth and Westminster at the taile of a boat is a punishment that most terrifieth them whiche are condemned therto . . . as in theft, so with adulterie and whoredome, I would wish the parties trespassant to be made bond or slaves unto those that received the iniurie [injury] . . . or be condemned to the gallies, for that punishment would prove more bitter . . . than halfe an houres hanging or standing in a sheet be the weather never so cold.

Such punishments may have been but a trifle to the court which handed them out and to the wealthy bourgeoisie who no doubt thronged to watch such spectacles (although they would have provided most of the victims if Harrison's views had become law), but for the 'simple weemen' in the stews they were anything but. It will perhaps be useful in the next chapter to consider in more detail the position of English women at this point in time.

NOTES

1 *Statutes of the Realm*, 2 & 3 Edward VI (1548), Vol. 23, p. 72.

2 'Latimer's Third Sermon before Edward the Sixth', in G. E. Corrie (ed.), *Sermons of Bishop Hugh Latimer*, Parker Society, p. 196.

3 William Stow, *Remarks on London*, 'Kent Street in Southwark'.

4 F. J. Furnivall (ed.), *John Awdeley's 'Vacabunds'*, E.E.T.S. Extra No. IX.

5 Alexander Barclay (1474-1552), *Mirrour of Good Manners*.

6 *Vulgaria Stanbrigiana* (ed. B. White), E.E.T.S. Orig. Ser. 187.

7 *William Horman's Vulgaria* (ed. M. R. James), Roxburghe Club, 1926.

8 *Tudor Proclamations at the Society of Antiquaries.*

9 William Harrison, *Description of England* (1587), in F. J. Furnivall (ed.), *Shakespeare's England*.

10 Phillip Stubbes, *Anatomie of Abuses*, in F. J. Furnivall (ed.), *Shakespeare's England*, pp. 59-60.

11 *C.P.R.*, 4 Edward VI (1550), Vol. III, Part II, p. 199, 7 May.

12 *C.P.R.*, 4 Edward VI (1550), Vol. III, Part II, p. 249.

13 In Old English the word 'goat' meant a kid or female goat and was a nickname for lustful women and whores much in use until about 1400. The male was a 'bucca' (buck).

14 William Harrison, op. cit.

15 Sir David Lindsay of the Mount, *Ane Pleasant Satyre*, line 1363, in *Works* (ed. Douglas Hamer).

16 Henrie Brinckelow, *Complaynte of Roderick More* (ed. J. M. Cowper), E.E.T.S. Extra No. XXII.

17 John Bale, *The Vocation of John Bale*, quoted by William Becket, op. cit.

18 Buret, op. cit., states that Katherine's father had syphilis, although 'not confirmed'.

19 G. E. Corrie (ed.), *Sermons of Bishop Hugh Latimer*, op. cit., p. 244.

20 William Harrison, op. cit., Part II, p. 226 ff, 'Sundry kindes of Punishments'.

X

'Englisshe Women be hotte as goattes'

In the preceding chapters we have seen many examples of the bitter fulminations against and denigration of English women as tempt-resses and arch-inducers to lewdness of every description. Up to the time of Henry VIII, the focus was on the fornications of lecherous monks; but by the time that Edward VI had established Protestant-ism, the animus had swung back against the women themselves. By the end of the century one hears Rowlands's well-known cry,[1] 'I knowe nott what shoulde be the cause why so innumerable harlots and Curtizans abide about London.'

Now the bald fact is that English women were no more or less sexually activated than women anywhere else in the world. In the old agricultural and peasant communities sex was a matter of course, openly practised and taken for granted; when animals are copulating all round the methods of procreation are not secret from the smallest child. Prostitution as an organized institution was unknown: the women who preferred to 'live by their bodies' were independent and recognized as such, even if deplored by some. Few women aspire to whoredom solely for money; the vast majority accept – even if they are not wholly satisfied by – the sexual opportunities given in marriage.

The open-mindedness of English women in the Middle Ages is demonstrated by Chaucer's Wife of Bath's earthy language and sexuality, and by 'The Tale of Ten Wives'. We have demonstrated, over the course of the centuries, the vagaries of England's rulers and the economic and political adventures into which they dragged the nation, wiping out hundreds of thousands of the menfolk, reducing the countryside to desolation over and over again and compelling the women to trek to the urban areas to seek food, sustenance and work. There never was a time after William the Conqueror when there was enough work for all the women in the towns and cities.

In the countryside women were busily involved in agriculture and domestic industries. A considerable number were engaged in certain

trades. Some were involved in crafts, either as their husbands' help-
meets or on their own account. Ale-brewing, for example, was a
woman's craft — 'brewster' is the female appellative to this day.
Wherever the family-industry system prevailed women had an
assured position; on her husband's death the widow usually carried
on. Trades like millinery and dressmaking and a profession — midwifery — were open to all.

But with the development of early 'capitalism' their opportunities
began to diminish. Outlets for their individual productive capacities
declined. Even before 'Jack of Newbury' (John Winchcombe the
Clothier, 1450-1520) there were 'factories' of a sort, presaging organized factory labour. The family wage gave way to the individual
wage, and while the men began to organize themselves for the labour
market, the women were not able to do so. The wage-earner tended
to work away from home and this helped to exclude women from
participation in their husband's employment.

The overall growth in the national wealth enabled many upper-
and middle-class women to withdraw from the labour market alto-
gether, to become housewives and even to employ servants themselves.
But hundreds of thousands of the poorer women were thrown onto
their own resources in an environment that had, as yet, no capacity
to employ them. The decline in the cottage industries and the daily
absence of the breadwinner also resulted in a loss of educational
opportunities for girls, and produced generations of women endowed
with a lower mental and moral calibre: it left the men with even
greater dominance. Hence the direct physical and psychological
influence which English women had over their menfolk when at home
diminished as the men drifted away to work outside the home.

By the time Henry VIII came to the throne, for countless
thousands of women the only remaining alternative was to peddle
their bodies, and for the best pickings they had to flock to the conur-
bations. Many were innocent and were seduced by the city 'slickers'.
Many became kept women and priests' whores. Still more became
ambulant independent prostitutes. A substantial number found their
way into the brothels, whose numbers had expanded greatly since
Henry V's ordinance of 1417 and notwithstanding several more
ordinances against prostitution in the interim.

The houses on the Bankside, although still limited in number, were
undoubtedly larger by now than when they had first been licensed in
1161 and brothels had sprung up like weeds in the surrounding areas
despite all fulminations and injunctions against them. On the Bankside, too, the bear- and bull-baiting rings and the cockpits attracted
thousands of unattached men daily to the waterside; and by the end
of the sixteenth century the opening of the playhouses brought

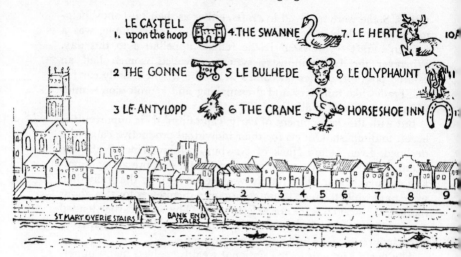

Reconstruction of the Bankside in 1547 (see plate 10).

thousands more flocking to this central place of amusement. The number of brothels in the peripheral areas of the City itself had also increased mightily.

Hundreds of watermen operated all hours of the day and night (despite the prohibitions) bringing men over the water from the City to the delights of the Bankside. At this time there were some three thousand wherries licensed on the Thames. The more pusillanimous men would go to one of the eighteen licensed whorehouses; the vast majority would patronize those run by private enterprise, doubtless because both the amenities and the women there were more appetizing. The hundreds of taverns could likewise supply places for assignment and beds for fulfilment.

The fierce competition would certainly have ensured brothels of greatly different categories. Some of them must have been of considerable luxury, and since many were owned or managed by Flemish and Dutch whoremistresses of great expertise and experience, regular customers could have been expected and catered for to their particular requirements.

It is pertinent to observe at this point that by the time Henry VIII closed down the licensed houses, much of their usefulness and hence their profitability had been eroded by those in private hands, since these could more quickly respond to consumer preference than the bureaucratically controlled establishments. There were assuredly

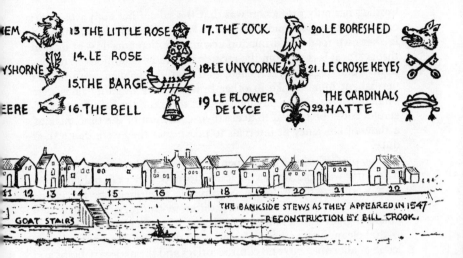

EM 13 THE LITTLE ROSE 17. THE COCK 20. LE BORESHED

YSHORNE 14. LE ROSE 18 LE UNYCORNE 21. LE CROSSE KEYES

15. THE BARGE

EERE 16. THE BELL 19 LE FLOWER DE LYCE 22 THE CARDINALS HATTE

THE BANKSIDE STEWS AS THEY APPEARED IN 1547
RECONSTRUCTION BY BILL CROOK.

GOAT STAIRS

brothel 'clans' struggling for hegemony and monopoly; the records of 1505-6 support this contention.

In a private brothel, treatment depended solely upon the girl's own ability and popularity with the customers and hence the money that she brought in. The life was hard, the discipline strict, the extortions vast. Within three or four years the girl would be worn out, even if she were lucky enough to avoid venereal disease. With the lack of hygiene and sanitation all diseases were a hazard, and the periodical outbreaks of plague meant at best death, at worst a living death. If she caught V.D. she would be thrown out; she might perhaps get some sort of treatment from the Lock hospital, but that was a mixed blessing because cross-infection through ignorant treatment was frequent.

The prostitute who survived the course would leave after this brutalizing work with little more than her few personal belongings. She might then 'trade on her own bottom' until she wasted and died; in a few instances she might be befriended or get married. After all, Pope Innocent III had recommended that decent men should marry a harlot so as to redeem her. She might become a Madam, but in most cases she would end up as a servant to other prostitutes. She was at all times the prey of lecherous priests and monks, of corrupt and venal constables and court officers, as well as poor and rich rakes.

The only advantage of work in a brothel was a roof over the head, and food and clothing, deducted from one's earnings. In the licensed brothel, her only protection was that the sale of her body was legal; otherwise the whore had her room as long as she paid for it, and paid for her own food and drink and accommodation outside – at least in theory, for it is clear from the records that these conditions were constantly and regularly breached, and that the women were in fact permanent inmates like in other brothels. The monthly fines were small in comparison to paying a double rent, and the bailiffs and constables could be trusted to avert their eyes most of the time, making a show of efficiency at intervals to prove that they were doing their duty.

Two professions were still open to women: midwifery and nursing. The latter was regarded as the lowest form of service fit only for low-class women – the Florence Nightingale syndrome was far in the future. Midwifery was in quite a different category. Midwives had amassed great skill and a certain degree of medical knowledge, such as that clean linen and clean hands were desirable. Most had a knowledge of abortifacients and contraceptives and the necessary herbs and simples. If the midwife was successful, there was no cavil from grateful patients; but if things went wrong, the old 'crones' (women perhaps still in their late thirties or early forties!) could be burnt for witchcraft, even when their only 'crime' was burning pungent old rags or washing in some dangerous antiseptic substance. Anything untoward was regarded as suspect by the clergy and the emerging monopoly of male practitioners, now becoming physicians and surgeons, from colleges to which women were not admitted.

To the prostitutes and brothelkeepers a good trained midwife was a great help against the hazards of the 'game'. Firstly all births were unwelcome: they were dangerous, but more importantly they interfered with working capacity and hence with profits. A brothel girl would lose her job (in the Stewes pregnant women had to be ejected forthwith) for customers preferred not to copulate with pregnant women.

Moreover the Madam could not permit any pregnancy or disease to interfere with the earning capacity of her 'commodities'. Where a Madam might rarely show compassion, her own master – including many a rich City burgess or Alderman, or even a Lord Mayor of 'gret ffame' – would be ruthless, greedy and rapacious. They would not allow their manageresses to endanger their profits. These Madams were running a flesh-peddling business on efficient businesslike lines; no interruption in their production lines would be permitted. They were not necessarily inhuman: a good, clean, contented girl was a great asset, and if she needed only a little regular attention, such as could be done by a midwife, it was preferable to throwing her out and training a replacement. Satisfied regular customers were the mainstay of all brothels; many men used the same girls for months or even years. When the brothel could not afford a full-time physician, a good midwife was an excellent substitute.

There was but one drawback. Older, experienced midwives might not tolerate interference or challenge, and would gain a reputation as a scold. If they escaped burning for witchcraft they stood a good chance of finding themselves on the ducking-stool for no other reason than some woman's bloodymindedness or the hatred of some fanatical or frustrated priest.

One further point must be noted before we conclude this wretched saga. The century 1550-1650 witnessed a population explosion in which the numbers almost doubled. This, together with the constant inflation and rising prices, created an impossible situation. Small wonder therefore that the brothels in Tudor times never went short of 'fresh meat'. The streets were packed with women and girls soliciting. The numbers of 'kept women' grew beyond count. The supplies of women were vast, yet the demand was never satisfied. Platten[2] re-marked on this in 1599: 'although close watch is kept on them [the whores] swarms of these women haunt the town in the taverns and playhouses.' He also mentioned in passing that there were children's brothels in which girls aged from seven to fourteen were supplied.

Rowlands, Latimer, Harrison, Stubbes, and all those who fulmin-ated against the women, knew equally of the state of the poor. They all raised their voices against the terrible poverty of their times. But not one had mercy or compassion for the common prostitutes. They were women, and women were not only God's frailest vessels but 'hotte as goattes', always luring men on to lust and lechery. It never seems to have occurred to any of them that it was God himself who had so created the sexes that without carnal copulation mankind would cease immediately. Nor did it strike them that the male partner was equally culpable – if that is the correct adjective to use when dis-cussing the Almighty's fundamental design for the reproduction of the species.

The political and economic complexion of Southwark meanwhile was also changing. Industry was taking root and with it a steady working-class element reinforced by large numbers of Protestant refugees from Spanish and French oppression. By 1580 there were more than a thousand Dutch families in Southwark, mainly decent, hardworking artisans, craftsmen and traders. They had introduced brewing, amongst other 'factory' crafts. Southwark's age-old 'inde-pendent' tradition was exemplified by a strong 'puritan' streak which was to manifest itself fiercely in Oliver Cromwell's time. Of course, the ranks of these Dutch immigrants also included highly-trained bawds and whores. By the turn of the century they were settling in the area of Paris Garden, where (according to some) the Manor House became known as 'Hollands laager', later to be called 'Holland's Leaguer' and become the most famous whorehouse of its time.[3]

The great property development on Bankside was to start about 1570, get into stride at the turn of the century, and turn into a gold rush between 1600 and 1660, when nearly every garden was overbuilt with rows of jerry-built tenements. The buildings along the waterfront were to be described by Thomas Dekker in 1612 as a 'contynuall row of ale-houses', although Ben Jonson, who knew the Bankside intimately, was nearer the truth in his *Epigram 'on the New Hot Houses'* in 1616:

> Where lately harbour'd many a famous Whore
> a purging bill, now fix'd vpon the dore,
> Tells you it is a hot-house: So it ma'
> And still be a whore-house. Th'are Synonyma.[4]

NOTES

[1] Samuel Rowlands, *Greenes Ghost Hunting Coniecatchers.*
[2] Clare Williams, *Platten's Travels in 1599*, p. 134.
[3] E. J. Burford, *Queen of the Bawds.*
[4] Ben Jonson, *Works* (ed. William Giffard), Vol. VIII.

XI

'Vulva Regit Scotos ... ac tenet ipsa Britannos'

Elizabeth I was no stranger to the Bankside. She visited the bear-gardens frequently, occasionally even forcing foreign diplomats, who had no love for the sport, to witness these bloody and degrading spectacles where the bears, chained to a post, were baited by dogs until bear or dogs were torn to pieces. Such was her infatuation with this sport that she ordered that 'players of enterludes' be restrained from 'reciting their plays on all other dayes of the week [because] the players cause great hurt to the game of bear-baiting and the like pastimes maintained for the Queenes pleasure'.[1]

Elizabeth's first act was to abrogate all her sister's laws and re-instate all those of her father; this of course meant that the Bankside Stewes were once again illegal. She does not appear to have taken any specific action against those being carried on in quasi-clandestine fashion as inns or taverns, and she made no legislation against prostitution as such. She did, however, reintroduce her father's laws against 'the moste horrible and detestable vyce of buggerie,'[2] bringing back all the old penalties for this crime.

When she came to the throne in 1558 England had been torn by years of religious upheaval and it is to her great credit that within a few years she had restored secular government. The state power of the Catholic faction had been broken and Protestantism had come to stay. But a change of religion made little difference to the condition of the poor. Protestantism did not change the public attitude to the fallen, especially not fallen women.

Although Elizabeth must have known that the evils of poverty and prostitution were in part caused by the lack of accommodation and housing, she set her face against developments in London and Southwark which tended to relieve the situation. She could not, of course, restrain the property developers from building houses and tenements on land sold to them by her father, but her *Proclamation Prohibiting Further Building in London*[3] shows that although she was aware that overcrowding drove the poor to begging 'and worse' she was deter-

147

mined (like the City authorities centuries earlier) to thrust it outside her immediate responsibility. It was sufficient for her to deplore the state of the poor publicly, and then forget about it.

The overcrowding was worsening yearly. The enclosures, which had started in the time of Henry VII and had been aggravated by Henry VIII's seizure of the Church lands and their distribution to rich magnates anxious to become even richer, had caused a great land shortage and forced thousands of people off the land. The Tudors' habit of summarily dismissing soldiers and sailors exacerbated the situation, since they were left penurious and driven to vagabondage and crime. Many a brave and worthy soldier met his end on the gallows.

There was another side to London life, however, as this description by a foreign visitor during Elizabeth's reign shows:[4] 'I have heard within these forty years when there were not of these haberdashers that selles French or millen [Milanese] cappes, glasses, knives, daggers, swordes, gyrdles . . . not a dozen in alle London. Nowe . . . every street is full of theym and their shoppes glytter and shyne . . . that it is able to make a temperate man to gase on theym and buy somewhat though it serve no purpose.'

Against this panegyric one must set the fact that the observer goes on to say that clothiers and drapers made bad cloth, stretching it unfairly in dark shops where the customer could not properly examine what he was purchasing; and goldsmiths were selling 'golde whiche is naught or ellse at least mixt with other drossie rubbage or refuse mettall.'

He added that vintners adulterated their wine, and butchers sold bad meat to those who were compelled by poverty to buy in small quantities. In some cases the merchants were making 300 or 400 per cent profit.

From 1562 onwards the Bankside properties were changing hands frequently and being divided up. Tenements were erected in what had been gardens: 'there continue to be erected great number of tenements called pennyrents in Southwark . . . wherein are placed a great number of very poor people . . . having no trade nor honest endeavour to maintain themselves nor pay their rents . . . [they] daily beg in the City.'[5]

Later[6] it is stated that because of the great multitude of such 'base tenements and disorderly houses' being built, there was a great increase in 'dissolute and insolent people . . . dwelling in poor cottages who frequent inns, ale-houses, taverns, bowling alleys and brothels.'

The building-over of the Bankside gardens led to the appearance of a large number of alleys, most following the ancient demarcation lines. By the turn of the century there were no less than eighteen of these alleys, most running from Bankside through to Maiden Lane, and criss-crossed with even narrower alleys. Later these congeries became known as 'so-and-so's Rents', with the landlord's name appended.

The names of these alleys help to locate the sites of some of the stews. Starting from the most easterly, next to *The Castle-on-the-Hoop*, were Mayland's Rents, Olyphaunt Alley, Tallow Chandlers' Rents, Horseshoe Alley, Griffin's Rents, Bullhead Alley, Rose Alley, Bear Gardens, Unicorn Alley, Tapping's Rents (or Plough Alley), Cordwainers' Rents, Boars Head Alley, Crosse Keyes Alley, Cardinals Hat Alley, Rockett's Rents (Pike Gardens or Pike [Pye] Alley), Mason's Stairs and Love Lane. This list cannot be more than approximate for the alleys changed names with the owners, or vanished completely.

To give an indication of the scale of the development let us consider in some detail the history of one property. We have traced *The Castle-on-the-Hoop* back to 1306 when the whole very large property which bounded on Deadman's Place, Maiden Lane and Bankside had belonged to the Stapleton family. In 1559 Vincent Amcottes bought the property, which by that time included *The Bulhed* at its western edge. It then comprised a wharf, some houses and four cottages. He divided the property in 1562, and that part which had been sold to John Cheyne was sold twenty years later to John Drew, now comprising not only *The Castle*[7] but also *The Gonne* and three messuages or tenements with the gardens. These were later known as Drew's Rents, and when John Drew died in 1595 he left forty shillings to his tenants on Bankside 'to make merry withal'. It is not known whether the light ladies who had helped to make him prosperous were included in the treat.[8]

In 1580 the Amcottes family sold the eastern portion of the property to Richard Spire.

Also in 1580 *The Swanne* and *The Bulhed* were leased to William Weyle, having in the meantime been converted into five tenements. In 1585 the two brothels were sold to John Trehearn and by the time he transferred in 1604 to Roger Cole, there were now four more tenements on the site. By 1685 they are described as 'seven messuages . . . formerly contained within one called the Bull or Bulhed'.

Somewhere between *The Castle* and *The Bulhed* lay *The Antilope*, so that by the end of the century there stood on this on original *Castell* site no less than five brothels besides many other tenements.

Sometime before 1616 the whole property came into the possession of Sir John Bodley Kt., who had a lease on it for twenty-five and a half years at £21 10s. per annum. In that year the freehold was bought by Sir Mathew Brend, who promptly sold it to Hillarie Mempris,

'Cityzen and Haberdasher of London'. He gave a lease to James Monger (the Elder), 'Cittizen and Clothworker of London', who built a brewhouse on that part adjacent to the Globe Theatre; he prospered and extended his brewery eastwards to the rear of *The Castle*. Meanwhile Mempris sold the freehold of the brewery to John Partridge for £400 and it stayed in the Partridge family until 1854.

In 1658 *The Castle* was renamed *The King's Head*; the building was burnt down in 1676 and rebuilt on the same site.

By 1674 the brewery had come into the ownership of James Child. He was in trouble with the Grocers' Company because he was practising 'the Art and Mistery of brewing' without having transferred to the Brewers' Company. Eventually, after having been involved in 'vexations and suites', he paid, with rather bad grace it seems, '£5 and a buck and a doe in season to the Wardens' and on 9 November, 1671 was 'translated' with due ceremony before the aldermen in the Guildhall. This venture became the famous Child's Brewery and prospered exceedingly, and in the course of its expansion acquired *The King's Head*, which it rebuilt and refurbished about 1750 and renamed it *The Anchor* (probably because it was a tap from the brewery at its rear, through which freshly brewed beer was poured directly into the customer's glass at the tavern bar), the brewery by this time having been renamed the Anchor Brewery.[9]

Working one's way along the Bankside it is possible to reconstruct from the records a picture of the changes of ownership, function and architecture that occurred over the years, up till the latter part of Queen Elizabeth's reign.

The Crane, in the possession of the Tallow Chandlers' Company since 1504, was, so far as is known, functioning as a brothel until some time before 1633 when it was converted into a 'sopehouse' (either a warehouse or a soap factory) and departs decorously from the evil company it had been keeping hitherto.

Next to it stood *The Hert*, separated by the narrow width of Olyphaunt (sometimes also called Elephant) Alley from *The Olyphaunt*. In the Token Books for the parish for 1598[10] it is stated that Elephant Alley was sometimes identified with *The Vine* which, 'before the Dissolution [of the monasteries in 1539] belonged to the Sisters of St Margaret's'. This gives *The Vine* a much longer pedigree than had been thought and must certainly take it back at least to the beginning of the century. It again reveals that religious ladies – as with the nuns of Stratford – had no qualms about owning brothels.

In 1598 too, there was a *Red Harte* in Deadman's Place just around the corner from the Bankside, and this 'brew hous . . . is now called *The Elephant*'. The Bankside *Elephant*, however, has its secure and permanent niche in history, for in Act III, Scene II of Shakespeare's

Twelfth Night Antonio says: 'In the south suburbs, at the Elephant, is best to lodge.'

Next was *The Horseshoe*, standing in (or probably straddling) the alley of the same name, which exists to this day. It has a very long history, going back to at least 1409 when it was the property of the Cordwainers' Company.[11] About the end of 1531 there is a record – 'super le bank al.dict le Stues-side [on the Bank otherwise called the Stewesside] to John Fitz' – which purports to be a transfer of the property by someone named Allen; and about 1580 much of the property in and around the alley belonged to Gilbert Rockett. A lease dated 5 November, 27 Elizabeth I (1585) between Gilbert Rockett and Thomas Trehearn runs: 'of a messuage in the bankside . . . to the east of the messuage called at the signe of the Horse shoe for 41 yrs at £8 per year.' In 1593 the actor William Sly lived in the alley.

In 1596 appears a note about 'a messuage called the Horseshoe heretofore called the Sugar Loaf and two others lately erected', which gives *The Sugar Loaf* a longer provenance than thought originally. It is but fair to say that *The Horseshoe* is never spoken of as a brothel, only as an inn of good repute. The alley was also very convenient as 'Ye way leading through Horseshoe Yard unto ye Playhouse called Ye Globe'.

Then there is the very curious affair of the Clink in Horseshoe Alley. The records of the Cordwainers' Company show that in 1628 they let to John Pidgeon 'a messuage thentofore used for the goal [sic] or prison called the Clinck, sometime in the tenure of Mathew Hancock, afterwards of Thomas Mason and late of Marcus Stone, in Horseshoe Alley.' This house, which stood on the corner of Maiden Lane, can be traced back in the Token Books to 1617, when it is not, however, mentioned as a prison. The Clink prison was next to the Bishop's Palace at the far eastern end of the Bankside, so this can only have been an annex, or perhaps a house rented by the Keeper either as extra room or, more likely, to house those prisoners who could pay for extra luxuries. How long it remained as 'the Clink' is not known, and although in the next century when there are several mentions of the Clink being moved 'to a house on Bankside' it is probably this one that is still being referred to.

In 1633 the Cordwainers took over from Henry Draper, who was in possession, 'the Sugar Loaf Inn formerly called the Horseshoe on Bankside, with an orchard, garden and bowling alley' which stretched back to Maiden Lane, and in the following year the owner was summonsed for keeping the bowling alley open on Sundays. The freehold still remained in the Fitz family, for Sir John left it to his daughter Mary, who conveyed it to a kinsman, who in turn sold the whole property in 1695 to William Smith. Thereafter on the site of the old

Sugar Loaf was an inn called *The George*, and the whole area was known as Smith's Rents.

Next hereabouts stood the ancient *Leonem*, the lease of which had been conveyed to Roger Fitz in 1505. By 1528[12] this property comprised 'seven messuages seven gardens and one wharf'. In 1605 there is a reference to 'two tenements le ram et le Lyon and eight cottages' still in the possession of the Fitz family, and by 1671 these 'ten messuages' too have passed to William Smith.

Next door to *The Lyon and Ram* must have been *The Hertishead* (or *Hartyshorne*) which does not appear in any record after 1510.[13] Then came Bullhed Alley.[14] Across this alley stood *The Beere* and next to it *The Little Rose*, which in 1574 belonged to Philip Henslowe, to whom these lands reverted in 1579 on the expiry of two leases. Rose Alley, which exists to this day, was adjacent to *The Little Rose*.

To the rear of these properties (all of which seem to have been part of the original *Rose* estate of the nuns of Stratford at Bow) was built the famous Rose Theatre which opened in 1587. Rose Alley ran through to Maiden Lane and was an entrance to the theatre.

Almost immediately adjacent to the theatre were the Bear Gardens, which were approached through Bear Gardens Alley (which exists to this day)[15] although at that time the entry to the Bear Gardens would also have been through the gateway of the triple brothel *The Bell*, *The Barge* and *The Cock*, all of which belonged to Henslowe. Hereabouts was *The Beerhouse* (which can either have been the Beer House, or the Bear House in which bears were kept). The probability is that *The Beer* (or *Bear*) brothel mentioned in 1505 stood here.

There is a good deal of confusion over the exact sites of the bear gardens, and there is some evidence that at different times over the centuries there were no less than five of them, extending from the Bear Gardens westwards as far as Mason's Stairs.[16]

In 1574 there is another mention of '*The Barge*':[17] 'John Paynes widow, [conveys] to Francis Puckryche of Grynwich . . . a messuage sometime called the Barge . . . between the tenement called The Roose towards the east . . . and upon the Beare Howse towards the south now in the occupation of William Glover and Joan Gravesende for 21 years. This indicates that *The Bee(a)rhouse* stood nearer to Maiden Lane, and is thus more likely to have been the abode of the animals than the building fronting on Bankside.

In this connection there is a unique document[18] with details of a transaction in December 1590 disposing of 'the Bear Garden' and its livestock.

THOMAS BURNEBYE of WATFORD . . . and RICHARD REVE Cit.and

Glazier of London . . . all the tenements lately belonging to JOHN NAPTON deceased . . . together with the BEARE GARDEN including:

IMPRIMIS. 1	Brinded Bull	the pryce v.L	[£5]
1	Blacke Bull called Danyen	iv.L	[£4]
1	greate Beare called Tom Hunckes	x.L	[£10]
1	greate Beare called Harry of Thame	viii.L	[£8]
1	Red Bull called Jugler	iiii.L	[£4]
1	greate Beare called Sampson	viii.L	[£8]
1	greate Beare called Jeremy	viii.L	[£8]
1	beare called Danyell	viii.L	[£8]
1	she-beare called Bosse	v.L	[£5]
1	yonge he-beare Whitinge	iii.L	[£3]
1	olde she-beare Nan	xxx.s.	[30s.]
1	horse & the ape	xl.s.	[40s.]
1	Puddinge boate	iii.L	[£3]

(Incidentally in 1576 there is mention of a Bosse Alley[19] 'at the Banck-side', next to the Great Pike Gardens. Perhaps the she-bear was named after some contemporary worthy?)

The Bell is mentioned in the Token Books for 1598 as being 'next Stewes rents'. *The Barge* was the most westerly of the triple brothel. That they were all considered as one entity is evidenced by a deed[20] dated 8 April, 1574 devising 'certayne capytall messuages and tene-ments called le barge le bell and the cocke'. *The Bell* may be that same brothel mentioned in 1390[21] as 'the bell . . . in the Bishops lordship at the Stuves'.

When and how *The Cock* was first built or identified is not known, but it is clearly not one of the original eighteen.

The adjoining estate comprised the famous *Unicorne*. Its boundary was straight up against that of *The Rose* complex. At the Bankside end there appears to have been a small enclave facing the Thames, in which nestled a tavern called *The Shipp*. It is mentioned in the *Travels* of John Taylor, 'the Water Poet', in 1630 as 'the Ship on Bankside . . . a tavern for drinking'. At some period it was also called *The Galleon*.

That portion of the old prioress's estate which included *The Uni-corne* was very extensive, stretching from Bankside through to Maiden Lane and along Bankside to Goat Stairs. In 1537 Henry VIII had leased to Henry Polsted (Polstead) '. . . the tenements known as the Vnycorne and the Rose which before then had belonged to the Prioress of Stratford-atte-bogh.'

In 1552 the whole property was divided up. The houses known as *le Rose* and *The Unicorne* were leased to John Davison. How long he held them is not known, although in 1604 a John Davison appears in the Token Books as the Keeper of the Clink Prison, and members of the Davison family were for many years afterwards closely connected with the Clink both as keepers and property owners.

In a Crown lease of 1596 there is granted 'to Edward Addison, Waterman and Joan his wife [some land] adjoining Bear Gardens and Unicorne Alley . . . and including a wharf.' On this land they built a row of tenements known later as Addison's Rents, and in one of these tenements lived the dramatist John Fletcher (1579-1625). He also lived variously at *The Unicorne* and for a short while at *The Cardinal's Hat* before dying of the plague in 1625, the year of King Charles I's accession.

In 1597 Philip Henslowe acquired the lease (which had been exchanged in a deal between the Crown and Polstead) and in 1625 the Crown mortgaged *The Unicorne* to Edward Alleyn, together with the Pike Gardens. This property, together with *The Bell*, *The Barge* and *The Cock*, went into the marriage settlement of Alleyn's second wife, the young Constance Donne, daughter of the eminent Divine Dr John Donne, Dean of St Paul's. All four were active brothels at that time.

From the lease in 1667, when Sir C. Sydenham sold the property to John Squibb, we learn for the first time its actual measurements. The Bear Garden comprised about half the property, measuring 330 feet (the length of the present Emerson Street) with a width of 166 feet.

To complete the saga of *The Unicorne*, the property was converted into glasshouses in 1693 and in 1750 these in turn were converted into a number of shops – one a colourman's – and foundries; there was also a small alleyway, called Crown Court, now disappeared.

The next brothel in line was most probably *The fflower de lyce* (*le Fleur de Lys*), which would imply some very early connection with a Dauphin of France. The house of resort called *The Dolphin*, already mentioned, is probably also a corruption of the word 'Dauphin'; it may commemorate some visit at an early time of the French Crown Prince.[22] Apart from the references in 1505-6 nothing is known of its history or actual location.

A little further along would have been *The Boar's Head*[23] and then *The Crosse Keyes* which lay alongside an alley of that name. Their exact locations and their further history is likewise unknown.

The last in the row of Stewes houses was *The Cardinal's Hatte* with its adjoining narrow alley. (This is now No. 49 Bankside.) Its history is the most fascinating of them all.

A '*Cardenallshatte*' first appears in Gracechurch Street in the City in a document dated 1316, and clearly had been there long before, perhaps even commemorating Pope Innocent III's foundation of this insignia in 1245. The one on Bankside can be traced back to 1360 (see page 100) and must have been established long before then. Cardinal Ottoboni came to England in 1266 and his striking red robes and splendid hat, carried on a gold cushion before him in procession, would certainly have made a great impression. Alternatively the name may have commemorated the first Englishman to be created a cardinal, Thomas Boyce in 1310. It became a very popular inn sign thereafter.

The Bankside establishment is documented in 1361[24] and 1447,[25] the spelling in each case being a little shaky – *'le Cardenalshat'* and *'le Cardynall hatte'* – and in 1463 it is mentioned in the accounts[26] of John Howard, Duke of Norfolk, who was to die on Bosworth Field fighting for Richard III. The entry reads: 'Item the xxx day of julle [July] my mastyre delyveryd to Sawnsam att the Cardenallys Hatt ffor my sayde lorde [of Norfolk] iij*li*.vj*s*.viij*d*.' An even more revealing item is found in these accounts under the date 23 May, 1465: 'item.the xxiij of may my mastyre lent to my lorde of Norffolke whan he lay att the stewes,xx*s*.'

Then, as we have seen, in 1468 *The Cardinalles Hatte* on Bankside became the property of the Prior of Merton as a result of his swap for *The Popes Hed* in the Borough High Street. He does not appear to have kept it very long for in 1470[27] it was sold by one William Hille of March in Cambridgeshire to 'John Merston [and others named] . . . a voyd plot of grounde by le Stewesside,' and the location is pinpointed as having 'the prioress's land [the Prioress of Stratford -at-Bow] on the east and Maiden Lane on the south.' On this 'voyd grounde' John Merston built *The Cardinals Hatte* in 1470.

If the site was vacant it must mean that the original building had been demolished – it would in any case have been in poor condition since it was already more than a hundred years old. The most likely explanation is that soon after 1468 the Prior must have sold the property to William Hille, who demolished the existing building, cleared the site and sold it to John Merston, who then built another building and gave it the original name, since it was well known and was to be used for the same purpose. The site is clearly that on which the Elizabethan and subsequent buildings were constructed. There is no record of any other messuage of the same name in Southwark.

John Merston also acquired land on the other side of the site, earlier known as the Great Pike Gardens, later Bannaster's Gardens, also on the Stewesside, which at this period ran westward along the riverside as far as *The Falcon* (which was the boundary of the Clink Liberty), while the Great Pike Gardens stretched southwards almost to Maiden Lane.

John Skelton, the famous satirical poet of the reigns of Henry VII and Henry VIII, had something to say about this hostelry and he speaks with authority since he is supposed to have been the paramour of Long Megg of Westminster, the legendary whore and bawd associated with Paris Garden. Skelton was a particular enemy of Cardinal Wolsey, of whom he wrote in 1522:[28]

> ...while he doth rule
> all is warse and warse.
> The Devill kiss his arse.

Later in the same poem he observes 'They shoot all above the mark ... at the Cardinal's hat' and some verses later he warms up with:

> What newes? what newes? ...
> but at the naked stewes
> I understand how that
> the Sign of the Cardinal's Hat,
> that inn is now shut up ...
> with Gup Whore, gup now gup.[29]

Thus Skelton gives us the incidental information that in 1522 this famous whorehouse was closed up. He must be referring to John Merston's brothel, which was also that raided in 1519 by Wolsey's minions.

There is then a gap in its history until 1579 when the great property developer Hugh Browker, Notary of London, built – or more probably rebuilt – *The Cardinal's Hatte* and leased it to John Raven, who managed it until his death in 1596. His widow kept it going until 1599 when it was in the possession of John Powell who ran it till 1615. Until this time it was still a brothel.

When Thomas Mansfield (or Mansell) took it over in 1615 it was described as an inn and as such was visited in 1617 by Edward Alleyn. His diary records that on 'December 12.I went to London [from Dulwich] and supped at the Cardinals Hatt wt.Mr Austen Mr Archer and Mr Ordes. 4.0 shillings. December 17.Dinner at Cardinalls Hatt wt.Vestry men. 3.0 shillings. Supper ther wt.Mr Austen etc. 2s 6d.' Since at this time Alleyn was a churchwarden of St Saviour's, it is hardly likely that he would have entertained the vestrymen in a whorehouse, although, as the Token Books show, vestrymen did not refuse contributions from the whorehouses for the parish funds.

Mansfield died in 1618 and bequeathed the property to his wife, who in 1624 leased it to Melchizedek Fritter, who is noted in the Token Books[30] at 'A cardinals Hat on ye Bankside. Brewer . . . hys half penny'.

In 1630 John Taylor, the 'Water Poet', who had been involved in a dispute with the Watermen, who had accused him of double-crossing

them, wrote 'They [the Watermen] reported that I took bribes from
the players to let the suit fail and that I had a supper with them at the
Cardinall's Hat on the Bankside.'[31] However, in his 'Travels' later on
he mentions other hostelries on Bankside, but not *The Cardinal's Hat*
nor *The Unicorne.*

For some reason, the name was changed after Fritter's death in
1673; when his widow gave it up to Sarah Humphreys in 1686 the
deed calls it *The Cardinal's Cap.* Under that name she bequeathed it
to her son John Leake in September 1686, and in turn to his son, also
John Leake. They were of course only tenants: the property still
belonged to the Browker family until they sold out in 1667 to Thomas
Hudson, who, dying in 1688 left it with all his other messuages on
Bankside to his sister, Mary Greene, in whose family it remained for
many years.

The house was rebuilt in whole or in part in 1710, as its present
facade is of that date,[32] but it is thought that one or two of the rooms
are part of the old Elizabethan structure of 1579 (the cellars are
certainly of that period). It is now known as Cardinal's Cap Wharf,
having been utilized earlier for smuggling by a sea captain. The pond
in the back garden may be a vestigial remain of the ancient King's
Pike Ponds. The garden still extends a considerable way back and its
wall runs the length of the Cardinal's Cap Alley. The visitor may
observe from this surviving alley how very narrow all these alleys
were originally.

The legend that Sir Christopher Wren stayed there while designing
and building St Paul's cannot be substantiated, since he stayed in a
house next to *The Falcon*, which is much further up the Bankside. He
may have eaten there occasionally, since Fritter's reputation as a
gastronome was high.

With *The Cardinal's Hat*, the tally of the original brothels is complete, although in ancient times the 'Stewesside' stretched past this
point as far as Love Lane, which infers the existence of several more
brothels. There were certainly some inns: one was *The White Hind*,
another *The White Lion*, and there was yet another *Boar's Head*
along an alley of that name.

There is also a record of a brothel called *The Fish Pond House on
Stewes Side*[33] and an illustration of this establishment shows a very
handsome late-Tudor double-fronted building with fine carvings over
and on each side of an imposing gateway leading to the ponds in the
courtyard. This building, which stood just opposite Mason's Stairs, is
described also as 'the Gate house and romen [rooms] buylded over the
Gate roome entryinge into the greate Pyke gardeyne at the Bankside.'
It is now the site of the cul de sac leading into the Bankside Power
Station.

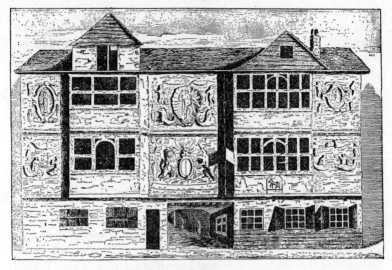

The Fish Pond House, c. 1600.

The precise locations of the houses known as *The Lyly* and the *Thatched House* are unknown. The first is mentioned in a most curious connection [34] – 'payde to Charles Tayler bayley of the Clynke the x of Octobre for quyt rent for the howse . . . and other ij tenements on the bank syde callyd the Lyly' – so that the likelihood is that it stood much further east, perhaps near the Bear Gardens, and that it was a substantial plot with two houses.

Others whose location cannot be pinpointed are *The Sarazinshed* (Saracen's Head – perhaps a reminder of Richard the First's crusades); and another, described in Sarah Humphrey's will in September 1686 in connection with some property in Mosse Alley (near Love Lane), called *The Maidenhead*. It is pertinent to reflect that this would certainly have been the only maidenhead in the whole district.

In 1561 there is another mention [35] of a tavern, close to *The Castle-on-the-Hoope*, called *The Vine*: 'the house on the bank-syde leeying in the hands of William Bennington and the house of Jhon [sic] Smythe of the vyne.'

Finally, there is a reference in 1649 to 'all that messuage known as the three tunnes lately a tavern between a certaine alley heretofore called Bulhead Alley and now Robinhood Alley.' [36] This Bulhead Alley was the one adjacent to Henslowe's whorehouse *The Little Rose*, and some considerable distance away from *The Bulhed* brothel adjacent to *The Castle-on-the-Hoope*. The potential confusion will illustrate the difficulty of pinpointing the locations more accurately.

These alleyways between the tenements were dirty and muddy – the inhabitants still doing their easements in the ways – and were still lit only by cressets stuck on the walls, although candle lamps were beginning to be introduced and householders to be compelled to affix one to their own walls.

The hundreds of sleazy tenements were masked by the rows of late-Tudor facades along the Bankside itself and the roadway in front was cobbled and widened sometime before 1618 into 'a broade carte waie leadynge unto the bancke Ande [end] . . . the breadth of this [allows] turne Cartes at fronte.' A new phenomenon, the coach, was not only to revolutionize transport but also vastly to improve access to Bankside. This was much resented by the Watermen, whose spokesman John Taylor went on record that:

> When Queen Elizabeth came to the Throne
> a Coach in England was then scarcely known :
> then t'was as rare to see one, as to spy
> a tradesman that had never told a lie !

By 1625 hackney-coaches[37] had become very common, and doubtless their drivers knew the way to the Bankside brothels as well as their rivals the boatmen.

Another important social shift helped to swell the business of Bankside's taverns, inns, ale-houses, stews and bear-gardens, and in their time, the theatres. This was the large number of wealthy country noblemen who had been compelled to flock to London. William Lauder[38] graphically described their plight: 'So manie of us as yee knowe, that have departed out of the countrey of late have bene driven to give over our households, and to kepe either chamber in London or to wayte on the Court uncalled, with a man and a lackey . . . where he was wont to kepe half a score of cleane men in his house.'

These men obviously found time hanging heavily on their hands, and gambling and whoring became essential pastimes. Sir John Harington, the Queen's favourite young cousin, summed it up:[39] 'Men cannot always be discoursing, nor women always pricking in clouts [embroidering] and it was boring to listen to old courtiers [reminiscing] of well spending that day when the King [Henry VIII] went to Bullen's [to Anne Boleyn].' 'Ill-breeding with ill-feeling, with no love but that of the lusty god,' he said, drove men to cards and dice to relieve the tedium.

Perhaps the most succinct description of Elizabethan court life is in the satirical collection of epigrams and poems entitled *Skialetheia*,[40] attributed to Edward Guilpin :

> My lord, most court-like lyes in bed till noone,
> Then, all high-stomackt riseth to his dinner:
> Falls straight to dice before his meate be downe
> Or to digest, walks to some femall sinner . . .
> This is a lords life, simple folkes will sing. . . .

All the amenities and diversions of the Bankside made up what was popularly known as the teachings in the 'Bear's Colledge'. The gossip of this college, though, would have been about their sovereign. After all, many of her royal contemporaries doubted Elizabeth's virginity. One anecdote[41] was that on 2 April, 1566, the Queen came secretly from Greenwich to Southwark attended only by two of her ladies. They descended the stairs at St Marie Overie (just in front of Winchester House) and boarded a 'whiry' (wherry) with a single pair of oars and were rowed quietly across the river to the landing stage at *The Three Cranes* in the Ward of the Vintry.

On this same day the Earl of Leicester had entered the City 'accompanyd with lordes knyghtes pencionars & a gret numbar of gentylmen & others with ye quenes ffoottmen and his owne also alle in theyr riche cotes & to ye nombar of 700.'

The Earl awaited the Queen at the Earl of Oxford's house, but becoming impatient he left there before the Queen arrived and went with all the train over the bridge into Southwark 'ffor that shee was not come when he came thether.'

At the top of *The Three Cranes* stairs the Queen had 'entryd a cowche coveryd with blewe and so rode . . . to mett wyth ye earle of Leycestar'. Then, changing her mind, she chose to go back the way she had come, overtaking Leicester, at which point 'shee cam owte of hir coche in ye highe way and shee imbrased ye earle & kyssed hym thrise & then they rose togyther to Grenewytche.'

When they recalled that the Queen had the full measure of the Tudor temper and that the Earl was so sure of himself that he could go on without waiting for her and still get such a loving reception, it was clear to the gossips at least that their relationship was more than platonic.

Her skilful procrastination earned her respect for her politics, but did not manifest itself equally in respect for her sex. The lampoons of the time were often witty and usually made imputations against her putative virginity, the more so in comparison with the number of women rulers active in Europe at the time. The most scabrous, but clever, is the salacious verse attributed to the French satirical poet D'Aubigné (1552-1630), who passed it on to a well-known publicist of the woes of Gallia, François Hotman:[42]

VULVA regit Scotos
VULVA ac tenet ipsa Britannos
Flanderos et Batavos
nunc notha VULVA regit;
VULVA regit populos
quos regnat Gallia portu,
et fortes Gallos Italia VULVA regit.
Huic furiam furiis VULVAM conjugite Vulvis
et naturae capux omnis regna capit.

This anti-feminist diatribe infers a sinister plot between the queens of Scotland and England in a vulvular conspiracy supported by Margaret Duchess of Parma (illegitimate daughter of the Spanish Emperor Charles V), who ruled over the Netherlands, Catherine of Austria (his sister), who was Regent for King Sebastian of Portugal, and Catherine de Medici who exercised great power from Florence.

Virgin or not, Elizabeth remained unmarried until her death in 1603. She was described in 1598 by Paul Hentzen,[43] tutor to a visiting German noble, as 'very majestic, her face oblong, fair but wrinkled, her eyes small yet black and pleasant, her nose a little hooked, her lips narrow and her teeth black . . . she wore some false hair and that auburn, her hands were small, her fingers long, her stature neither tall nor low, her air stately, her manner of speaking mild and obliging.'

By contrast, another foreigner, the Frenchman de Maisse,[44] had observed in his journal that 'she is very avaricious and when some expense is necessary her Councillors must deceive her . . . she thinks very highly of herself and has little regard for her servants and Councillors: she mocks them and often cries out against them.' Physically, he describes her much as Hentzen did, adding that her face was very wrinkled with age, her teeth yellowed and uneven, with so many missing that one could not understand her easily. But he conceded that 'she kept her dignitie'.

NOTES

1 *Acts of the Privy Council*, Vol. **XXI**, p. 324.

2 *Statutes of the Realm*, 5 Elizabeth I (1552-3), Vol. 23, p. 447.

3 Proclamation No. 815, 44 Elizabeth I (1602).

4 W. B. Rye (ed.), *England as Seen by Foreigners in the Days of Queen Elizabeth and James I.*

5 *Remembrancia*, II. 102, under the date September 1595.

6 *Acts of the Privy Council*, Vol. XXV, p. 230, 1 Feb., 1596.

7 *Wills in the Prerogative Court of Canterbury*, Vol. XXV, p. 132, Scott 9, 1582.

8 He left it to his son John, who fell into financial trouble and had to sell to James James, Apothecary of London, all of Drew's Rents, which then comprised fourteen tenements. James James (or his son) died in 1689 and his legatee, James Coych, sold it to Walter Gibbon, who in 1725 sold it to the brewer Edmund Halsey, then lord of the manor. (See also p.183)

9 B. W. Cockes and L. W. Cook, *Three Centuries*.

10 William Rendle, *Inns of Old Southwark*.

11 *Deed Poll*, 10 Henry IV (1409), 10 June: 'of John Hill Cittizen and Fysshemongere . . . to George Byckes and William Schuborne five gardens at the stewes'.

12 Chancery Proceedings, C. III, 65-67 (1528).

13 In *Hyckescorner* (*c.* 1510), op. cit. p. 188, occur the words: 'There shall be no man play doccy [doxy] there at the Bell, Hartshorn or elsewhere, without they have leave of me.' 'To play doxy' was to make use of the whores.

14 There may have been an old bull-baiting site here, perhaps known as Bull Yard, later Bull Head, but it had no connection with *The Bulhed* brothel, which was much further east, next to *The Swanne*.

15 The Bear Gardens Museum stands almost on the spot today.

16 W. W. Braine, *The Site of the Globe Playhouse*.

17 *Ancient Deeds*, Vol. VII, C. 8582, 16 Elizabeth I (1574), 11 Nov.

18 *Ancient Deeds*, Vol. VII, C. 8581, 33 Elizabeth I (1590), 15 Dec.

19 *Ancient Deeds*, C. 8348, 19 Elizabeth I (1576-7), 20 Jan.

20 *Ancient Deeds*, Vol. V, A. 12582, 17 Elizabeth I (1575), 8 Apr.

21 *C.P.R.*, 11 Richard II (1390), p. 280.

22 On 2 June, 1216 the Dauphin of France, Louis, arrived in Southwark at the invitation of the barons, with a view to occupying the throne of England and ousting King John. His march from Southwark over the Bridge was acclaimed by the population 'with great enthusiasm' (*Flores Historiacum of Mathew of Westminster* [ed. H. R. Luard]).

23 At some time between 1590 and his death in 1626, *The Bores Head* was owned by Edward Alleyn. In *Alleyn's Papers*, p. xvi, it is stated that this brothel was 'formerly kept by his brother John'.

24 *C.L.B.*, Book I, 35 Edward III (1361), p. 154.

25 *Ancient Deeds*, Vol. II, B. 2088, 25 Henry VI (1447).

26 Thomas H. Turner, *Manners and Household Expenses of England in the 13th and 15th Centuries*, p. 153.

27 *Ancient Deeds*, Vol. VI, C. 4711, 10 Edward IV (1470).

28 John Skelton, 'Why come ye not to court?' in *Poems*, op. cit.

29 The modern equivalent of 'gup' is 'gee up!', as to horses, i.e., get going.

[30] *Token Books of the Corporation of Wardens of St. Saviour's*, 1624.

[31] John Taylor, *The True Course of the Watermen's suit concerning the Players*, p. 9. This was a pamphlet (*c.* 1613) explaining the matter.

[32] Hampton & Sons, *Catalogue of Sale of Cardinal's Cap Wharf* (No. 49 Bankside), 13 July, 1937.

[33] William Taylor, *Annals of Ste Marie Overie*, citing *C.C.R.*, 5 Elizabeth I (1563).

[34] *Churchwardens' Accounts of St Saviour's*, G.L.C. Records Room.

[35] V. M. Book I, G.L.C. Records Room.

[36] W. W. Braine, op. cit.

[37] From *hacquenie*, Old French, meaning a slow or ambling nag.

[38] William Lauder, 'Examination', in *Minor Poems* (ed. F. J. Furnivall), p. xxv.

[39] Sir John Harington, *Nugae Antiquae*.

[40] Edward Guilpin, *Skialetheia, or the Shadow of the Truth in certayne Epigrams and Satyres*, Epigram No. 25.

[41] J. Gairdner (ed.), *Three 15th Century Chronicles* (from the Lambeth MS. 306), Camden Society, p. 137.

[42] Iwan Bloch describes this as a 'malicious satire' and states that it was composed by Théodore D'Aubigné for François Hotman in 1561; this cannot be correct for in 1561 D'Aubigné was nine years old. It was probably composed about 1580. Hotman (or Hotoman) was a powerful propagandist who wrote mainly in Latin, and this effusion is probably in his *Historia tragica de furoribus Gallicae*. I have not been able to inspect a copy to verify.

[43] Paul Hentzen in W. B. Rye (ed.), *England as seen by Foreigners. . . . ,* p. 101. Original (1598) in Latin, translated in English by Richard Bentley in 1754.

[44] Hurault de Maisse, *Ambassade de H. de Maisse en Angleterre,* Paris, L.A. Prevost-Paradol, 1855. De Maisse was Henry IV's ambassador to the English court, 1595-8.

XII

'Elizabeth was King. Now is James Queen.'

Elizabeth's successor James I was a character of such different calibre that the unkind – and also quite untrue – saying became popular: *'Rex fuit Elizabeth: nunc est Jacobus Regina'*.

Sir Anthony Weldon described him thus:[1] 'He was of middle stature, more corpulent through his clothes than in his body . . . the clothes being quilted . . . and stiletto proof. His eyes large, ever rolling . . . his beard very thin, his tongue too large for his mouth . . . his skin was soft as Taffeta Sarsnet . . . because he never washed his hands, only rubbed the fingers' ends with the wet end of a napkin. His legs were very weak . . . his fingers ever fiddling with his codpiece . . . he would never change his clothes until worn out to very rags.'

Sir Anthony found him very witty in a deadpan fashion, and 'very liberal of what he had not in his own grip . . . [he] would rather part with an hundred pound he never had . . .than twenty-one shillings within his own custody.'

Of the drunken and profligate nature of his court there is ample reference elsewhere. His widespread granting of titles for cash led Sir Francis Bacon to observe that he had created within two months as many knighthoods as Elizabeth had bestowed in ten years. These new and old ladies and gentlemen of the court 'frequently became dead drunk and rolled on the floor'.

Under James's benevolent, if drunken eyes the Bankside amusement parade flourished as never before. His attitude may be seen in his Proclamation of 1618 when he ordained that after divine service 'oure goode people be not disturbed, letted or discouraged . . . from such as dauncing, either men or women . . . leaping, vaulting or any such harmless recreation.' This wise monarch had calculated that by allowing such wholesome sports he would prevent 'filthy tiplings and discontented speeches in their ale-houses.' Here indeed he was well ahead of his time.

The King was known to frequent from time to time the 'Holland's Leaguer', the high-class brothel run by Dame Elizabeth Holland in

Old Paris Garden.[2] He was of course followed by almost all his courtiers. The goings-on in Southwark did not escape the eagle eye of contemporaries like Thomas Archer, who in 1613[3] noted that the Bankside panders would procure women for a 'dumbe man' (a simple or bashful man) but warned that 'these bee no bashful Companions . . . their common talk will be of Rebaldry . . . they will hie to some blinde Brothell house . . . where for a Pottle of Wine, th' embrassement of a painted Strumpet and the French Welcome [a dose of the pox] for a Reckoning, the yonge Man payeth 40/- or better.'

Paradoxically, the chorus of Puritan fulminations against woman-kind grew louder under the tolerant King. The outcry was provoked in part by the dress of women of this period. Fashions had changed every few years or so; early in the Tudor period dresses were up to the neck, later the bosom was exposed; and the exposure of the breasts became even more marked in the Jacobean period. In 1565 John Hall had written : [4]

> That women theyr breasts dyd show and laye out,
> as wel was yt mayd whose dugs were stoute:
> which usance at fyrst came upp from the stues
> which mens wyves and daughters after did use.

At about the same time Charles Bansley[5] made the same point equally succintly:

> for a stewde strumpet can not so soone
> gette vp a lyghte lewde fashyon,
> but everie wanton jelot [jilt] wyll lyke itt well
> and catch it vp anon.

Robert Burton[6] (1577-1640) complained that 'opin brest and sing-ing . . . aren toknes of horelinge', and in another work describes the women in question, 'theyre fyngres ful of rynges, theyre neckes naked almost vntoe the reynes [kidneys]'. Thomas Dekker[7] describes the Bankside whores in 1612: '. . . the dores of notorious *Carted Bawdes* . . . stand night and day wide open, with a paire of Harlots in Taffata gownes [like two painted posts] garnishing oute those dores, beeing better to the house than a *Double Signe*.'

Throughout history it has been found that fashions often originate amongst courtesans and prostitutes; it is instructive to see this con-firmed once again. All the strictures, however, were directed at the wives and daughters of the middle and merchant classes whose chastity had to be safeguarded. Women of the working classes were taken for granted and no one bothered much about their dress; by general repute they were prone to lewdness and regarded as natural whores, so such attire was to be expected of them. In any case, whores were likely to be less conservative in their dress; or perhaps more adventurous. Not surprisingly, the bare-breastedness of English women found great favour with visiting foreign gentlemen and is much remarked upon in their reports home.

Another interesting article of Bankside fashion is commented on in the satirical booklet *Quippes for the Vpstarte Newfangled Gentlewoman*: [8]

> These Holland smockes, so white as snowe
> and gorgets brave, with drawn-work wrought,
> a tempting ware they are, you knowe
> wherewith (as nets) vaine Youth are caught.
> But many times they rue the match
> when Pox and Pyles by whores they catch!

There is a mass of information in this late-Elizabethan and Jacobean period to be gleaned from the works of the playwrights, all of whom describe in detail the theatres and the whorehouses, as well as contemporary habits and dress. The popular appetite for reading was ravenous among all classes and much of the reading matter was highly indelicate when it was not actually pornographic, albeit it was often disguised in pseudo-moralistic forms. The cheap little blackletter booklets and pamphlets changed hands with incredible rapidity and their lightheartedness disturbed the puritanically inclined, who were seeking to induce a decent moral climate. Roger Ascham remarked that more papists were made by the merry books of Italy than all the earnest religious books of Louvain. He was referring particularly to the host of booklets purporting to be by or after Peter Aretino; but he could also have had in mind the rumbustiously explicit works of the Frenchman François Rabelais.

These cheap duodecimo books reached the poorer people and undoubtedly educated them in current events, raising the standard of political and religious understanding and stimulating the festering unrest.

The glories of the Elizabethan age had brought little respite to the poor. They remained a faceless mass, lurking in the wings, making 'discontented speeches in their ale-houses', and waiting for the cue that would bring them to the centre of the stage. Thousands were in prison for debts they had no hope of repaying. Philip Stubbes (1543-1591) [9] had written how it broke his heart to walk through the streets and hear the complaints of poor prisoners in durance for debt, and likely to stay in prison all their lives, without the meanest kind of meat or drink and often without clothing on their backs, 'lying in filthy strawe and loathsome dung woorse than anie dogge', and wishing for death to come and relieve them of their 'shackles gyves and iron bandes'.

Conditions were much the same in all the prisons, including the Clink and Bridewell. It is to the everlasting credit of many a simple English man and woman that they left money in their wills for the relief of prisoners, and they could daily be seen giving food and clothes, pushing them through the gratings at street level, to these indigent and starving wretches, most of them the victims of obdurate creditors.

The activity of the Bankside was being documented in 1602-3 in a curious set of verses by Bishop Joseph Hall:[10]

> To see the broken Nuns, with newe shorne heads
> in a blinde cloyster, tappe the idle beads;
> or louzy Cowles come smoking from the Stewes
> to raise the lewd rent that to their lord Accrewes,
> (who with rank Venice doth his pompe advance
> by trading of ten thousand Courtezans.)

The expression 'louzy cowles' may refer to some Catholic priests still having recourse to sexual satisfaction in these whorehouses and the bishop infers that *couillage* was still being rendered to the pope; but it may also be a sideswipe against the Bishop of Winchester keeping a lot of whores in a red-light district much as the papacy maintained thousands of whores in Rome in emulation of those who were making Venice famous. The phrase 'come smoking from the Stewes' is particularly powerful and brings to mind the old Roman gibe that men emerged *redoles adhuc fornices* (with the stink of fornication on their clothes).

In 1603 it was reported to the Privy Council that a plague had begun in the City 'and especially in Southwark . . . and it is feared that nexte yeare it will be very contagious'. It swept through the tenements on Bankside and was to become a regular feature of life there, waxing and waning in intensity, for another fifty years.

The Bankside was then described as the haunt of all vagrants and masterless men, 'theeves, horsestealers, whoremongers, cozeners, conycatchers', and the criminal elements who infested the theatres and bear-baiting rings. Thomas Dekker described the Bankside as being 'a contynuall alehouse'.

Henrie Chettle[11] (perhaps referring to Philip Henslowe) told of 'dy houses turned into whorehouses' because such large profits could be earned by prostitution that the dyers, who had taken over many

premises after 1550, found it better to change their type of business.
In these tenements, says Chettle, exorbitant rents were charged for
the smallest attics, and the tenants were always in debt. They were
enjoined to take their provisions and fuel 'on trust' at their landlord's
shop; at the weekend they would then have to pawn their clothes to
pay the rent and bills, and the same landlord would also be the pawn-
broker.

Great lords, like Queen Elizabeth's cousin Lord Hunsdon, were not
above dabbling in this immoral traffic. In 1603 he is recorded as
having leased out a mansion in Paris Garden to a famous Madam,[12]
setting down the terms on which men and women were to be received.
If she allowed men to bring in too many women, or if the women
brought in more than a specified number of men in a day, the lease
could be forfeited. It says much for the entrepreneurial skills of this
lady that she was still in possession some thirty years later.

The Bankside of this time was portrayed by Bishop Hall, with its

> mydnyghte Playes, or Tavernes of New Wine.
> Hie, ye white Aprons, to your landlord's sign:
> when all save toothless age or infancy,
> are summond to the Courte of Venerie.

Here the Bishop not only recalls the aprons of a bygone age, but lets
out the truth about brothels disguised as inns, each with its own stable
of wenches, wearing white aprons to indicate that their services were
for hire. (A hundred years later the Fleet Street prostitutes were to be
so attired, for the delectation of the 'cits'.)

Not unnaturally the Bankside tavern keepers were anxious to keep
their monopoly. It appears that up to about 1617 there had existed
'from time immemorial' a short cut from the High Street, across St
George's Fields, to Bankside, thus establishing a 'right of way'. The
locals had enjoyed this ancient amenity until some fifteen months
previously when 'some innholders of the borough . . . have chained up
the waye . . . to the bankside taverns.' The High Street tavern keepers,
as tenants of the Bridge House Wardens of the City of London, had
asked for support from their powerful patrons, and requested one
Ralph Rathbone, a surveyor, to make a survey and a plan, for which
on 30 May, 1618 he was paid 41 shillings with a further 11 shillings on
25 November, 1620 'ffor drawing the mapp of St Georges his fieldes'.
To bolster their claim further they made an appeal to the Privy
Council[13] that 'The LORD MAYOR & Aldermen RECOMEND . . . the
petition of the inhabitants of Southwark against a road leading from
Southwark to two new inns on Bankside, the road proving a way of
escape to malefactors.'

Their plea was rejected after years of litigation. The High Street men smouldered and tried again in 1637, by barring the way. This time the two new innkeepers were the plaintiffs and again the Privy Council upheld their rights.[14] Rathbone's map is invaluable for details of Southwark; it shows the spur called 'the road to the banke' and at the junction of Bank End with Clink Street the name 'Clink' appears, next to a pillory and stocks.

It is difficult to visualize exactly what the Bankside looked like at the beginning of the seventeenth century. Infuriatingly, Visscher's panorama of 1616[15] clearly delineates all the *backs* of the houses and their gardens. A painting by Claude de Jongh[16] dated 1630 shows a very small section of the river bank adjacent to London Bridge; the ramshackle buildings are all in the late-Tudor style, and the muddy foreshore is littered with driftwood and other debris. The Bankside houses must have looked very much like these, with inns and taverns interspersed with shops and a few dwelling houses, and of course, the brothels. Architecturally, it must have been a hotchpotch of designs, for there would still have been some of the buildings and gardens which had existed from ancient times, some Elizabethan open-fronted shops with their outside swinging signs, and some dye-houses with smoking tubs of materials and men and women splashing busily away with their arms coloured up to the elbows, exchanging noisy chitchat and abuse with neighbours and passers by.

By then the ancient brothels would have been functioning as inns, some having been rebuilt since about 1570 in the new Tudor style and much enlarged. One or two may have still retained the whitened fronts required by the ancient regulations, although these would have been regarded as a quaint relic of bygone days or pointed out to avid foreign tourists, perhaps as an inducement to step aside and visit one of the brothel houses in any one of the alleys.

At the turn of the century, and before the great spate of tenement building, the larger brothels had been built like great inns, with large courtyards around which the whole establishment revolved. The reception rooms were on the ground floor facing onto the courtyard, which was entered through a great arch big enough to allow coaches to pass. Next to the reception rooms would have been a restaurant and, of course, a bar – or perhaps several, to cater for clients of different status and means. The women's chambers would have been upstairs opening onto the gallery which went round three sides of the courtyard. At a later period, the gallery and the rooms would be enclosed. There might also have been suites of two or three rooms for the regular wealthy clients, who would (as in Italy today) transact their business and entertain their clients therein.

Where there was a watercourse or 'sewar' – one ran the length of

Maiden Lane at the rear of the Bankside gardens – the human refuse
was voided into it; otherwise the chamberpots would have been taken
out and emptied onto the dunghill at the rear of the premises to await
the gong-farmer. Nearby would have been the stables in which the
clients' horses were looked after by the ostler and where (later, after
1618) their coaches might be parked.

Doubtless the servants' quarters would have had their quota of girls,
although these would have been somewhat shop-soiled and consequently cheaper to suit the leaner purses.

Some of these Elizabethan and Jacobean brothels were quite
luxurious. Those owned by the famous Elizabethan actor Edward
Alleyn (later to found Dulwich College on the profits made from his
many whorehouses on Bankside) were stripped to furnish his new
residence at Dulwich. 'All the wainscot, hangings, pictures, carpets,
presses, chairs, tables, fforms and stools . . . all shelves desks seats . . .
and six pewter chamber potts' were transferred to his new mansion.

There is in fact a first-hand description of such a brothel in 1614 in
a satire,[17] which as usual commences with a warning. The bawds are
described first:

> . . . now ceaz'd with age and both of them turn'd Bawds,
> old Hackney-women, they hire out their jades –
> a crew of whores far worse than Crocodiles,
> killing with feign'd Tears and forged Smiles.

Then, in contrast, comes the description of the luxuries to be enjoyed:

> But if some Gallant, whose outside doth holde
> greate expectation of goode store of Golde
> . . . to see thir choysest beauties him they bring
> . . . into a private room, which round aboute
> is hung with pictures: all which goodlie Rout
> is framed with Venus's fashyon, female all . . .
> and then good Bacchus' grape
> flowes in abundance . . . provocative to stirr up appetite
> to brutish luste & sensuall delightes
> must not be wanting. Lobsters' buttered thighs,
> Hartichoke, Marrowbone, Potato Pies,
> Anchoves, Lambes artificiallie drest stones,
> fine Gellies of decocted Sparrows' bones:
> or, if these faile, th'apothecaries's trade
> must furnishe them with rarest Marmelade,
> candid Cringoes & riche Marchpane stuffe
> . . . but then these daynties must be washe'd down well

with Wine, with Sacke with Sugar Eggs and Muskadine
with Allegante, the blood of Venerie.

It will be seen that there was no lack of aphrodisiacs, but one must
remark upon the dish made from lambs' testicles as something quite
out of the ordinary even in such a menu as this. It is also curious to
find that 'Marmelade' (by which is meant jam) and also 'Marchpane'
(marzipan) are stated to be the province of apothecaries. For the first
time too, Alicante wine is advertised as best to stir the blood to venery.

This satire is, incidentally, directed against the courtiers of James
I and certain City magnates who frequented these stews. It also provides the information that incest and sodomy were rife at court and
were protected by 'the Moste Powerfull', that is James himself.

In such a place (and this description would almost certainly fit a
brothel like *The Unicorne*) hand-picked girls, each with some peculiar
expertise to ensure the complete gratification of the most exigent (and
aged) clients, well-spoken, clean and even speaking a foreign language
or two, and capable of playing an instrument or singing, would have
been found. There were gaming rooms for diversion when sexual
energies were flagging, an excellent kitchen with wines of the best
quality, sumptuous waiting rooms, and comfortable beds with clean
linen.

Above all, the Madam, reinforced by the presence of a resident
'phisitian', saw that the strictest standards of personal hygiene were
observed and that there were no 'vitious smells'. Finally, there was a
beautiful and secluded garden, perhaps with a pond, for promenading
or relaxation from the arduous business of fornication. Maximum
enjoyment was guaranteed, albeit at maximum expenditure.

At the lower level the brothels were more functional, although good
fare and, especially, large quantities of liquor were always to be had.
The quality of the entertainment would have been lower and the
turnover much quicker. In these establishments time was money; the
girls had to ensure the maximum number of customers in the working
day. In the lowest class of brothel, there would have been no entertainment but plenty of liquor, and the girls worked till they dropped
from fatigue. (No contemporary statistics are available, but some
modern research discovered that in a high-class brothel a girl might
serve ten to twelve men in a night, in the lower-class houses thirty was
the average, while in the lowest category fifty-seven is known.)

One thing was common to all brothels: the customer would be
fleeced. The contemporary literature is full of the tricks and strata-
gems used to deprive the customer of all his money; even going so far
as having him waylaid and robbed on his departure, and in some cases
murdered.

What was not common to all, however, was the degree of cleanliness and hygiene maintained. This deteriorated the cheaper the establishment. The customers and the girls in these haunts had no other option but to avoid expense, with all the consequent risks, and it is remarkable to observe how much this was taken as a normal risk of life, a sort of 'what's a little pox among friends?' philosophy prevailing.

It should not be thought that all whores and Madams were ill-favoured, sluttish creatures. Most of them seem to have been good-looking and many were very beautiful. Contemporary prints – always designed to point to a moral – invariably depict Madams as gross and ugly, bulging and big-breasted. They certainly were not; such a figure, except in the lowest haunts where nobody cared about appearances, would have been inimical to business. Many bawds were still lovely, and the majority were handsome, mature women. But in the main they were also hard and unscrupulous, having realized that it was better and safer to peddle the flesh of others than their own, though not averse to participating in the (profitable) fun when it suited them.

They were, above all, businesswomen running an enterprise that had to produce constant profits to withstand the demands of corrupt constables, magistrates and judges and other official hazards. They had also to cope with the bully-boys running protection rackets. There were ever-present hazards from disease – and especially the dreaded plague. The fire-risks were terrible; and on top of this there was the annual Shrove Tuesday rampage of the London Apprentices, which included, as a very ancient tradition, the sport of whore-bashing and the pulling-down (literally in the case of the older, flimsy, wood and thatch houses) of the brothels themselves. Above all there was the hourly threat of arrest and incarceration in the Clink or Bridewell, with its beatings and other savageries. By contrast, carting and the pillory were more easily shrugged off: they left no marks on the skin. Marks on the conscience or reputation were invisible to the customers.

In general, however, whoring was not a long or profitable profession for the women themselves; one aspect of their life is summed up in a verse in the *Poor Whores' Complaint to the Apprentices of London*[19] (1668):

> Our Rents are great, our clients go apace,
> and we forsaken are in ev'ry place.
> None pities us nor hearkens to our moane,
> but ev'ry Shag-bag casts at us a stone. . . .
> Besides all this, with hot encounter, We

too many of us, scab'd and mangy be.

A part of this complaint was also directed at the quacks who preyed on them with false cures for the venereal diseases. Many of these were Dutch and Flemish tricksters, who battened on the credulous women and then ran away home when things went wrong.

Nevertheless, in the intervening centuries great advances had been made in medical knowledge. The two principal diseases of Venus's servants had now been differentiated and named. Various methods of alleviation or cure were being used, all of them based on some mercurial compound, applied directly to the skin or used in hot sweating baths. For some reason, Leather Lane in Holborn was the principal centre for these mercurial sweat baths, which were later much patronized by the diseased noblemen and noblewomen of King Charles II's court. The treatment, from their descriptions, appears to have been almost as bad as the disease, but it certainly seems in many cases to have had some curative results.

Pregnancy was a whore's most constant daily hazard. By this time a number of other contraceptive measures were undoubtedly being used as well as the time-honoured but certainly ineffective method of 'pyssynge harde into the chamber pott'. That most basic of contraceptives, the sheath, had been used in the Middle East for centuries, utilizing the intestines of the sheep. But it was not until the seventeenth century that it was introduced in Europe. The Italian anatomist Gabriele Fallopio (1523-62) devised a sheath as a protective against syphilis. His own words introducing this remarkable 'invention' bear repetition: 'As often as a man has intercourse, he should use a small linen cloth made to fit over the *glans penis* and draw forward the prepuce. It would improve matters if it were moistened with a little spit or a lotion. If you are afraid that syphilis will get into the pipe of your penis, then take the linen sheath and after slipping it over your prepuce, thrust it into the woman's vulva.'[20] He goes on to state that 'I tried this experiment on more than a hundred men ... and not one of them was infected.'

Fallopio thought it would be useful to carry one of the sheaths in one's pocket, but, perhaps because they were so cumbersome and rough, they did not come into general use until much later. That experiments were still being made to improve them is shown by Madame de Sevigny's complaint (about 1650) concerning a sheath 'made of goldbeaters' skin', which she qualified with the sage remark that 'it was armour against full enjoyment and only a spider's web against the danger of infection.'

In England these contraceptives were not 'invented' until the time of Charles II, when they were called 'condoms' or 'cundums'. Some authorities trace the invention to a London doctor called Conton, who used lambs' intestines, dried and well oiled to make them soft and pliable. Others swear that it was a Colonel Condum who came up with the sheath in order to protect his troops from disease. As the likely carriers of the disease were French women, they became known as 'French letters'; the French, of course, called them 'English letters'.

Whoever the inventor – and at least one of these two gentlemen, Conton or Condum, must be a fiction – all are agreed that the condom appeared during Charles II's reign (the word first appears in print in 1665) and some say that it was invented at his instigation. Whatever the case, it was much appreciated by his court: the Earl of Rochester even wrote a ballad, *A Panegyrick vpon Cundum*, in which he recommmended its use far and wide in the king's dominions as a specific against pregnancy.

Sheaths, despite these recommendations from high places, did not catch on and it is unlikely that they were much used in the Bankside houses. Even in the next century Boswell was complaining that they were very uncomfortable to use. There were no female pessaries either – the first effective pessary was not introduced until 1881. For the whores, then, it was still the old method of hearty pissing and a wipe down with wine or vinegar, or practising *coitus interruptus*. While most favoured by the women, this latter method would not have been popular with the customers. Most whores probably just crossed their fingers and took a chance against pregnancy and disease.

There were many remedies advanced, but few of any value. An example is that given in 1603 by a Doctor Vaughan: 'In the morning make water in an Urinall, that by looking or it you may ghesse some what of the state of your bodie.'[21]

Tudor and Jacobean men, as we have seen, often observed the maxim laid down in 1303[22] that 'Frenche men synne yn lecherye & Englys men yn enuye', and while this may be true, it was also true that Englishmen expected their wives to be constantly concupiscent. Observe, for instance, the old saying, 'Women be farre more lecherous thann men: one rooster can serve thrice five hens but thrice five men cannot satisfy one woman !', a pleasant conceit that has served menfolk everywhere very well since the dawn of time.

It has served to hide the fact that in those days life expectancy was very short: only 10 per cent of the population reached the age of forty and females had a shorter life span than men. The women in the stews were doomed to an even shorter life because of the mode of life thrust upon them and the probability that if they lived longer, dissipation and disease would take a further toll and by the age of forty they would be old hags. It is perhaps this fact that led contemporary writers to stress their 'old age' when in fact they were prematurely aged. Often they were suffering from a venereal disease, and frequently tuberculosis into the bargain. Indeed so many diseases were rife that they were taken for granted as a normal part of life, and perhaps the historian is more touched by their condition at this distance in time than the actual sufferers were.

This was the reality behind the facade of 'Merry England'. Some of the whores, it is true, became rich; many of those who became bawds became very rich. Officially repudiated, despised and vilified as they were, they flourished because the same nobility and gentry who disparaged them in public, utilized their services in private. In return, the women were able to earn money by blackmail and even at times to marry well above their station; in concubinage they could go as far as royalty itself. So that whether they operated under licence or as freelances in unlicensed houses, they were an integral part of life, and leech-like they flourished in good times and bad. The abysmal wastage of the flower of English womanhood was the price society paid, but then in those days women were still regarded as expendable chattels. The ultimate refinement was yet to come. Brothels for female children were to be invented in Queen Anne's reign, and to be an institution noted by many a foreign visitor.

That young girls of twelve and thirteen were prostituted on Bankside goes without saying. There was no minimum age of consent, and families of professional prostitutes were bred and born into the trade. Parents sold their children into prostitution from the age of eleven. All this was consistent with the concept of female children being not only chattels but useless mouths to feed, a burden on the family or wage earner. Yet there is no evidence in all the mass of documentation as to the existence of any child-brothel on Bankside.

While King James lived, there was little attempt to check the escalation of brothelry and prostitution. In every section of the community money was the key, and for money almost any enormity could be practised; although towards the end of his life even this tolerant King was compelled to make some protest at what was going on in some of the London suburbs,[23] and eventually to tighten up the bail arrangements because so many defendants and bondsmen jumped bail. But neither ordinance referred to Bankside and the King still visited the theatres there and upon occasion is stated to have visited that ancient house called *The Bulhead*. His visits to 'Holland's Leaguer' were no secret either, and must give the lie to the canard that he was homosexual. He died in 1625 of a combination of diseases ranging from stones in the bladder to dental caries; despite a life of debauchery, gluttony and drinking, he had somehow escaped the venereal diseases.

NOTES

1 Sir Anthony Weldon, *The Secret History of the Court and Character of King James I*, 1651.

2 E. J. Burford, op. cit.

3 Thomas Archer, *Look On Me, London*, 1613.

4 John Hall, *The Court of Virtue*, 1565.

5 Charles Bansley, *Pryde and Abuse of Women* (1540).

6 Robert Burton, *Anatomie of Melancholie*, 'Artifices and Allurements of Love'. See W. C. Hazlitt, *English Popular Poetry*, Vol. IV.

7 Thomas Dekker, *The Bel-mans nighte walkes whervnto is added O per se O*, Chapter IX 'The Infection of the Suburbes', 1612.

8 Stephen Gosson, *Quippes for the Vpstarte Newfangled Gentlewoman*, 1595.

9 Philip Stubbes, *Anatomie of Abuses*, in F. J. Furnivall (ed.), *Ballads from MSS*, Vol. I, p. 33.

10 Bishop Joseph Hall, *Virgidimarium*, Lib. IV, 'Satire I', p. 56.

11 Henrie Chettle, *Kinde Harte's Dreame* (1592).

12 E. J. Burford, op. cit.

13 *C.S.P.D.*, 16 James I (1619), pp. 24-5, 16 March.

14 *C.S.P.D.*, 12 Charles I (1637), p. 113, item 88.

15 In the British Museum Print Room.

16 In the Iveagh Bequest at Kenwood House, London.

17 J. M. Cowper (ed.), *Times' Whistle* (1614), Satire No. 6 'The Practice of Bawds', E.E.T.S. Orig. Ser. 48.

18 Abraham Flexner, *Prostitution in Europe*.

19 J. L. Ebsworth (ed.), *The Bagford Ballads*, Vol. II, No. 45. A 'shag-bag' is a tramp.

20 Gabriele Fallopio, *De Preservatione a Carie Gallica*, 1564.

21 'Fifteen Directions for Helthe', in Frances Seagar, *The Babees Boke* (ed. E. Rickert), E.E.T.S. Orig. Ser. 32, p. 253.

22 Robert de Brunne, *Handlynge Synne* (ed. F. J. Furnivall), E.E.T.S. Orig. Ser. 119, p. 131.

23 *Middlesex Sessions Books*, 20 James I (1622), 4 Dec.

24 Ibid., 21 James I (1624), 13 Jan.

XIII

The End of the Beare's Colledge

King Charles I came to the throne in 1625. His outlook was completely at variance with that of his tolerant brother, and this became
immediately apparent at his first Parliament[1] when the Lord Chief
Justice was ordered forthwith to attend to the matter of certain bawdy
houses in the suburbs of London. Again, however, the Bankside
escaped the royal antagonism. Quite why is not so easy to understand.
It might have been that the King deemed it inexpedient to interfere
with the Bishop's Liberty of the Clink. Moreover, the other brothel
areas were round the City of London like a fringe, almost unbroken
from the north-west to the south-east, and the City authorities needed
some assistance in cleaning them up. It is unnecessary to remark that
the attempt was doomed to complete failure.

To give King Charles his due, whatever his political and religious
views, he was a monarch of unimpeachable morals, the like of whom
had not been seen in England since Edward VI some seventy-five
years previously. Perhaps he was too busy with his other principles to
worry overmuch about the activities on Bankside; that these were not
seriously impeded is indicated by a couplet in 1638:[2]

> Come, I will send for a whole coach or two
> of Bankside ladies, and we shall be Joviall.

This at least demonstrates that despite the calamity which had
befallen Holland's Leaguer in 1631-2 when it had been besieged by
the troops and finally closed down, there still remained on Bankside
a great many willing ladies, even by the coachload, securely
ensconced in the taverns there.

The fate of the Bankside was perhaps presaged by the return of the
plague in 1625. The theatres carried on and so did the bear gardens,
but attendances declined. Another, more subtle change was also
taking place. That was the effect of the great Dutch and Flemish
immigration of the previous fifty years, which had begun to indus-

trialize large areas and to create an established, sober, artisan class.

More important still was the change in the political complexion of Southwark. It should be remembered that amongst those who rejoiced at the victory over the Armada in 1588 were all the Dutch and Flemish Protestant refugees, and with the advent of another Catholic king – or at least a pseudo-Anglican who openly strived to bring back Catholicism – they were more determined than ever to adhere to their brands of puritanism. In the stern struggle between King and Parliament which was to lead to the Civil War and ultimately to Charles' decapitation, Southwark was a stronghold for Parliament, and frequently at odds with the City of London on this issue. The degree to which the Dutch Madams and quacks were involved is not known; they were in any case pledged to eschew political or racial discrimination, even 'jewes and turkes' were acceptable. Apartheid was no part of the harlots' creed, as the greatest whoremistress[3] of them all remarked : 'I make no scruple but give free traffique to all nations. If you have payd your dues, you may putt in !'

But before these momentous events, came another disaster for Southwark in the form of one of the most virulent outbreaks of the plague ever to strike the borough. In 1630 the authorities ordered all the theatres to close and the players to disperse, which they did to such good measure that they never returned to the Bankside again. The bear gardens were closed, as were the bowling alleys and other diversions, but curiously there is no mention of the closure of the inns and taverns. If the pattern of previous outbreaks was followed, it could be expected that the normal 'let us be merry for tomorrow we die' attitude would enable the prostitutes to carry on, but on this occasion the deaths from plague were very numerous and doubtless everybody who could get away did so. The Bankside never fully recovered from this blow. Strangely enough the next-door Paris Garden escaped the worst of the plague – perhaps there was more open space and not so many crowded tenements there – and was in a position of some advantage when the epidemic had passed.

In April 1644 Parliament closed all whorehouses, gambling houses and theatres. The players were whipped at the cart-arse, fined for using oaths, or sent to prison. The maypoles were pulled down wherever they could be found, on the ground that they incited the peasantry to lust. Nude statues, when not broken up, had their genitals covered with leaves and scrolls; some were clothed to hide their nudity. Austerity was the word, piety the rule.

When the crunch came, the Roundheads could count on a firm base in Southwark. On 1 October, 1645[4] the Committee of Militia instructed the Committee of Southwark to levy 1,465 recruits for Sir Thomas Fairfax's army 'to be ready to go [to Reading] with the militia of London.' It was a very large number for just a suburb.

Already in 1640 Parliament had enacted that prostitution was no longer a crime but only a nuisance, grossly indecent if carried on in public. The Commonwealth was to make adultery a felony for which (on a second conviction) the penalty was to be death.[5] In fact even Puritan juries revolted against this: a man of eighty-nine was executed for adultery in 1653 and another man in 1656 for incest with his brother-in-law's daughter; after that the juries refused to convict.

It is not to be thought that the Roundheads were all kill-joys. There was unanimity only in their fight against the King. The ranks of soldiers were filled by ordinary men, and not all of them marched to the sound of psalms. There were many Roundhead songs and ditties which if not actually indecent, as most marching songs are, were very far from being pious.

Cromwell himself was no saint; he is reputed to have enjoyed extra-connubial bliss with Bess Dysart (an open and confessed harlot and very likely a nymphomaniac), who was later to become Duchess of Lauderdale. Of her, says the ballad, 'She is Besse of my heart, she was Besse of Old Noll, she was once Fleetwood's Besse, and she's now of Atholl.'[6]

Nor were the inns and taverns closed down, for they were an essential part of daily life; perhaps their sexual activities were somewhat muted but the records show clearly that even the Commonwealth could not stamp out whoredom in its many manifestations, nor the practice of bawdry.

Then a series of blows struck Bankside, not the least of which was the sale, between 1647 and 1649, of the lands belonging to the Bishop of Winchester to a number of property developers, including Thomas Walker.

On 26 September, 1648[7] Thomas Walker bought 'the mansion in Southewarke...called Winchester Libertie...alias the Clink Libertie ...three and a half acres...nine messuages...and the Clink Gardens [stretching] to the Cage on the west of the cawsey [causeway] leading from the Stewes Bank towards the Clink Gate,' for the sum of £4,380. In March 1651 he bought several more houses and tenements belonging to the Manor of Southwark for £456 13s. 4d. By this purchase he also made himself Lord of the Manor of the Clink Liberty, and proceeded almost immediately to pull down, rebuild and alter many of the old hostelries, filling up the gardens and cleared spaces with tenements.

In 1647 the Brew House and Bear Gardens on the Bankside were sold to Sarah Palmer for £1,783 15s. 0d. and on 24 March of the same year Thomas Rollison bought 'the ffaulcon on the Stews Bank' for £484.

It was the beginning of the end. A few brothels carried on bravely; *The Bell* was still standing, and so were *The Barge* and *The Cock, The Unicorne* and some others whose names are unknown. For example, in 1652 John Polgreene was accused at the Surrey Court Sessions 'of kepeinge a notorious disorderly house [on Bankside] by keping wenches to stand at his dore to beckon to Flemings and other lewd persons into his house where bawdery is suspected.'

After the King's execution in 1649 the Puritan hand became more oppressive. In 1653:[8]

> The Bear Baiting and playing for Prizes ... hitherto practised in Southwark ... which have caused great Evills and Abominations, [are] to be suppressed from this time
> *signed*   Colonel Pride.

It seems that this injunction was ignored, for in 1655, 'Seven beares have been shot to death by souldiers next the Hope Theatre.'

In the following year Thomas Walker pulled down the Hope and built tenements all over the site.[9]

Bankside might be down but it was not completely out. The Surrey Court Sessions for 1663-5 saw a stream of people charged with various immoral practices and sexual improprieties. Among them:

RICHARD DOVER Innkeeper of le Bankside. July 1663. fined x*s.*
ROBERT GARDINER Innkeeper of *The Angel* in Peper alley.Bankside. fined.xij*d.*
ROBERT YOUNGER Innkeeper of *le fflouer de luce* on Bankside. fined xij*d.*
ABRAHAM KESIER Kept a Disorderly House on Bankside. Sept.1.1664.fined x*s.*

(The mention of the very ancient *fflower de luce* on the Bankside as late as 1663 is most interesting; its name does not appear in any other document since that of 1506. Unfortunately this still gives no clue as to its exact location but it does prove that the name and the game were still the same.)

Those that remained on the Bankside were now operating from the warren of tenements which honeycombed the area behind the taverns and shops, using the inns as places of assignation. But in 1665 the disaster of the Great Plague decimated the population of Southwark, and scarcely was it over when the Great Fire broke out, destroying half of London and a great number of the rebuilt blocks of houses on the northern side of London Bridge.[10] It is from this time that the Bankside as the centre of whoredom collapses, although it was to be cited as its epitome for another two centuries to come.

That a few brothels survived the disasters may be seen from Pepys' note of December 30, 1666, when King Charles sent his men to scour the brothels 'and bid all the Parliament men there' to get back to the House of Commons immediately to save one of his Bills.

From a smudged and rather pornographic pamplet published in 1660[11] there are indications that three of the most famous procuresses of that time, who were to make their mark later in Charles II's reign, had some connection with the Bankside in the 1650s, for by 1660 they are already well established and supplying the court with fresh nubile goods before moving on to more commodious and central premises. These were Mother Cresswell, Damon Page and Priss Fotheringham and their exploits merit a book all to themselves.

The return of King Charles II in 1660 gave the Bankside a fillip, but the theatres did not return and the main amusement centre was once again the bear gardens, which in turn stimulated the more ancient pastimes in the locality, although during the Commonwealth a great many whores had emigrated permanently to Westminster, Covent Garden and to the outer purlieus of the City. Many had emigrated even further afield, to Flanders and especially to Venice, where they were greatly esteemed, although occasionally in trouble for minor matters like murder.

A considerable number had been coerced or cozened into going to the American colonies[12] to serve the sexual requirements of the women-starved settlers, and it is but fair to say that the great majority were enabled to start new lives, get married and become the mothers of many a respected daughter of the American revolution – a proof, if it were needed, that commercial prostitution thrives mainly on the subjection of women in poverty.

After 1666 the surviving houses on London Bridge began to deteriorate, and although all those destroyed in the fire had been replaced within some twenty years, the merchants had begun to move away. Sam Lee's *Directory* of 1677 lists only eight on the bridge, while twenty-seven were now listed on Bankside. Then the better class of tenants began to move out also, so that after the turn of the century the houses on the bridge, much neglected, were let out as lodgings attracting a much lower class of persons; by 1720 the houses were chiefly occupied by makers of pins and needles[13] but this is almost certainly a euphemism for prostitutes. The historian Walter Harrison[14] says that the bridge 'was exceedingly disagreeable . . . the line being broken by a great number of closets that projected from the buildings' and overhung the parapets. Pennant, in his recollections of London life, said that it was 'narrow darksome and dangerous to passengers . . . [the inmates of the houses] soon grew deaf to the noise of the falling waters, the clamours of watermen or the frequent shrieks of drowning wretches.'

The popularity of the Bankside bear gardens is attested to by Samuel Pepys who went there on 14 March, 1666 'to see the Bull's tossyng of dogges . . . a very rude and nasty pleasure', which nonetheless did not stop him from going again yearly until 1699. They were still in full spate in 1670 when John Evelyn visited them on 16 June, noting in his diary: 'I went to the Bear Gardens where there was cock-fighting, dog-fighting, bear and bull baiting, it being a famous day for all these butcherly sports, or rather, barbarous cruelties . . . one of the bulls tossed a dog full into a lady's lap in one of the boxes at a considerable height from the arena . . . I most heartily weary of this rude and dirty pastime which I had not seen in twenty years before.'

By the year 1700 the Bankside had lost almost every trace of its murky past; it was turning into a bleak warehouse and wharf area, with a few dye-houses and a number of public houses serving mainly the watermen and labourers who loaded and unloaded barges and other vessels. A number of breweries had also been established in the immediate hinterland, surrounded by slums.

A few reminders of the past remained. The site of the ancient *ad leonem* and its successor *The Lyon and Ram* was now covered by Smith's Rents, by which name it was still known in 1745.

The *Three Tunnes*, first heard of as a tavern in 1649, was still in business, although its neighbouring Bulhed Alley had been renamed Robinhood Alley – perhaps because visitors there were still being relieved of their purses.

The Bear and *The Bell* were still operating and are last heard of in 1791 when they were sold to Michael Blind for development. There is one further reference to *The Bulhede* in the report of The Warden of the Great Account[15] (undated but probably *c*. 1750): 'John Taylor Esq., pays yearly for the back part of the late Bulls Head Tavern now occupied by Mr. Joshua Lockwood commences Ladyday 1735 clear of Taxes.term of years 61.expires 1796. £11.'

The Horseshoe, as we have seen, had been renamed *The Sugar Loaf*, but the name Horseshoe Alley was retained – indeed it is so called to this day. In 1745 there stood at the junction of the alley and Bankside 'a dye house owned by Arclay and Child' [16] and this would seem to have been the fate of the tavern.

One other most ancient landmark also survived until 1750. This was the Clink prison which had been Bankside's constant and faithful companion since the time of William Rufus. Beginning as the Bishop's prison in the Liberty, it had housed incontinent women and recalcitrant monks as well as various minor rascals. Then later, from about 1500 as 'The Clink' it had accommodated debtors, thieves and murderers, and the same ladies and their friends. It became in the end a dismal debtors' prison. For a time it had also lodged, with some degree of luxury, the Royalists who had fallen foul of the Commonwealth. This was probably its heyday. In 1720 when it had almost completely lost its *raison d'être* and was in great decay, it was removed to a site across Deadman's Place adjacent to the Anchor Brewery, which stood on the site of the ancient, disreputable 'Castle of Southwark' (as it was affectionately called), and was to go up in flames at the hands of Lord George Gordon's rioters in 1780.

The other landmark was *The Castle* itself, by then known as *The King's Head*. In 1734 it was incorporated in Ralph Thrale's expanded brewery and shortly afterwards reconstructed, although leaving much of its 1676 structure, and renamed *The Anchor*. Thrale's son Henry was the great friend of Dr Samuel Johnson, whose affections also embraced Mrs Hester Thrale, and through whom the Thrales have been immortalized. Dr Johnson even became chairman of the brewery for a short time before it was sold to Robert Barclay and John Perkins.

Barclay Perkins Brewery is also gone, but *The Anchor* remains at No. 1 Bankside. It is a quirk of history that the only other ancient building still standing in that otherwise undistinguished street is the even older *The Cardinal's Cap* (now No. 49), no longer an inn, but with its 1710 facade clearly to be seen.

With a little imagination – and perhaps with this book in hand to fill in the gaps – a visitor may walk the Bankside from No. 1 to No. 49 and conjure up all the scenes of its colourful and rumbustious past, and at the end of the stroll be the wiser for having learned of an aspect of English life ignored by orthodox historians. The glory has departed but thanks to The Clink and The Globe the memory lingers on, to remind us that *Sic Transit Ingloria Mundi*.

NOTES

[1] *Journals of the House of Commons*, Part I, Vol. I, p. 807, 9 July, 1625.

[2] Thomas Randolph, *Poems with the Muses Lookynge Glasse* (1638), in F. J. Furnivall (ed.), *Ballads from MSS.*, Vol. I, p. 25, citing Nares' *Old Plays*.

[3] Dame Elizabeth Holland.

[4] *Middlesex Sessions Books*, Vol. dxi, p. 170, 1 October, 1645.

[5] 'For adultery and inceast. The death penalty. For ordinary fornication, three months.'

[6] James Maidment, *A Book of Scotch Pasquils*.

[7] *Act of Sale of Church Lands*, MS. Rawlinson B. 236, Bodleian Library,

[8] *Middlesex Sessions Books*, Vol. xxxvi, p. 307, 5 May, 1653.

[9] Thomas F. Ordish, *Early London Theatres*, p. 240.

[10] Gordon Home, *Old London Bridge*, pp. 240 ff.

[11] *The Wand'ring Whore*, Issue No. I, 1660.

[12] Walter H. Blumenthal, *Brides from Bridewell*, Rutland, Va., 1962.

[13] Thomas Pennant, *Some Account of London*, pp. 317-20.

[14] Walter Harrison, *History of London*, p. 24.

[15] M. Concanen and A. Morgan, op. cit., p. 148.

[16] Ibid., p. 235.

BIBLIOGRAPHY AND REFERENCES

Unless otherwise specified, place of publication is London.

Alexander, William, *History of Women*, Murray, 1779.

Ancient Deeds, Calendar of, Vols I - IV, HMSO, 1890-1915.

Anglo-Saxon Chronicle, ed. Benjamin Thorpe, Rolls Series No. 23, 1861.

——, ed. R. Flowers and H. Smith, E.E.T.S. Original Service, No. 208, 1941.

Against Vagrant Whores in the City, Proclamation, Letter Book L, Guildhall, London.

Anonimalle Chronicle, see Knighton.

Archer, Thomas, *Look on Me London*, 1613.

Astle, Thomas, *The Will of Henry VII*, Private Publication, 1775.

Aubrey, John, *Brief Lives*, ed. Andrew Clark, Oxford, Clarendon, 1898.

Awdeley, John, *Vacabunds*, see Viles and Furnivall.

Baker, Sir Richard, *A Chronicle of the Kings of England* (1643), Sawbridge, 1674.

Bansley, Charles, *Pryde and Abuse of Women* (1540), and *Schole House for Women* (1540), Russell-Smith, 1864, see Hazlitt.

Barclay, Alexander, *Eclogues*, see E.E.T.S.

Becket, William, 'The Antiquity of Venereal Diseases', *Transactions of the Philosophical Society*, Vol. XXX, December 1717.

Bede, The Venerable, *Historia Ecclesiastica*, ed. Thomas Miller, E.E.T.S. Original Service, Nos. 95-6, 1890-8.

Blair, William, *Prostitutes Reclaimed*, Seeley, 1809.

Blakman, Joannes (John), *Collectorum Mansuetudinem et bonarum monum Regis Henrici VI* (Compilation of the Mildness and Good Character of King Henry VI), ed. M. R. James, Cambridge University Press, 1919.

Bloch, Iwan, *Sexual Life of our Times*, trans. M. Eden Paul, Rebman, 1908.

——, *Sexual Life in England, Past and Present*, F. Aldor, 1938.

Boast, Mary J., *Southwark*, Southwark Borough Council, 1969.

Braine, W. W., *The Site of the Globe Playhouse*, Hodder, 1924.

Brinckelowe, Henrie, *Complaynte of Rodericke More*, see E.E.T.S.

Brunne, Robert de, *Handlynge Synne*, see E.E.T.S.

Buret, F., *Syphilis in Ancient and Prehistoric Times* (Vol. I: Syphilis in

Ancient Times; Vol. II: Syphilis in Mediaeval Times), trans. A. H. Ohmann-Dumesnil, Philadelphia, Davis, 1891.

Burton, Robert, *Anatomie of Melancholie* (1621), Longmans, 1827.

Busino, Orsino, *Anglopotrida, see* Furnivall.

Calendars:

Of *Close Rolls (C.C.R.)*, Henry III - Henry VII, HMSO, 1902-63.

Of *Coroners' Rolls of the City of London (C.Cor. R.)*, 1300-1378, ed. R. R. Sharpe, R. Clay, 1913.

Of *Early Mayor's Court Rolls (C.E.M.R.)*, 1298-1307, ed. A. H. Thomas, Cambridge University Press, 1924.

Of *Inquests Post-Mortem (C.Inq. P.M.)*, Records Commission, 1806-28.

Of *Letter Books of the City of London (C.L.B.)*, 1275-1497, Books A - L ed. R. R. Sharpe, Guildhall, 1899-1912.

Of *Letters and Papers of Henry VIII (L & P)*, ed. J. S. Brewer, HMSO, 1875.

Of *Memoranda Rolls (C.M.R.)*, 1326-1327, HMSO, 1969.

Of *Pleas and Memoranda Rolls of the City of London (C.P.M.R.)*, Vols I - IV, ed. A. H. Thomas, Cambridge University Press, 1930-43.

Of *Patent Rolls in the Tower of London (C.P.R.)*, Henry IV - Richard III, ed. Sir T. D. Hardy, Records Commission, 1902-35.

Of *State Papers (Domestic) (C.S.P.D.)*, ed. W. J. Hardy, Records Commission, 1856-95.

Of *Wills in the Court of Hustings (C.W.H.)*, 1258-1688, ed. R. R. Sharpe, City of London Corporation, 1889-90.

Camden Society, Publications of, Old Series:

28. *Promptorum Parvulorum (c.* 1440), ed. Alfred Way, 1843.
34. *De Antiquis Legibus Liber*, ed. T. Stapleton, 1846.
42. *Henry Machyn's Diary*, ed. J. G. Nicholls, 1848.
45. Sir Roger Twysden, *Government of England*, ed. J. M. Kemble, 1849.
57. *Ancren Riwle*, ed. J. Morton, 1853.
72. *Romance of the Blonde of Oxford,* ed. C. R. de Lincy, 1858.
77. *Narratives of the Days of the Reformation*, ed. J. G. Nichols, 1859.
95. Peter Levins, *Manipulus Vocabulorem* (1570), ed. H. B. Wheatley, 1867.

——, New Series:

11. Charles Wriothesley, *A Chronicle of England During the Reign of the Tudors* (1485-1559), ed. W. D. Hamilton, Vol. I 1875, Vol. II 1877.
28. John Stow, *Three Fifteenth Century Chronicles* (from the Lambeth MS. 306), ed. J. Gairdner, 1880.
30. *Catholicon-Anglicum* (1483), ed. S. J. Herrtage, 1882.
39. *Reports of Cases in the Courts of the Star Chamber 1631-2*, ed. S. R. Gardiner, 1886.

Chettle, Henri, *Kinde Hartes Dream* (1592), Hy. Kempe, 1602.

Cockayne, Thomas O. (ed.), *Leechdoms, Wortcunnings and Starcraft of*

Early England, Longmans (for the Rolls Series), 1864.

Cockes, B. W., and Cook, L. W., *Three Centuries*, Barclay Perkins, 1951.

Collier, J. Payne (ed.), *Edward Alleyn's Papers*, Shakespeare Society No. 18, 1843.

——, *Philip Henslowe's Diary*, Shakespeare Society No. 28, 1845.

Colvin, H. M., *History of the King's Works*, HMSO, 1963.

Concanen, M., and Morgan, A., *History and Antiquities of St Saviour's Southwark*, Parsons, 1795.

Cotgrave, Randle, *French-English Dictionary*, Dolle, 1673.

Cranstoun, James (ed.), *A Lewd Ballet*, in *Satirical Poems in the Times of the Reformation*, Scottish Texts Society, 1891.

Cunningham, Peter, *Handbook of London*, Murray, 1849.

——, *Some Account of the Revels at the Court of Queen Elizabeth and King James*, Shakespeare Society, No. 7, 1842.

Danyell, Samuel, *Collection of the Historie of England*, N. Okes, 1618.

D'Archenholz, Baron J. W., *Picture of England*, Jeffery, 1789.

Delaporte, L. J., *La Mesopotamie, les Civilisations Babylonienne et Assyrienne*, Paris, 1925.

Devil Vpon Crutches (1690) by 'A Gentleman of Oxford', Philip Hodges, 1755.

Dekker, Thomas, *The Belman of London*, Butter, 1608.

——, *The Bel-mans nighte walkes wherevnto is added O per se O*, Creede, 1612.

Dion Cassius, *Roman History*, trans. T. E. Page and W. H. D. Rouse, Loeb, 1912.

Dolley, R. H. M., 'Notes on the Anglo-Saxon Mints in Sudbury and Southwark to the Time of Aethelred II', *British Numismatic Journal*, Vol. 8, 1955-7.

Du Cange, Domino, *Glossorium*, ed. G. A. Henschel, D. Nutt, 1884.

Dufour, Paul, *Mémoires Curieux sur l'histoire des Moeurs et de la Prostitution*, Brussels 1853, Paris 1854.

Dugdale, William, *Monasticum Anglicanum*, R. Dodsworth, 1686.

Dunbar, William, 'Ane Brash of Wowing', in *Poems* (1503), ed. W. Mackay Mackenzie, Edinburgh, Porpoise Press, 1932.

Dunning, Gerald C., *A Mediaeval Jug Found in London Decorated with Human and Animal Figures*, Paris, Private Publication, 1971.

Early English Texts Society (E.E.T.S.), Original Service:

20. Richard Rolle de Hampole, *English Prose Treatyses*, ed. G. G. Perry, 1866.
30. William Langland, *Pierce the Ploughmans Crede*, ed. W. W. Skeat, 1867.
32. Frances Seagar, *The Babees Boke* (1557), including Wynkyn de

Woorde, *Boke of Keruynge* (1413); *Boke of Curtasye* (Sloane MS. 1986); Richard Weste, *Booke of Demeanoure*; and John Russell, *Boke of Nurture*, ed. E. Rickert, 1868.

33. *Book of the Knight de la Tour Landry*, ed. Thomas Wright, 1868.

48. *The Times' Whistle or Nerve daunc' of seven satires*, ed. J. M. Cowper, 1871.

61. *Thomas de Ercildonne* (Thomas the Rhymer), ed. J. A. Murray, 1875.

74. *The English Works of John Wyclif*, ed. F. D. Matten, 1880.

75. *Catholicon-Anglicon* (1483), ed. S. J. H. Herrtage, 1881.

89. *Book of Vices and Vertues* (Stow MS. 240), ed. F. Holtzhausen, 1888/1921.

95, 96, 110, 111. *The Venerable Bede*, ed. Thomas Miller, 1890-8.

102. Lanfrancus, *The Science of Cirurgie*, ed. R. Fleischacker, 1894.

119. Robert de Brunne, *Handlynge Synne*, ed. F. J. Furnivall, 1901.

131, 136. *Layamons Brut*, ed. F. W. D. Brie, 1906-8.

148. *A 15th Century Courtesy Book*, ed. R. W. Chambers, 1914.

175. *Eclogues of Alexander Barclay*, ed. Beatrice White, 1928.

187. *The Vulgaria of John Stanbridge and the Vulgaria of Robert Whittinton*, ed. Beatrice White, 1932.

207. *Liber de Diversus Medicinum*, ed. Margaret Ogden, 1938.

208. *Anglo-Saxon Chronicle*, ed. R. Flower and H. Smith, 1941.

223. Wynkyn de Woorde (ed.), *Tretyse of Love*, ed. J. H. Fisher, 1951.

——, Extra Service:

VIII. Sir Humphrey Gilbert, *Queen Elizabeth's Academie*, ed. F. J. Furnivall, 1869.

X. *Breviary*, ed. F. J. Furnivall, 1910.

XII. Henrie Brinckelowe, *Complaynte of Roderick More* (1542), ed. J.M. Cowper, 1874.

XIII. Symon Fysshe, *A Supplycacyon for the Beggers* (1529), ed. J. M. Cowper, 1871.

LXXI. *The Towneley Mystery Plays*, ed. G. English, 1897.

LXXXV. *The Poems of Alexander Scott*, ed. A. K. McDonald, 1902.

XCI. *The Macro Plays*, ed. F. J. Furnivall, 1904.

CII. *Promptorum Parvulorum sive Clericoscum Dictionarus Anglo-Laterans*, ed. E. L. Mayhew, 1908.

CX. *Mirroure of the Worlde*, trans. W. Caxton, ed. O. H. Prior, 1913.

CXVIII. John Skelton, *Magnyfycence and Other Poems*, ed. R. L. Ramsey, 1908.

Ebsworth, J. W. (ed.), *The Bagford Ballads*, Hertford, The Ballad Society, Nos. 14-16, 1877-8.

Eckenstein, Lina, *Women Under Monasticism*, Cambridge University Press, 1896.

Ekwall, Eilert, *Concise Oxford Dictionary of English Place Names*, Oxford, Clarendon, 4th edn. 1966.

——, *Early London Personal Names*, Gleerup, Lund, 1947.

——, *Early London Street Names*, Oxford, Clarendon, 1954.

Enguerrand de Monstralet, *Chroniques* (1390-1453), trans. Thos. Johnes,

Bohn, 1849.

Erasmus, Desiderius, *Colloquia*, ed. N. Baily, Gibbins, 1900.

Fabyan, Robert, *Chronica Major* or 'The Great Chronicle of London', ed. A. H. Thomas and I. D. Thornby, G. W. Jones, 1938.

Fallopio, G., *De Morbo Gallico*, Patavia (Padua), L. Bertelli, 1564.

Fleta Seu Commentarius Juris Anglicani (1503), ed. Sir T. Clarke, 1753.

Flexner, Abraham, *Prostitution in Europe*, New York, New Century, 1918.

Foedera, Conventiones, Literae et Cuiusque Generis Acta Publica, ed. Thomas Rymer, Records Commission, 1806.

Fort, G. F., *History of Medical Economics in the Middle Ages*, New York, Bouton, 1883.

Froissart, Jean, *Chronicles of England*, trans. Thomas Johnes, W. Smith, 1862.

Furnivall, F. J. (ed.), *see* E.E.T.S.

——, *Bagford Ballads*, Hertford, Ballad Society, 1876.

——, *Ballads from MSS.*, Hertford, Ballad Society, 1876.

——, *Love Poems and Humorous Ones*, Hertford, Ballad Society, 1874.

——, *Shakespeare's England*, including Philip Stubbes, *Anatomie of Abuses*; Orsino Busino, *Anglopotrida*; and William Harrison, *Description of England*, New Shakespeare Society VI, Trubner, 1877.

Gale, Thomas, *Historia Britannicae-Saxonicae, Anglo-Danicae Scriptores*, Oxford, Sheldon, 1691.

Garfield, John, *The Wand'ring Whore*, Nos. 1-6, 1660-63.

Gascoigne, Thomas, *Liber Loci et Libro Veritatum*, ed. J. E. T. Rogers, Oxford, Clarendon, 1881.

Gay, John, *The Beggar's Opera*, Longmans, 1881.

Giles, J. A. (ed.), Matthew de Paris, *Chronica Major*, Bohn, 1852.

——, William of Malmesburie, *Gesta Regum Anglorum*, Book IV, Rolls Series, 1887-8.

Gosson, Stephen, *Quippes for the Vpstarte Newfangled Gentlewoman*, 1595.

Greene, Robert, *Theeves Falling Oute*, Bell, 1621.

Guilpin, Edward, *Skialetheia in Certayne Epigrams and Satyres*, 'Printed by I. R. for Nicholas Ling and are to bee solde at the little weste doore of Poules', 1598.

Hale, William Hale (ed.), *A Series of Precedents and Proceedings in Criminal Cases; Extracts from the Act Books 1473-1640 of the Ecclesiastical Courts in the Diocese of London*, Rivington, 1847.

Hall, Edward, *Chronicle – 1540*, Johnson, 1809.

Hall, John, *The Court of Virtue* (1565), ed. R. Fraser, Routledge, 1961.

Hall, Bishop Joseph, *Virgidimarium or Satyres* (1597), Harrison, 1602.

Hall, J. R. Clark, *Saxon Dictionary*, Sonnenschein, 1894.

Halliwell, J. O., *Dictionary of Archaic and Provincial Words*, Smith, 1872.

Hamilton, R. Claude (ed.), *Chronica Domini Walterus de Hemingburghe*, Royal Historical Society, 1847.

Hampton & Sons, *Catalogue of the Sale of the Cardinal's Cap Wharf*, 1935.

Hardy, Sir John (ed.), *Norman Rolls*, Public Record Office, 1881.

Harman, Thomas, *A Caveat or Warning*, 1567.

Harrington, Sir John, *Nugae Antiquae*, Fredk Lene, 1759.

Harrison, Walter, *History of London*, Cooke, 1776.

Harrison, William, *Description of England* (1587), *see* Furnivall.

Harvey, Gabriel, *Pierce's Supererogation*, Jno. Wolfe, 1593.

Hazlitt, W. C. (ed.), *Remains of the Popular Poetry of England*, Russell-Smith, 1864.

——, *A Select Collection of Old English Plays, by Robt. Dodsley*, Reeves, 1874.

Hearne, Thomas (ed.), *Cartulary of the Augustine Priory of the Holy Trinity, Aldgate, by William of Newburghe*, Oxford, Sheldon, 1719.

Hemingburghe, Walter de, *see* Hamilton, R.C.

Henslowe, Philip, *Diary*, in J. P. Collier (ed.), *Edward Alleyn's Papers*, q.v.

Herrtage, S. J. H., *see* E.E.T.S.

Higden, Ranulph, *Polychronicon* (*in John Trevisa's translation*), ed. J. R. Lumby, Rolls Series, 41, 1865.

Hindley, Charles (ed.), *The Roxburghe Ballads*, Reeves and Turner, 1874.

——, *The Works of John Taylor*, Reeves, 1872.

Holinshed, Raphael, *Chronicles of England Ireland and Scotland*, ed. J. Johnson, 1807.

Home, Gordon, *Old London Bridge*, Bodley Head, 1931.

Horatius Flaccus (Horace), *Satires*, ed. A. H. Bryce, Port, 1907.

Hovenden, Roger de, *Chronica*, ed. Bishop William Stubbs, Rolls Series, 51, 1868.

Howes, John, *MS. 1582*, ed. S. V. Morgan, Private Publication, 1904.

Hughes, P. L., and Larkin, J. F., *Royal Tudor Proclamations*, New Haven and London, Yale University Press, 1969.

Hunter, Joseph (ed.), *The Great Pipe Roll of the Exchequer, 31 Henry I*, Records Commission, 1833.

Huntingdon, Henricus de, *Historia Angliorum*, ed. T. Forester, Bohn, 1847.

Hyckescorner, *see* Hazlitt, *A Select Collection.* . . .

Jacob, Giles, *New Law Dictionary*, Strahane & Woodfall, 1772.

Jacobs, Joseph, *The Jews in Angevin England*, Oxford University Press, 1893.

Jonson, Ben, *Works*, ed. William Gifford, 1816.

——, *Bartholomew Fair*, 1616.

Juvenalis, Decius Junius (Juvenal), *The Sixteen Satires*, ed. William Gifford, 1802.

Kemble, J. M. (ed.), *Codex Diplomaticus aevi Saxonici*, English Historical Society, 1839.

Knighton, Henrie, *Chronicon* (including the *Anonimalle Chronicle*), HMSO (for the Rolls Series), 1889.

Kurath, Hans, and Kuhn, Sherman H., *Middle English Dictionary*, Ann Arbor, University of Michigan Press, 1961.

Lacroix, Paul, *Manners, Customs and Dress in the Middle Ages*, Chapman & Hall, 1874.

Lambert, Bernard, *History and Survey of London*, Hughes, 1806.

Laneham, Robert, *Letter from Killingworth Castle* (1575), J. H. Brun, 1821.

Lanfrancus, *see* E.E.T.S.

Langland, William, *Piers Plowman*, *see* E.E.T.S.

Latimer, Hugh, *Sermons of Bishop Hugh Latimer*, ed. G. E. Corrie, Cambridge, Parker Society, 1884.

Lauder, William, *Minor Poems*, ed. F. J. Furnivall, E.E.T.S. Original Service No. 41, 1870.

Lea, H. C., *History of Sacerdotal Celibacy*, Williams & Norgate, 1907.

Le Pileur, L., *Documents sur la Prostitution en XIII siècle*, Paris, H. Champion, 1908.

Lewinsohn, Richard, *History of Sexual Customs*, trans. A. Mayce, Harper, 1958.

Liber Albus, *see* Riley, H. T.

Liber de Antiquis Legibus, *see* Riley, H. T.

Lindesay, Sir David, of the Mount, *The Answer quhilk Scher David Lindesay maid to the kynges flytinge*, ed. Douglas Hamer, Edinburgh, Scottish Texts Society, 1931.

——, *Ane Pleasant Satyre*, in *Works*, ed. Douglas Hamer, Edinburgh, Scottish Texts Society, 1931-6.

Lindsay, Ralph, *Etymology of Southwark*, Smith-Elder, 1839.

London County Council, *Survey: Southwark Bankside*, L.C.C., 1949.

Louth, The Venerable Archdeacon John, of Nottingham, *Reminiscences*, *see* Camden Society.

Luard, H. R. (ed), *Annales Monastici* (of Waverley Abbey), Rolls Series, 36, 1864.

——, *Chronicles of Matthew de Paris*, Rolls Series, 57, 1872.

——, *Flores Historiarum of Matthew of Westminster*, Rolls Series, 95, 1890.

Lupton, Daniel, *London and the Countrey Carbonadoed*, N. Okes, 1632.

Machyn, Henrie, *Diary*, *see* Camden Society.

Mackay, Charles (ed.), *Collection of Ballads and Songs of London*, Percy

Society, No. 7, 1841.

Macro Plays, The, see E.E.T.S.

Magna Rotuli Scacciarum, see Hunter, Joseph.

Maidment, James (ed.), *A Book of Scotch Pasquils*, Edinburgh, Paterson, 1827.

Maitland, William, *History of London*, Osborne, 1760.

Malcolm, J. P., *Anecdotes of London Manners and Customs*, Longmans, 1808.

Malmesburie, William de, *Gesta Regum Anglorum, see* Giles, J. A.; *Eulagium Historiarum*, see Rolls Series, 9.

Mancini, Dominic, *The Usurpation of Richard III* (1461), trans. and ed. C. A. Armstrong, Unicorn, 1936.

Manning, Owen, and Bray, William, *History of London*, Vol. III, 'Southwark', J. White, 1804.

Matthew de Paris, *Chronica Major, see* Giles, J. A.; *Chronicles of, see* Luard, H. R.

Matthew de Westminster, *Flores Historiarum, see* Luard, H. R.

Middlesex County Records, 3 Edward IV – 4 James II, ed. J. C. Jeaffreson, 4 Vols, Middlesex Committee, 1888-92.

Middlesex Sessions Books, Calendar of, 1689-1709, ed. J. W. Hardy, Middlesex Committee, 1905.

Middlesex Sessions Books, Calendar of, New Series, 1612-18, 4 Vols. Middlesex Committee, 1935-41.

More, Sir Thomas, *The History of Richard III*, ed. J. R. Lumby, Oxford University Press, 1883.

Moryson, Fynes, *An Itinerary of Travel in Twelve Countreys*, ed. J. Maclehose, Glasgow University Press, 1907.

Monier-Williams, M. F., *Records of the Tallow Chandlers' Company*, Whittington, 1897.

Munimenta Gildhallae, ed. H. T. Riley, Rolls Series, 12, 1849-62.

Murdoch, J. R. (ed.), *Bannatyne MS. of Alexander Scott: Ane ballet maid to the Derisioun of Wanton Women*, Edinburgh, Hunterian Society, 1896.

Nash, Thomas, *Pierce Penniless his Supplicacyon to the Deuill*, Shakespeare Society, No. 12, 1842.

Nicholas, N. H., *Harley MS. 565. A Chronicle of London, 1089-1483*, Longmans, 1827.

Nicolas, Sir Nicholas (ed.), *Privy Purse Expenses of Elizabeth of York* (1503), Pickering, 1830.

Northbrooke, John, *Treatyse against Dicing Dauncing Players and Enterludes* (1577), Shakespeare Society No. 14, 1843.

Ordish, Thomas F., *Early London Theatres*, Elliott-Stock, 1894.

Otway, Thomas, *Venice Preserv'd*, 1682.

Overall, W. H. (ed.), *Remembrancia 1579-1640; 1660-1664*, City of London. 1870-8.

Ovid, *Ars Amatoria*, ed. T. E. Page and W. H. D. Rouse, Loeb, 1914.

——, *Fasti*, ed. Sir J. G. Frazer, Loeb, 1951.

Pennant, Thomas, *Some Account of London*, Faulder, 1791.

Pichon, Baron J-F, *Le Menagier de Paris*, Paris, Société des Bibliothèques Françaises, 1846.

Pinchbeck, Ivy, and Hewett, Margaret, *Children in English Society*, Routledge & Kegan Paul, 1969.

Pipe Roll Society, Publications of:

Ancient Charters, ed. J. H. Round, No. 10, 1888.

Cartae Antiquae William I – Henry III, ed. Lionel Landon, New Series, 1939.

Memoranda Roll John I (de Finibus Judiarum), ed. H. G. Richardson, New Series, 1943.

Ploss, H. H., and Bartels, M., *Woman*, trans. E. J. Dingwall, Heinemann, 1935.

Pliny the Elder, *Naturalis Historia*, ed. J. Bostock and H. T. Riley, Bohn, 1855.

Poole, A. L., *From Domesday Book to Magna Carta*, Oxford University Press, 1951.

Prerogative Court of Canterbury (Births, Christenings, Wills), 1383-1604, 4 Vols, British Records Society, 1893-1901.

Privy Council, Acts of the, ed. J. R. Dasent, HMSO, 1890-1960.

Promptorum Parvulorum . . . , see E.E.T.S., see also Rolls Series.

Rabutaux, M., *De la Prostitution en Europe depuis l'antiquité jusque'a le fin de l'xvi siècle*, Paris, Duquesne, 1869.

Rae, James, *Deaths of the Kings of England,* Manchester, Sherratt & Hughes, 1913.

Randolph, Thomas, *Poems with the Muses Lookynge Glasse*, 1638.

Rendle, William, *Southwark in the Time of Shakespeare*, privately printed pamphlet, in the Minet Museum, 1878.

——, *Old Southwark and its People*, Royal Society of Literature, 1878.

Rendle, William, with Norman, Philip, *Inns of Old Southwark*, Longmans, 1888.

Reynold, Roland, *Character of a Town Miss*, 1680.

Richardson, H. G., *Memoranda Roll of John I*, Pipe Roll Society, N.S. No. xxi, 1943.

Riesman, David, *Syphilis*, New York, Paul Hueber, 1935.

Rigg, J. M., *Calendar of the Plea Rolls of the Exchequer of the Jews (1218-1277)*, 2 Vols, Jewish Historical Society, 1905-10.

——, *Select Pleas, Starrs and Other Records of the Exchequer of the Jews (1220- 1284)*, Quaritch, 1902.

Riley, H. T. (ed.), *Liber Albus*, Trubner, 1861.

——, *Liber de Antiquis Legibus*, Griffin, 1863.

——, *Memorials of London and London Life, 1276-1419*, Longmans, 1868.

——, *Munimenta Gildhallae* (includes the *Liber Customarum* in the Cotton MS. Claudius D. II, British Museum), Longmans, (for the Rolls Series), 1849.

Robertson, S. J. (ed)., *Anglo-Saxon Charters*, Oxford University Press, 1956.

Robinson, Hastings (ed.), *The Zurich Letters, 1541*, Parker Society, 1842.

Rochester, John Wilmot, Earl of, *Poetical Works*, 1688.

Rolls Series, The (The Chronicles and Memorials of Great Britain and Ireland During the Middle Ages, published under the direction of the Master of the Rolls):

9. *Eulagium Historiarum sive Temporis Chronica ab urbe condito usque ad AD mccclxvi, a monacho quodam Malmesburiensi exaretum*, ed. F. Scott Haydon, 3 Vols, 1858.

12. *Munimenta Gildhallae*, ed. H. T. Riley, 1849-62.

14. *Promptorum Parvulorum sive Clericoscum Dictionarus Anglo-Laterans*, ed. Thomas Wright, 2 Vols, 1859-61.

23. *The Anglo-Saxon Chronicle*, ed. Benjamin Thorpe, 2 Vols, 1861.

28. *Chronica monasterii S. Albani*, ed. H. T. Riley, 12 Vols, 1863-9 (includes *Thomae Walsingham quondam monachi S. Albani a historia Anglicana*, 2 Vols, 1863-4; and *Gesta Abbatum monasterii S. Albani a Thoma Walsingham regnante Ricardo secundo*, 3 Vols. 1867-9.

35. *Leechdoms Wortcunnings and Starcraft of Early England*, ed. Thomas O. Cockayne, 3 Vols, 1864-6.

36. *Annales Monastici*, ed. H. R. Luard, 5 Vols, 1864-9.

38. *Chronicles and Memorials of the reign of Richard I*, ed. William Stubbs, 1865-6.

41. *Polychronicon of Ranulph Higden including the English translation by John Trevisa*, ed. J. R. Lumby, 9 Vols, 1865-6.

44. *Historia Angliorum Mattheis Parisiensis monachi S. Albani*, ed. Sir F. Madden, 3 Vols, 1866-9.

46. *Chronicon Scotorum (1133-1150)*, ed. W. M. Hennessey, 1866.

51. *Chronica Rogeri de Hovedon*, ed. Bishop W. Stubbs, 4 Vols, 1868-71.

52. *Willelmi Malmesbiriensis monachi de gestis pontificum Anglorum*, ed. N.E.S.A. Hamilton, 1870.

57. *Matthaei Parisiensis monachi S. Albani Chronica Major*, ed. H. R. Luard, 7 Vols, 1872-85.

59. *Anglo-Latin Satirical Poets and Epigrammatists of the 12th Century*, ed. Thomas Wright, 2 Vols, 1872.

76. *Chronicles of the reign of Edward I and of Edward II*, ed. William Stubbs, 2 Vols, 1882-3.

84. *Roger de Wendover Liber qui dicitur flores historarium* ('The Flowers of History'), ed. H. G. Hewlett, 3 Vols, 1886-9.

92. *Chronicon Henrici Knighton (vel Cnitthon)*, ed. J. R. Lumby, 2 Vols, 1889-95.

95. *Flores Historiarum of Matthew de Westminster*, ed. H. R. Luard, 3

Vols, 1890.

Rotuli Parliamentorum ut et Petitiones in Parliamento, 6 Edward I – 19 Henry VII (1278-1503), Records Commission, 1783-1830.

Round, J. H. (ed.), *Ancient Charters*, Pipe Roll Society, No. 10, 1888.

Rowlands, Samuel, Dr. *Merrie Man, his Medicine against Melancholy*, 1607.

——, *Greene's Ghost Haunting Coniecatchers*, 1602.

Roxburghe Ballads, The, see Hindley, Charles.

Rye, William B., *England as Seen by Foreigners in the Days of Queen Elizabeth and James I*, J. A. Smith, 1865.

Rymer (Rhymer), Thomas the, see E.E.T.S.

Sabatier, A., *Histoire de la Législation sur les femmes prostituées et les lieux de débauche*, Paris, 1821.

Salzmann, L. F., *Building in England to 1540*, Oxford University Press, 1967.

Scott, Alexander, *Poems*, see E.E.T.S.; *Bannatyne MS. of*, see Murdoch, J. B..

'Shrubbe', *Histrio-Mastix or The Players Scourge*, Sparke, 1633.

Skelton, John, *Poems*, see E.E.T.S.

Skinner, Stephen, *Etymologicon Linguae Anglicane*, ed. Thomas Henshaw, Roycroft, 1671.

Smith, John Thomas, *Antient Topography of London*, M'Creery, 1810-15.

Spelman, Sir Henry, *Concilia Decreta Leges Constitutiones*, Wilkins, 1736.

Statutes of the Realm, 1 Henry I – 13 Anne, Records Commission, 1810-22.

Stevenson, Joseph, *Church Historians of England*, including John of Wallingford's Chronicle, Seeley, 1864.

Stevens, T. P., *Winchester House in Southwark*, S.P.C.K., 1945.

Stow, John, *Surveigh*, ed. C. L. Kingsford, Oxford, Clarendon, 1908.

——, *Three 15th Century Chronicles, Memoranda from the Lambeth MS.*, Camden Society, New Series No. 28, 1880.

Stow, William, *Remarks on London*, St Aubyn, 1722.

Stratmann, F. H., *Dictionary of Middle English*, Oxford, Clarendon, 1891.

Stubbes, Philip, *Anatomie of Abuses*, see Furnivall, F. J.

Surrey Quarter Sessions 1659-1668, ed. D. L. Powell and H. Jenkinson, 3 Vols, Surrey Record Society, 1934-8.

Tacitus, Caius Cornelius, *Annales*, ed. G. Ramsay, Murray, 1904..

——, *De Germania*, ed. H. Furneaux, Oxford, Clarendon, 1894.

Talbot, C. H., and Hammond, E. A., *Medical Practitioners in Mediaeval England*, Wellcome Institute, 1965.

Talk of Ten Wives on their Husbands' Ware (Porkington MS. 10), *c*. 1460, in the Brogyntyn (Porkington) Collection, National Library of Wales, Aberystwyth.

Talmont (ed.), *De Finibus Judiarum* (Memoranda Roll, King John, Vol. 1),

Pipe Roll Society, New Series No. xxi, 1943.

Taylor, John, *A Common Whore*, 1622.

——, *Prayse and Vertue of Jayles and Jaylers*, 1623.

——, *The True Course of the Watermen's Suit Concerning the Players*, 1613 (?).

——, *Works* (1630), Manchester, Spencer Society, 1870-8.

Taylor, William, *Annals of St Marie Overie*, Nicholas, 1833.

Thorpe, Benjamin, *Ancient Laws and Institutes*, Public Record Office, 1840.

Timbs, John, *Curiosities of London*, Longmans, 1868.

——, *London and Westminster*, Bentley, 1868.

Towneley Mystery Plays, see E.E.T.S.

Traill, H. Duff, *Social England*, Cassell, 1892.

Trevelyan, G. M., *English Social History*, Longmans, 1946.

Tudor Proclamations at the Society of Antiquaries, Oxford University Press, 1897.

Turner, Thomas H. (ed.), *Manners and Household Expenses of England in the 13th and 15th Centuries*, Roxburghe Club, 1841.

Udall, J., *State of the Church of England in a Conference between Diotrephes and Tertullius etc.*, Edw. Arber, 1879.

Viles, Edward, and Furnivall, F. J., *Rogues and Vagabonds of Shakespeare's Youth* (includes John Awdeley's *Vacabunds*), New Shakespeare Society VI, No. 7, 1880.

Villanova, Arnoldus de, *Regimen Sanitatis Salerni*, trans. Thomas Payne, T. Berthelet, 1541.

Virgil, *Catalepton*, ed. H. Ellis, Dodsley, 1783.

Vulgaria, of William Horman, ed. M. R. James, Roxburghe Club, 1926.

——, of J. Stanbridge, *see* E.E.T.S.

——, of R. Whittinton, *see* E.E.T.S.

Walcott, Mackenzie E. C., *William of Wykeham*, Manchester, D. Nutt, 1852.

Walford, Edward, *London Old and New*, Cassell, 1877.

Walsingham, Thomas, *Chronica Monasterium St Albaniensis*, ed. H. T. Riley, Rolls Series, 28, 1867.

Warner, Sir G. F., *Catalogue of MSS. of Edward Alleyn*, Longmans, 1881.

Weber, Henry (ed.), *The Seuen Sages: A Metrical Poem from the 13th Century*, Edinburgh, Constable, 1810.

Welch, Charles, *History of Tower Bridge*, Smith Elder, 1894.

Weldon, Sir Anthony, *The Secret History of the Court and Character of King James I*, 1651.

Wendover, Roger de, *Flores Historiarum*, see Rolls Series, 84.

Wheatley, H. B., *London Past and Present*, Murray, 1891.

Whitelock, Dorothy, *English Historical Documents*, Eyre & Spottiswoode, 1955.

Whitwell, J. R., *Syphilis in Early Days*, H. K. Lewis, 1940.

Wilkes, John, *Essay on Woman*, Private Publication, 1871.

Wilkins, David, *Leges Eadgari*, 1721.

Wilkinson, R., *Londina Illustrata*, Herbert, 1808.

Williams, Clare, *Platten's Travels in 1599*, Jonathan Cape, 1937.

Wingent, R. M., *Historical Notes on the Borough of Southwark*, Ash, 1913.

Winstanley, Roger, *Poor Robin's Vision*, 1677.

Wood, Anthony, *History and Antiquities of the Colleges at Oxford*, ed. John Gutch, Oxford, Clarendon, 1786.

Wright, Leonard, *A Display of Dutie*, 1614.

Wright, Thomas, *Anglo-Saxon Glossary*, Mares, 1859.

——, *A History of Domestic Manners*, New York, Appleton, 1862.

——, *Vocabulary of Anglo-Saxon English*, Private Publication, 1884.

——, *Womankind in Europe*, Gronbridge, 1869.

Wriothesley, Charles, *A Chronicle of England . . .* , *see* Camden Society.

Wyclif, John, *English Works*, see E.E.T.S.

Wynkyn de Woorde, *Cock Lorell's Bote*, ed. F. Rimbault, Percy Society, 1843.

——, *Hyckescorner*, in Hazlitt, W. C. (ed.), *A Select Collection . . .* , *q.v.*

Yearsley McLaren, *Le Roy est Mort*, Unicorn Press, 1935.

Yonge, C. D. (ed.), *Flores Historiarum of Roger de Wendover, collected by the (Supposed) Matthew de Westminster*, Bohn, 1853.

Zurich Letters, The, see Robinson, Hastings.

INDEX

Individual brothels are listed under brothels; *brothel owners, lessees and managers under that heading.*

Adminius, 12
Addle Street, 18
Addison, Edward, 154
Ad Sorores IIII (The Four Sisters), 22
Aedgifu (Edith), 32
Aedile, 18, 19, 20, 22
Aelfred (Alfred), King, 14, 28, 29, 54
Aelfric, Archbishop, 104
Aethelberht, King of Kent, 25, 27, 28
Aethelred, King, 30, 31, 33
aldermen, of the City of London, 90, 95, 107, 131, 144, 168
Aldgate, 22, 68
Alleyn, Edward, 154, 156, 162, 170
ambulatrices, 21
America, 21, 181
Angles, 24
Anglo-Saxon Chronicle, 25, 40
Anonimalle Chronicle, 81
Ansonius, D. Magus, 20
Anu, 53
Apollo, 16
Apothecaries, Society of, 162
apprentices, 172
aprons, 49, 51, 168
Aretino, Peter, 166
Ascham, Roger, 166
asylum, right of, 61, 96
Athens, 18, 54
Attys, 17
Augustine, St, 25-7
Augustus Caesar, 11
Avignon, 67

Babylon, 54

Bacon, Francis, 164
bailiffs, 45, 47-9, 51, 55, 73, 75, 89, 91, 92, 95, 117, 119, 123, 144
Ball, John, 77
Bannaster's Gardens, 100, 155
Bank End Stairs, 136
Bankside Alleys: Addison's Rents, 154; Bear Gardens, 149, 152, 154; Boar's Head Alley, 149; Bosse Alley, 153; Bullhead Alley, 149, 152, 158; Cardinal's Cap Alley, 149, 157; Cordwainers' Rents, 149; Crosse Keyes Alley, 149, 154; Crown Court, 154; Drew's Rents, 149, 162; Griffin's Rents, 149; Horseshoe Alley, 149, 151, 182; Love Lane, 149, 157, 158; Mason's Stairs, 149, 152, 157; Mayland's Rents, 149; Mosse Alley, 158; Olyphaunt Alley, 149, 150; Pike (Pye) Alley, 149; Plough Alley, 149; Rockett's Rents, 149, 151; Rose Alley, 149, 152; Robinhood Alley, 158; Smith's Rents, 151, 182; Stewes Rents, 153; Tallow Chandlers' Rents, 149; Tapping's Rents, 149; Unicorne Alley, 149, 154
Barbarossa, Frederick, 63
Baselee, William, 123
bawds, *see* brothel owners and lessees
Bawds of the Bank, 76, 122
beadles, 44
bear-baiting, 15, 64, 123, 126, 134, 141, 147, 180
Bear Gardens, 123, 135, 141, 147, 149, 152, 153, 154, 159, 177, 178,

181, 182
Bear's Colledge, 160, 177
Beaufort, Henry, Cardinal, 95
Becket, Thomas à, 9, 44, 62
Bede, the Venerable, 25
Bedford, John, Duke of, 95, 98
Benedict III, Pope, 103
Berengaria, Queen, 63
Bermondsey, 37, 65, 73
Billingsgate, 14
Black Death, The, 74, 75, 86, 172;
  see also plague
Boadicea, Queen, 15
boatmen, 56, 69
Bodleian Library, 42, 43, 92
Boleyn, Mary, 114
Borage, Will, 121
bordel, origin of term, 61, 73
Bordhawe, 69
Bordich (Bordych), 65, 69, 73, 124
Boteler (Butler), Elizabeth, 62, 97-8
bowling alleys, 123
Boyce, Thomas, Cardinal, 155
Bradwine, Thomas, 75
branding, 120
breasts, exposed, 165-6
Brend, Sir Mathew, 149
'brennynge', infirmity of, *see* venereal diseases
Brewers' Company, 150
brewsters, 86, 141
Bridewell Prison, 131, 132, 167, 172
Bristol, 110
brothels: *Angel,* 180; *Antilope,* 108, 115, 116, 131, 149; *Aulus Comitis,* 71, 108; *Barge,* 72, 79, 100, 108, 115, 119, 123, 152, 153, 154, 180; *Beere (Beareshedde),* 108, 115, 121, 152, 182; *Bell,* 79, 100, 108, 109, 123, 152, 153, 154, 162, 180, 182; *Blew Mead (Blue Maid),* 123, 131; *Boar's Head,* 108, 115, 116, 154, 157, 162; *Bulhede (Bull),* 71, 96, 100, 108, 121, 149, 158, 162, 175, 182; *Cardinalles Hat (Cap),* 100, 108, 121, 154, 155, 156, 162, 175, 182; *Castell-upon-the-Hoop (Castle),* 72, 96, 100, 108, 115, 116, 117, 118, 121,

149, 150, 158, 183; *Cock,* 100, 152, 153, 154, 180; *Crane,* 96, 119, 150; *Crosse-Keyes,* 108, 115, 121, 154; *Crosse-Keyes* (Southwark High St), 98; *Crown,* 131; *Dolphin,* 100, 154, 162; *Fishpond House,* 157; *Fflower de Lyce (Fleur de Lys),* 108, 115, 116, 121, 154, 180; *Galleon,* 108, 153; *Gonne (Gun),* 108, 149; *Greyhonde,* 95; *Half-Moon,* 123; *Herte (Hart),* 96, 99, 101, 108, 115, 116, 121, 150; *Hertyshed (Hartyshorne),* 108, 109, 115, 116, 152, 162; *Holland's Leaguer,* 146, 164, 168, 175, 177; *James,* 109; *Leonem, Ad,* 77, 108, 115, 116, 119, 152, 182; *Lion and Ram,* 119, 182; *Little Rose,* 71, 152, 158; *Lyly,* 109, 158; *Mermaid,* 123, 131; *Olyphaunt (Elephant),* 108, 115, 116, 119, 121, 150, 151; *Pope's Head,* 100, 109, 111; *Rose (La Roserie),* 71, 72, 79, 96, 100, 108, 121, 123, 131, 135, 152, 153; *Ship,* 108, 153; *Six Windmills,* 181; *Swanne,* 108, 131, 149; *Thatched House,* 109, 158; *Unycorne,* 108, 115, 117, 121, 135, 153, 154, 171, 180; *Vine,* 150, 158; *White Hind,* 157; *White Lion,* 157; *Whyte Hart,* 131
brothels in Roman London, 13-14
brothel owners, lessees and managers: Aldersley, William *(Boreshed),* 115, 116; Amcottes, Vincent *(Castle),* 149; Allen, Robert, 122-3; Alleyn, Edward *(Bell* etc.), 154, 162, 170; Arnold, David *(Antylopp),* 115, 116; Aston, John, 121; Atkynson, Barthlimaeus, 121; Bartone, John, 121; Baylley, William *(Hertyshorne),* 116; Boyd, Thomas, 97, 98; Brank, John, 121; Byglay, Robert, 121; Canby, Capt., 119; Cathard, Robert, 121; Cosyn, John *(Bulhede),* 96; Cresswell, Elizabeth, 181; Curson, Margaret *(Herte),*

115, 116; Denote the Bawd, 74; Dogging, Robert, 121; Drew, John (*Castle*), 149, 162; Eierby, John (*Castle*), 118; Erswyth, William, 121; Fotheringham, Priscilla (*Six Windmills*), 181; Freeman, Joan (*Fflower de Lyce*), 115, 116; Frigg, John, 95; Gardiner, Joan (*Leonem*), 116; Gardiner, Richard (*Leonem*), 115, 116; Gardyner, Agnes (*Boreshed*), 116; Gardyner, Anne (*Boreshed*), 116; Goode, Christopher, 121; Gray, John (*Castle*), 115, 116; Gwynne, Ludovic (*Leonem*), 116; Harrison, 123; Henslowe, Philip (*Bell*, etc.), 152, 154, 158, 167; Herring (Hemyng), Henry, 121; Hurt, Joan, 76; Kent, Eleanor (*Beere*), 115; Kerbyrd, John, 121; Litelbaker, John (*Barge, Crane*), 118; Margaret, 97; Mosse, Katarin (*Fflower de Lyce*), 116; Murray, David à, 116; Murray, Robert à (*Barge*), 115, 116, 117; Page, Damarose, 181; Pluckrose, Nicholas, 74; Preston, John (*Antylop*), 116; Ratcliffe, Anna (*Crosse-Keyes*), 115; Rose, Thomas, 76; Sandes, John (*Castle*), 115, 116, 117, 118; Sarson, Joan, 90; Taylloure, John (*Leonem*), 116; Toogood, Margaret (*Hartyshorne*), 115, 116; Toogood, Thomas, 109, 116; Tydman, Joan (*Leonem*), 116; Walworth, Sir William (*Rose*), 78-9, 81; Wharton, Edward (*Olyphaunt*), 115, 116; Whitehorne, Henry, 104; Whyte, Rolyng, 121

Browker, Hugh, 156
buggery, 122, 130, 147
bull-baiting, 15, 123, 134, 141, 162, 182
Bunny, Thomas, 76
Burghal Hideage, 32

Cade, Jak, 98
Caesar, Julius, 9, 11, 12

Canterbury, Archbishops of, 9, 40, 71
Captain of the Stews, 117, 127
caprificus, see venereal diseases
carting, 78, 132, 138, 163, 172
Cato, 18
Catullus, 16, 20
celibacy, of priests, 40, 102
Chancery Lane, 65, 67
Charlemagne, 28
Charles I, 177
Charles II, 38, 56, 173, 174, 181
Charles the Bald, 28
charters, 34, 72, 131
Chaucer, Geoffrey, 83-4, 85-6, 140
Cheapside, 69
Chichely, Robert, 81, 90
Child, James, 150
children's brothels, 145, 175
Christian beliefs and Christianity, 25-7, 29, 31, 38, 40, 42, 52, 54-6, 61, 64, 70, 73, 75, 86, 99, 100, 103, 121, 124, 137
City Chamberlain, 97
Clement V, Pope, 71
Clement VII, Pope, 120
Clink Liberty, 9, 32, 38, 55, 75, 92, 100, 101, 115, 117, 121, 131, 177, 179, 182
Clink Prison, 38, 95, 98, 119, 132, 136, 151, 154, 158, 167, 172, 182, 183
Clink Street, 100, 169
Cnut (Canute), 30, 31
cock-fighting, 15, 141
Cock Lorells Bote, 114, 117
Cokkeslane (Cock Lane), 58, 67, 69, 78, 97
Colchester, 12
Commonwealth, The, 179, 181, 183
constables, 44-5, 48-9, 51, 92, 95, 96, 101, 143, 144
Constance, Great Council of, 90
Conton, Colonel, 173-4
contraception, 144, 173-4
Cordwainers' Company, 110, 151
couillage (*cullagium*), 38, 40, 65, 102-3, 167
Courts leet, 38, 42, 43, 55, 60, 76,

92-4, 97, 115, 121
Covent Garden, 181
Crayford, 24
Cripplegate, 18
Cromwell, Oliver, 64, 145, 179
Cromwell, Thomas, 122
Crusades, The, 41, 63
cucking-stool, 26, 46, 47, 57, 132, 138
custumaries, 9, 42, 43, 51, 53, 92, 93
Cymbeline, 11, 12

Danes, 28-32, 36, 40
Davison, John, 135, 153-4
Deadman's Place, 100, 101, 136, 149, 150, 183
De Maisse, H., 161
De Mulieram Affectibus, 33
Domesday Book, 27, 32, 36, 37
Domus Conversarum, 65, 71
Donne, John, 127, 154
Donne, Constance, 154
dress, 54, 73, 107, 134, 141, 163, 164
Dunstan, Archbishop, 29-30
dye-houses, 169, 182
Dysart, Bess, 179

Eadgar (Edgar), King, 29-31
Eadmund (Edmund), King, 34
Eadwy (Edwy), King, 29
Edward the Confessor, 32-4, 36-7
Edward the Elder, 54
Edward I, 68-71, 87
Edward II, 70-2, 131
Edward III, 72-5, 77, 100
Edward IV, 43, 94, 98-9, 107, 125
Edward V, 107
Edward VI, 125, 130-1, 133, 135, 136, 138, 140, 177
Egypt, 16, 17, 20
Eleanor la Belle, 42
Elizabeth I, 137, 147, 148, 151, 161-2, 164
Emerson Street, 154
Erasmus, 113
Eubulus, 15, 20
Evelyn, John, 182

Fairfax, Thomas, 178, 179

Fallopio, Gabriele, 173
Farringdon Ward, 58, 67
Fetter Lane, 67
Fish (Fysshe), Dr Simon, 124
Fishmongers' Company, 95, 118, 162
Flemings and Dutchmen, 22, 34, 37, 78, 97, 121, 125, 142, 145, 173, 177, 178, 180, 181
Fletcher, John, 154
focarii, 40-1, 102
fornication, 14, 22, 30, 31, 37, 52, 104, 140, 171, 183
Foulle Lane, 74, 123
Frances, Henry, 117, 127
Frankfurt, 97
Frankpledge, 116, 121
Freya (Frigga), 17
Fridayfeld, 17
Frithwald, King of Surrey, 27

Gardiner, Stephen, 117, 126, 137
Gaunt, John of, 86, 95
Gaveston, Piers, 70
Germany, 22, 26, 102, 103, 121
Gifford, Bishop of Winchester, 38
Glanvill, Ranulph de, 61
Globe Theatre, 151, 183
Gloucester, Humphrey, Duke of, 95
Goat Stairs, 136, 153
Godwin, Earl of Kent, 32, 37
Goldsmiths' Company, 95, 96
gong-farmers, 135-6, 170
Gordon, Lord George, 183
Gothic tribal customs, 26
graffiti, 21-2
Gravill Lane, 90
Great Fire of London, 180
Great Pike Gardens, 153, 154, 155
Grocers' Company, 150
Gropecuntelane, 34, 69
Guildable Manor of Southwark, 72, 123

Haberdashers' Company, 150
Hadrian, 19
harbours, 21, 25, 27, 32
Harley MS. 293, 42; MS. 1877, 42, 50, 125, 131

Harington, Sir John, 159
Harold II, 34-5
Harpocrates, 16-17
Hastings, Battle of, 34
Hengist and Horsa, 24, 25
Henry I, 39-41, 102, 120, 141
Henry II, 9, 41-2, 51, 54, 61, 62
Henry III, 64-5, 68
Henry IV, 79, 89
Henry V, 89-91, 95, 98, 102, 141
Henry VI, 43, 60, 91, 92, 95, 97, 98
Henry VII, 107, 114-5, 117-9, 148, 155
Henry VIII, 9, 38, 103, 118, 119-20, 122-7, 131, 135, 136, 140, 141, 142, 148, 155, 159
Hlothaere and Eadric, Kings of Kent, 27
Holborn, 114
Holland, Dame Elizabeth, 146, 164, 168, 175, 177
Hope Theatre, 180
Horace, 11, 20
Horus, 16
Howard, John, Duke of Norfolk, 155
Hungerford, Lord, 122
Hunsdon, Lord, 43, 168
Hyckescorner, 109, 162

indulgences, 38
inns: *Anchor,* 150, 182; *Beerhouse,* 152; *Belle,* 100; *Bernacle-upon-the Hoope,* 100; *Bull's Head,* 182; *Dolphin,* 154, 162; *Falcon,* 155, 179; *Galleon,* 153; *George,* 152; *Helme-upon-the-Hoope,* 100; *Horseshoe,* 95-6, 151, 182; *King's Head,* 150, 183; *Maidenhead,* 158; *Pecock,* 100; *Red Harte,* 150; *Sarazinshed,* 158; *Ship,* 153; *Sugar Loaf,* 151, 182; *Vine,* 150, 158; *White Hind,* 157; *White Lion,* 157; signs of, 126, 169
Innocent III, Pope, 143
Innocent VII, Pope, 143
inspection of brothels, 45, 59, 101
Isaac, Jew of Southwark, 65, 69, 73
Isis, 15-16; Isis jug, 16

Italy, 97, 103

Jack of Newbury, 141
James I, 164-5, 171, 175
Jericho, 17, 54
Jewish physicians, 34, 59; *see also* physicians
Jews, 14, 35, 38, 39, 63, 65, 67, 69, 70, 73, 86
John, King, 62-4, 102, 162
Johnson, Dr Samuel, 183
Jonson, Ben, 146
Joshua, 17, 54
Julian the Apostate, 19
juries, 92-4

Ka-Kum, 53
Kal-Ba, 54
Katherine of Aragon, 120
Kett, Robert, 126
King's Pike Garden, 135, 157
Knight's jug, 68

Lambeth, 17, 138
Lanctantius, Firminius, 16
Lanfrancus, Bishop, 39
Langland, William, 69, 74
Lateran Council, 103
Latimer, Hugh, 130, 138
laws, of Aethelberht, 27; of City of London, 22, 67, 132; of Canute, 30-1; of Edgar, 29-30; of Edmund, 34; of Visigoths, 26
Leechdoms, Saxon, 33-4, 59, 70
Leo X, Pope, 102
licences, 38, 40, 46, 54, 60, 102, 126
Lock Hospital, 70, 117, 131, 143
London, 1, 12-15, 17, 18, 21-2, 24-5, 34, 36, 54, 69, 76, 90, 92, 97, 99, 123, 131, 142, 147, 181
London Bridge, 16, 30, 32, 50, 56, 64, 72, 78, 87, 98, 123, 124, 126, 136, 162, 169, 180, 181
London jug, 66
Long Megg of Westminster, 156
Lord Mayor of London, 107, 119, 125, 130, 144, 168
Love Lane, Billingsgate, 68; Cripplegate, 18; Southwark, 74

lupanaria, 13

Magna Carta, 64
Maid (Maiden) Lane, Cripplegate,
    18; Southwark, 60, 74, 75, 90, 96,
    100, 123, 131, 149, 151, 152, 153,
    155, 170
Marshalsea Prison, 122, 123
Mary, Queen, 136-7
Medici, Catherine de, 161
Mellitus, Bishop of London, 26
Mercers' Company, 95
Mercury, 16
mercury baths, 173
meretrices, 21
Merton, John, Prior of, 100, 155
midwives, 144-5
Mincing Lane, 67
Mint, in Southwark, 32
Monford, Michel, 104
Montpellier, 67
morbus gallicus, morbus indecens,
    morbus turpis, see venereal
    diseases
Mutinus, 17

Nabu-Akhe-Iddin, 54
Naples, 65
Nashe, Thomas, 104
Nebuchadnezzar, 54
nephandam infirmitatem, see
    venereal diseases
Newgate Prison, 117
noctiluces, 21

Odin, 17
Odo, Bishop, 37
Ordinance for the Government of
    the Stews, 9, 42, 43-51
Ordinances: *of Boatmen,* 69, 80;
    of Cleansing the Streets and
    Lanes, 69, 80; *Contra Meretrices*
    Vagrant Circa Civitates, 107; *as*
    to the Dress of Common Women
    w'in the City, 73; *of Privies,* 63;
    of Punishment for Whores and
    Bawds, 78; *pour Remover les*
    Estues, 90; *of Thieves and*
    Whores, 69, 80.

Osiris, 16
ostlers, 45, 46, 57, 59, 92
Ottoboni, Cardinal, 155
Ovid, 20

Paris, 91
Paris Garden, Liberty of, 95, 123,
    131, 135, 136, 146, 165, 168, 178
Parliament, 44, 53, 56, 73, 79, 85,
    94, 130, 177, 178, 179, 181
Parr, Katherine, 127
Pepys, Samuel, 181-2
Perrers, Lady Alice, 77
phallus, 16-17; *phallophores,* 16
physicians: Arderne, John, 86;
    Anglicus, Gilbert, 59; Anglicus,
    Richard, 59; Berri, Gerard de,
    71; Elias le Mire, 86; Fordun,
    John de, 110; Isaac of London,
    59; Gaddesdon, John de, 70;
    Gilbert the Physician, 59; Lan-
    francus of Milan, 70; Josce fil
    Medicus, 59; Marchadeus, 64;
    Scotus, Michael, 59; Valesco de
    Tarentum, 87; Villanova, Arnold-
    us de, 86; Widman of Tübingen,
    113
pillory, 78, 124, 132, 172
plague, 172, 178, 180
Plautus, Titus Maccius, 14
Plautius, Aulus, 11-12
Pliny the Elder, 20, 21
Pole, Reginald, Cardinal, 137
Polsted, Henry, 123, 135, 153, 154
Polsted, Thomas, 135
Pompeii, 16, 20, 22
Poynings, Robert, 98
press gangs, 120, 125, 138
prisons, 46, 47, 48, 84, 93, 95, 98,
    119, 166
Privy Council, 79, 126, 167, 168, 169
proclamations, 120, 124, 125, 131,
    134, 147
property developers, 127, 135, 146,
    147, 149, 156, 168, 179, 180, 182
Protestants, 126, 136-8, 145, 147,
    178
Ptolemaeus, Claudius, 12
punishments, 117-8, 120, 131, 132,

138
Puritans, 126, 137, 163, 179, 180
putagium, 65

quacks, 173, 178
Queenhithe, 14, 21, 25, 109

Rathbone, Ralf, 168-9
Reynolds, Walter, 71
Richard I, 63-4, 158
Richard II, 77-9
Richard III, 107, 155
Richborough, 12
Rochester, Bishop of, 75, 124
Rochester, John Wilmot, Earl of,
   174
Rome, 22, 102
'Room of the King's Whores', 118
Rosamund, 41-2
Rose Alley, 149, 152
Rose Theatre, 152
Rouen, 37, 38, 39

Sadelyer, Sir Ralph, 123, 135,
St Giles in the Fields, 114-5
St Katherine's, 114-5
St Marie Overie, 30, 67
St Margaret's, 99-100, 101, 122, 150
St Paul's, 67, 137, 154
St Saviour's (Southwark Cathedral),
   124, 156
St Saviour's Dock, 27, 32
St Swithin of Winchester, 17, 30, 38,
   124
St Thomas's Hospital, 100, 123
Salisbury, Abbess of, 121
Salerno, 34, 86
Sancto Paulo, John de, 65, 71
sanitation, 84-5, 89, 101, 113, 121,
   132, 159, 170, 172
Saxons, 17, 24-5, 27, 30, 33-4
scolds, 93
Seneca, Lucius, 12, 14
Severus, Alexander, 19
Severus, Septimius, 19
Sevigny, Madame de, 173
Shakespeare, William, 150
Shore, Jane, 107
Shoreditch, 114, 115

signs, on brothels, 125-6, 169
Sink, The, 123-4
Sixtus IV, Pope, 102, 118
Skelton, John, 107, 119, 155
slaves, 14, 21, 53, 63, 85, 138
sodomy, 33, 39, 72
Solon of Athens, 18, 54
Southwark, 9, 11-13, 15-16, 20-5, 27,
   28, 32, 33, 34, 40, 61, 65, 67, 70,
   72, 74, 75, 77, 79, 86, 89, 94, 97,
   119, 131, 136, 144, 145, 147-8,
   155, 160, 162, 165, 167, 168, 178,
   180; Southwark High St, 21, 65,
   73, 79, 96, 123-4, 168-9
Stephen, King, 40-1
stews, 42, 61, 71, 74-5, 76, 77, 86,
   87, 90, 94-7, 99, 104, 107, 109-10,
   114-5, 117, 119, 121, 123, 124,
   125-6, 127, 130, 135, 144, 147,
   151, 153-5, 165, 171, 174
'Stewes Bank', 151, 155, 157, 179
Stratford-at-Bow, Priory of, 71-3,
   79, 123, 135, 150, 152, 153, 155
Sumerians, 53
Synod of Cambrai, 103
syphilis, *see* venereal diseases

Tacitus, Caius Cornelius, 18, 22, 26
Tallow Chandlers' Company, 118,
   150
Talk of Ten Wives, A, 105-6, 140
taxes, 18-19, 102
Taylor's Company, 135
Taylor, John, 153, 156, 159
tenements, 148-9, 152, 159, 168-9,
   179, 180
Testa, William de, Cardinal, 71, 100
Teutons, 17, 22, 24, 26
Tewkesbury, Battle of, 99
Thames, The, 11-12, 25, 29, 79, 138
theatres, 141, 147, 151, 166, 177,
   178, 180, 181
Theobaldus, Archbishop, 9, 44
Theodoric II, 19
Thrale family, 183
Thurston, Archbishop, 40
Titus Caesar, 14
Token Books, 150, 151, 153, 154,
   156

Toulouse, 67
Tower of London, 14, 36, 67, 114
Turks, 42, 63
Tutunus, 17
Twdr, Nest ap, 52, 120
Tyler, Wat, 75, 77-9, 98

Udall, Nicholas, 132

vagabonds, 107, 124, 131, 134, 139
venereal diseases, 11, 23, 33, 41, 70,
    86-7, 102, 110, 113, 118, 143, 173,
    175; 'ape-galle', 113; 'brennynge',
    41, 49, 50, 59, 113; *caprificus,* 20;
    gonorrhea, 77; *morbus gallicus,*
    133; *morbus indecens,* 19; *morbus
    turpis,* 19; *nephandam infirmita-
    tem,* 41, 49, 113; syphilis, 19, 20,
    41, 51, 68, 89, 102, 113, 114, 117,
    120, 127, 136, 137, 173
Venice, 118, 167; Venetians, 97,
    167, 181
Vespasian, 11
Vulgaria, 132-4

Wallingford, John of, 28, 31
Wars of the Roses, 98
washerwomen, 45, 57
Watermen, Guild of, 142, 154, 156-
    7, 159, 182
Weston, Hugh, 137
Westminster, 36, 38, 44, 56, 71, 73,
    114, 115, 138, 181
whipping, 78, 131, 132
white fronts, to brothels, 125-6, 169
'whore-bashing', 124, 172
Wilkes, John, 57
William I, 9, 34-8, 78, 91, 140
William II, 38-9, 182
William of Malmesburie, 39
Winchester, Bishops of, 17, 30, 37,
    41, 52, 53, 67, 71, 75, 85, 95, 98,
    99, 103, 117, 121, 126, 167; Lib-
    erty of the Bishops of, 15, 22, 38,
    42, 55, 57, 58, 67, 92, 119, 121,
    177, 182
Winchester, city of, 39
'Winchester Geese', 127, 137
Winchester Palace, 95, 98, 136, 151,
    179
witches, witchcraft, 54, 144-5
Wolsey, Thomas, Cardinal, 120,
    121, 122, 156
Woorde, Wynkyn de, 27, 112, 132
Wren, Sir Christopher, 157
Wycliffe, John, 87, 103